After You've Said Goodbye

After You've Said Goodbye

How to Recover
After Ending A Relationship

Trudy Helmlinger

Schenkman Publishing Company, Inc./
Two Continents Publishing Group, Ltd.
Cambridge   New York

Copyright © 1977
Schenkman Publishing Company, Inc.
Cambridge, Massachusetts

Distributed in the USA by The Two Continents
Publishing Group, Ltd., 30 East 42nd Street, New
York, New York 10017.

Library of Congress Cataloguing in Publication Data

Helmlinger, Trudy
    After you've said goodbye.

    1. Grief.   2. Separation   (Psychology)   3.
Adjustment   (Psychology)   I. Title.
BF575.G7H44   158'.2   76-22541
ISBN 0-8467-0214-2

A SPECIAL ACKNOWLEDGEMENT

From now on when I read the acknowledgements in a book, I'm going to pay closer attention to the words because I've discovered something while writing this book. Even when there is only *one* author listed, without the help of others, it would never exist.

Ms. Pat Musgrave and Mr. Duane Newcomb guided me towards trying to write. My publisher, Mr. Alfred Schenkman, made it possible and Ms. Karen Frisher, my editor, helped make it worth reading.

My co-workers, friends and family offered their kindness, suggestions and encouragement. And, my patients gave me the inspiration and continuous reaffirmation of "man's" ability to grow through the crisis of saying good-bye.

To each of them individually, my warm and special THANKS.

TO THE READER.

HOW THIS BOOK CAN HELP YOU START LIVING AGAIN

This book is written for a very *special* group of people: those who are affected by the death of an intimate relationship, have the guts to acknowledge that, and the courage to grow.

Right now you may be asking yourself a number of questions: Who am I and how do I fit into the world? What makes me a worthwhile person? What do I need to feel secure? Can I tolerate *not* always feeling safe? How much of me depends on someone else? The list may go on and on.

Here you will find guidelines to help you answer those questions for yourself and tools to let you win the emotional battles you may be currently fighting.

To get the most from this book, I suggest that you first skim through it. Then, pick out the chapters that best apply to you and use them.

Even though saying good-bye is painful, it *can* be the start of something new and exciting. The fact that you're reading this means that you're ready to let go of some of the pain and begin living again. So, let's get on with it!

Table of Contents

How to "brush yourself off."
How to start living again.
The other side of scary is excitement!
Experiments and Exercises.

Getting yourself in proper perspective.
How to give up ex-love's total perception
of you.
Developing your own self-perception.
Check out feedback from all friends and
acquaintances.
Matching inner and other directed per-
ceptions.
How to develop a priority list.
How to build on strengths.
How to corral and tame frailties.
How to protect your vulnerable spots.
How to develop your dormant talents.
How to use anger to get you moving.
Experiments and Exercises.

How to get positive feedback and support
from old friends, family and acquaintances.
How to get ego-building feedback from
new friends.
How to make yourself look better.
How to gain feedback at work.
Getting the most out of inspirational litera-
ture.
Gaining strength from others in a similar
situation.
Gaining courage from religion, if you're
religious.
How to find competent professional mental

health support.
Experiments and Exercises.

Trying to help each other through the crisis.
Getting back together with ex-love.
Trying to be friends.
Saving old love letters, mementos, etc..
Pulling in memories to fill the emptiness.
Checking up on ex-love.
Trying to get friends to take sides/pumping them for information.
Wishing it hadn't happened and hoping it'll change.
Beware of anniversary dates.
Panicking with free time: week-ends and such.
Falling in love with the first person you meet.
Experiments and Exercises.

How to put a limit on self-pity.
How to fight self-pity and self-doubt.
How to clear your eyes and look at whom you've lost.
How to determine what you've lost.
How to own ending as your choice too.
Common self-induced traps and how to avoid them.
Ways of reaching out to others.
On the thought of moving.
Experiments and Exercises.

Moving is no picnic either; problems en-

countered by those who left.
Causal factors of guilt.
Healthy ways of dealing with guilt.
How to get yourself in proper perspective.
How to equalize blame for dissolution.
Common self-induced traps.
Utilizing strengths to handle obstacles coming up.
Experiments and Exercises.

How to give yourself permission to grieve.
Ways of allowing self to feel pain.
Getting proper perspective on loss.
Techniques that help you let go of pain.
How to reach out to others for comfort/support.
How to bury the dead.
Unhealthy mourning practices.
How to stop grief from overwhelming you.
Experiments and Exercises.

Causal factors of depression.
How to figure out why you're depressed.
How to fight depression.
How to find ways to win.
The art of feeling better.
Pitfalls that reinforce depression.
Experiments and Exercises.

Causal factors of anger.
Traps that reinforce anger.
Owning anger: the first step towards breaking away.
How to gain control over your anger.
Dealing directly with what causes your anger.
Constructive ways to utilize anger.

Learning to let go of your anger by replacing losses.
Experiments and Exercises.

Causal factors of self-pity.
Common traps that reinforce self-pity.
Accept that you are feeling sorry for yourself.
Take responsibility for immobilizing yourself.
Give up the "doormat" syndrome.
Other ways to give up self-pity.
Get involved in interests outside of yourself.
Experiments and Exercises.

On the fear of being alone.
Understanding your own loneliness.
How to combat loneliness by yourself.
Fighting loneliness with environmental change.
Fighting loneliness with the aid of others.
Pitfalls to avoid in loneliness.
Experiments and Exercises.

Giving yourself permission to be free.
New and exciting vacations.
Fun ideas for around town.
Other singles and where to find them.
Dating again.
Assessing new loves.
Look before you leap again.
Experiments and Exercises

1:   Ending Does Not Equal Failure

The ambulance screeched to a halt in front of the emergency entrance of a large metropolitan hospital. Doors banging, the attendants scurried down the hallways with their stretcher carrying a young woman to the emergency room. In the next thirty minutes, several white coated doctors and nurses mechanically forced air in the patient's lungs, shoved plastic tubes down her throat and pierced her veins with needles connected to tubes and bottles of liquid.

The patient, Mary L., an attractive 25 year old elementary school teacher, had attempted to kill herself by overdosing. If it hadn't been for a friend who dropped in to visit Mary that night, and finding her unconscious, rallied the ambulance, Mary would be dead. She had eaten a bottle of aspirin, some over-the-counter sleeping pills and several prescribed pain capsules from a recent back injury. The friend, knowing that Mary was depressed after the break-up of a love affair, had dropped over to cheer her up.

When Mary woke up on the psychiatric ward and found that she was still alive, she sobbed desperately that her whole life was a failure—she wasn't even successful at killing herself.

Even though she had worked her way through college and with the help of scholarships had attained a teaching credential, she nevertheless felt she had failed by breaking up with her boyfriend of three years and moving out of his house into an apartment. Mary has a number of close friends, a warm supportive family, and is an extremely talented and creative person. Yet, with the dissolution of an intimate relationship, she has decided that she is a failure.

Mary's story is not unusual. The psychiatric hospitals and mental health clinics are bulging with relatively successful adults who identify themselves as failures because of the break-up of an intimate relationship.

Each year hundreds of thousands of people end such relationships. According to the Bureau of Statistics, one out of every three marriages ends in divorce, with an average marital life expectancy of 7.8 years. And the duration for unmarrieds certainly isn't any longer. Intimate relationships can no longer be viewed as units that last forever—realistically, they simply don't.

Although every single who was once part of a couple does not attempt suicide or obtain psychiatric help, few are able to shirk the awesome feeling in the pits of their stomachs that they have failed, and, are, therefore, failures.

And, frankly, we've been programed to believe this. As children we are taught that normal well-adjusted adults are married and live together forever. In our newspapers, we honor couples as "successful" who have been married for fifty years. When someone gets a divorce or breaks up an intimate relationship, it is not uncommon for us to wonder what went wrong and who was to blame.

The idea that together is success and apart is failure is reinforced day after day in our lives—in our churches, from our families and friends and through our mass media and court-rooms.

Is it any wonder then, that Mary or any of the rest of us who end a relationship decide we are failures? Actually, it takes quite a person to believe he has *not* failed as he walks out of a relationship.

Yet, authorities such as anthropologist Margaret Mead and many mental health professionals will agree that ending an intimate relationship does not necessarily equal failure of the intimates involved. Dr. Mead states: "We have come to admit that many marriages *should* end in divorce."

With that idea in mind, let us look at some of the more common relationships which end in dissolution and examine the idea that ending does not equal failure.

OUTGROWING A NEUROTIC RELATIONSHIP MEANS GOOD-BYE.

The *Parent/Child Relationship* is a very popular unit in which one partner assumes the role of the "protective", all knowing and ever present, parent figure. The other member takes the role of the child who is coddled and needs strict guidance and structure from the parent in order to function.

Bill and Nancy S. are in their early thirties, married for eight years and living in the suburbs of San Francisco. Bill is an OB-GYN physician and Nancy rarely dreams of thinking, reading, trying or doing anything without his permission or suggestion first. She rarely shops for anything other than groceries without him. And, often, he goes with her to help figure out what the "best" buys are. She is almost always a good, submissive child. And Bill often tells his friends that he trusts his wife completely. On those rare occasions when Nancy does assert herself, she uses child-like temper tantrums or pleadings, thereby reaffirming the parent/child relationship.

Maintaining this type of relationship is costly to both. The price Nancy pays for "Someone to Watch Over Me" is not being trusted or valued as a grown-up, and believing that she needs to be treated like a child in order to survive. Bill pays a high price too. Constantly taking care of and feeling responsible for another adult is draining. There is little time left over for him to take care of his own needs, nor is he able to obtain the occasional reassurance and comfort that he, too, will want from his wife.

In order for the *parent/child relationship* to endure, both members need to remain emotionally stagnant. Bill has to continue feeling that he should take care of and be responsible for his wife. Meanwhile, Nancy needs to continue behavior which reinforces the belief that she is too immature to survive without constant parenting.

If and when one member outgrows and no longer needs a *parent/child relationship* and the other member continues to maintain his previous role, the relationship is no longer viable.

> Bill began getting tired of taking care of Nancy's every need. "Baby talk" got old and Nancy's inability to function at more than a minimal level without his help became draining rather than flattering to him. He longed for the day he could go golfing on Saturday rather than shopping with Nancy. At home, he missed having an adult he could talk with about his needs or current world problems or his other interests. The nurses at the hospital began looking more and more attractive to him as he wished he could make Nancy more independent. Bill talked with her about this issue. Nancy whined. Finally, after several months of begging his wife, in vain, to become an adult, Bill left. He had outgrown the need to have another adult be "small" and totally dependent in order for him to feel "big" and capable. He was tired of carrying her. Nancy was not.

It would not be accurate to say that Bill was a failure because he left this relationship. All of us need to be loved by an adult and would like to feel that we have someone whom we can lean on once in a while for support and reassurance when we're down. At the same time, we all need to love someone whom we can trust—but not take care of as we would a child. Bill couldn't have a mutual relationship with Nancy; she had to be carried.

It is just as common in a *parent/child relationship* for the mate in the child position to outgrow her role and no longer need or desire a live-in parent.

> Nancy got bored staying at home all day and, at Bill's suggestion, enrolled in a couple of classes at the community college. The instructors and her classmates, not knowing that Nancy couldn't think for herself, asked her to do just that. And, she did, discovering, of course, that she had a good mind of her own. She then began making decisions about a number of things: what she should wear, how she should look, and, how she felt about problems in the community. Much to Bill's dismay, Nancy became a "liberated" woman: slowly she began taking the responsibility to take care of her own needs as a person rather than depending on her husband to make her feel fulfilled. Although this was emotionally healthier for Nancy, it did produce unresolvable problems in their relationship. Bill wanted Nancy to stay dependent on him without feeling dissatisfied. He was unable/unwilling to adjust to Nancy's growth—she was unwilling to give up her new sense of "wholeness".

To decide that Nancy is a failure because she grew out of this relationship is absurd. A seedling becomes a tree—if it's healthy. A child becomes a mature adult—if she's healthy. And Nancy had outgrown the need to be a coddled, irresponsible, immature marital mate because she was becoming a healthy adult.

The ending of a *parent/child relationship* is not failure; after all, none of us can or should promise that we will always remain the same. And although ending any intimate relationship is painful, no one can be blamed or labeled a failure for the growth that precipitated the time to say good-bye.

Another common neurotic relationship is the *To-Regain-My-Youth* variety.

Dick is a divorced college professor who struggled with his fears of growing older by attempting to look and act younger than his age. At 40, his curly black hair was beginning to whiten, firm muscular body was starting to sag and his college students began looking obnoxiously younger to him each year. Pressured by his unresolved fears of growing older, Dick initially handled his anxiety by altering his physical appearance (hairstyle and wardrobe) and dating one of his college students, Sally.

Sally is an 18 year old freshman who met Dick two weeks after she moved away from her "small town" home. Her parents had been quite protective towards Sally and part of her rationale for moving was to develop her independence. Being "on her own" was exciting—but also a little bit frightening and Dick's apparent sophistication and maturity was extremely appealing to Sally.

For awhile their relationship was romantic and enchanting. Dick was flattered by Sally's admiration and she felt extremely "mature" by dating one of her professors.

If you were in this kind of relationship, maybe you can remember feeling a little funny—but, excited too. And the relationship could have lasted forever if you both had stayed stagnant. As long as our hero is still panicked at growing older and needs to pretend he's not outgrown his youth, he will stay. Sally will continue to admire Dick's sophistication and maturity until she gains some of her own.

But growing up in this kind of relationship means good-bye.

Gradually, Dick became disenchanted with Sally's youth and her adolescent games. He no longer felt flattered by her admiration. He began feeling foolish, and ironically, much older than his actual age because of the contrast between them. Growing older, he acknowledged, has different challenges than growing up and he wanted to enjoy them with someone more mature. Once Dick decided to move forward, rather than regress, he ended his relationship with Sally.

Dick and Sally's love was understandably doomed from the beginning. The emphasis on youth in today's culture makes it almost inevitable that some of us will scramble away from growing older by running towards our adolescence again. And, it takes a hero to give that up and accept the challenges and wisdom of his own age.

CONQUERING THE FEAR OF LIVING ALONE MAY MEAN LEAVING.

The fear of living or being alone can produce overwhelming and immobilizing anxiety in many people. Therefore, many couples join hands and continue to hold on—no matter how painful—for fear of living alone.

If you are one of the many people who held on to a relationship long after there was any other reason, you remember how scary it was to even think of being without someone. Maybe you didn't love your mate and perhaps you even longed for a different kind of life, but it's hard to plunge into the unknown alone.

I'm sure you asked yourself all kinds of questions. How will I survive without someone with me? Will I ever find anyone else? What will happen to me if I get sick—who will care if I live or die? What does it mean if I live alone—am I unlovable?

Everyone's afraid of being alone and being unlovable. But, somehow, if you gather enough strength to begin finding answers to some of these questions you may find that you really do have the ability and guts to walk on your own without holding someone else's hand.

It won't be easy. Even if the only thing left in the relationship was another body in the house—at least, you felt connected to someone.

And now it would be unfair to call you a failure for being strong enough to walk out of a relationship that was dead and forge the unknown alone. Cowards hover in the corner for protection; heroes strike out on their own.

FINDING THE GUTS TO RISK FINANCIAL SECURITY OPENS THE DOOR TO GO.

It's a fact that two people living together can live cheaper than two people living separately. And anyone who has contemplated and/or actually lived on his or her own can attest to it.

But financial security meets more than survival needs for most of us. Often we decide that importance and self-worth are hinged on how much money we have and what we can buy with it. The statements: "The clothes make the man," and "Money can't buy happiness, but it buys very good substitutes" are widely repeated and often believed. As much as possible, we ignore the poor and admire the rich.

Is it any wonder, then, that couples stay together for financial reasons long after the emotional reasons for their unity are dead?

> Jim and Pat V. just hit their thirties. High school sweethearts, they married right after graduation. And, in thirteen years of marriage they have accumulated: three children (12 year old Mike; 9 year old Karen; and 6 year old Andy), a $30,000, three-bedroom house in the suburbs, a mongrel dog, a two year old stationwagon and assorted household goods, plus lots of bills. Jim is a life insurance agent and, in the past ten years, has worked his way up to the management level. Pat stays home with the children. The financial and emotional stress of caring for three children as well as themselves has gradually eroded whatever love Jim and Pat felt towards each other. They talked about their dying relationship, but decided they could not afford a divorce. On

his salary, Jim could not support two households; and, Pat, who had never worked, had absolutely no employment skills. Besides, with three children, the child care costs would devour whatever salary she could earn. It was too risky to split.

It's easy to understand why you might stay in a relationship like that, even if it's been dead for years. Having to worry about bills or wondering if you'll have enough money to afford what you need or want is a very debilitating situation. Especially if you've worked very hard to *finally* get to a position where money isn't one of your foremost worries. Naturally, it would take a lot of guts to risk financial insecurity again.

But if the financially dependent mate is able to gather the courage to risk living at a lower (perhaps minimal) standard of living, the relationship will end—if that is the primary reason for staying together.

> During one of the evenings that Jim was out late, Pat sat at the kitchen table, drinking coffee, wondering if she and the kids could make it without Jim. There really wasn't any reason to continue their relationship; they had long since ceased to be lovers or friends. And as far as the welfare of the children was concerned, it would be healthier to come from a broken home than to grow up on a battlefield. The thought of leaving the financial security she currently had was frightening. Jim would probably give child support, but she couldn't count on that paying for everything. She'd never had a job, but felt sure she could find one. She decided to try it. Two weeks later, armed with the courage of her decision, she and the kids moved into an apartment in the city.

Neither could be blamed for the relationship dying; it was inevitable.

To *finally* leave a dead relationship takes guts. And, if you have recently forged the same frontier, you know how hard it is to do. To walk away from financial security requires courage.

DISCOVERING YOUR PRINCE IS REALLY A FROG

The adage "love is blind" can be either beautiful or tragic—depending on what the lovers see when they open their eyes. If your Cinderella turned into a chimney sweep or your prince a frog, you know how disheartening that can be. For a while you may even be in shock. Then, you might decide to look for some magic, perhaps on a second honeymoon, to make it right again. In the end though, your Cinderella will still belch at parties or your prince will still give you warts. Endings are always sad, but it doesn't mean failure.

If you have vowed allegiance to yourself or your prince that you will never find a love as great as yours was, you might spend years trying to keep the fairy tale alive. But, when you finally gain enough insight and courage to admit you've been duped by your heart, you will take Cinderella back to her step-mother, or the prince back to the pond.

The failure, if there is any in this kind of relationship, is not in the ending, but rather in its beginning. It's not your fault that the fairy tale is over; it never was very real to begin with.

UNMARRIEDS LIVING TOGETHER.

The odds against an intimate relationship enduring without the bonds of matrimony can be overwhelming. Let's look at some of the facts:

(a) Most couples choose living together vs. marriage as an alternative. One or both of the partners assume that an intimate relationship will not last and, therefore, are unwilling to enter an "until death do us part" contract.

> Dave L., a 23 year old, medium built, dark haired, part-time college student and full-time clerk for the State of California fell in love with Sandy D., an attractive, 21 year old, blond secretary in his office. They talked about marriage but Sandy was reluctant to become Dave's wife. She had come from a broken home and witnessed many marriages crumble. There was no guarantee that their relationship

would last and Sandy was not about to take marital vows she wasn't sure she could keep. They decided to live together instead, and, so, moved into an attractive apartment in the city near their work.

Trying to "win" a long lasting relationship by beginning with the doubt that anyone, including you and your love, will succeed is stacking the deck against yourself.

(b) A living together situation or trial marriage, implies that the couple is testing its strength and ability to last. The primary objective in testing is to discover the breaking point, which every relationship or object has. And, as you probably discovered, if you were in this kind of relationship, you, too, have your frailties and breaking points. Did you really need to test that to find it was true?

(c) Testing the endurance of an intimate relationship without an avowed emotional commitment to permanence can be disastrous.

As their arguments became more prevalent, both Sandy and Dave began ending them with, "I don't have to stay with you" statements. After all, they concluded, there was nothing binding them together. Neither one had made any "for better or worse" commitments to each other.

Arguments like this hurt, especially if you started with the doubt that no intimate relationship lasts and added the fear that yours wasn't any different.

(d) The additional social pressures from friends and family members who may condemn an intimate relationship outside the bonds of matrimony can be an added burden to the unmarried couple.

If we live in a new age with all of our social values changing, why do our families still live in the Dark Ages? The answer is not as relevant as the result, which is an extra strain on you if you've living with someone out of the bonds of matrimony.

(e) If a couple decides their relationship will last, or are convinced that they want to commit themselves towards that goal, they usually join the ranks of the married.

(f) An intimate relationship held together by ambivalence and lack of commitment has difficulty surviving the bombardment of everyday stresses and strains.

> Sandy and Dave lived together for a year before they finally decided to call it quits. They had joined together feeling that intimate relationships didn't last—and, after a year, had convinced themselves that that was true for them, anyway. Neither had much of a personal stake in making it work: so, neither gave in very much to the other's needs or desires. In addition, Sandy felt living with Dave had alienated her from her family and she didn't wish to pay that price for a life with Dave.

Although there are a number of positives in the theory of trial marriage, the reality is, in today's society (and with our own internalized value systems regarding commitment and responsibility) living together and making it last is a highly risky wager at best. The intimates who live together are bucking overwhelming odds for permanency. And, perhaps, they know that when they decide to live together rather than marry.

The ending of this type of intimate relationship should not be seen as a failure, but, rather, perhaps, as expected. You did not fail if you ended a relationship of this kind. It was set up at the beginning to be temporary.

BUYING WOMEN'S LIB MAY MEAN SELLING THE LITTLE WOMAN ROLE.

> Harry and Madge had been married for 25 years when they finally agreed on divorce. Both had grown up believing in traditional roles for husbands and wives and had patterned their lives on those beliefs. Gradually, however, Madge began to alter her ideas and seek satisfaction as a "separate" individual. The idea that her husband was her Lord and Master slowly eroded and in its place was the

concept that both partners were important and valuable. As she changed her own value system regarding her role as a woman and wife, the marital relationship became strained beyond the point of constructive repair or mutual satisfaction.

Today, more than ever, the changing male/female roles are shattering the once seemingly peaceful marriages of people like Harry and Madge. As women like Madge revolt, rulers like Harry find that they no longer have their kingdom and subjects to command. Although, in rare instances, couples are able to renegotiate their relationship, the more common solution is dissolution.

Little women who become liberated are often very angry at their old Lord and Masters. And a dethroned king rarely steps down with grace.

Certainly the ending of this kind of relationship cannot be seen as a failure on either member's part. Harry and Madge grew up in one culture and suddenly began living in another. As our society changes its expectations, rights and responsibilities of the sexual roles, many more intimate relationships may explode because of cultural shock—not because of any failure on either member's part.

It takes quite a person to adjust to his/her new role in our changing society. Carrying the "I'm a failure" syndrome with you is an extra weight you need not carry.

GETTING OUT OF LIMBO MAY MEAN LEAVING.

It is hard to decide to do something big—like move to a new town, change occupations or end an intimate relationship, even a dead one. In fact, the decision to end an intimate relationship, even a very painful one, can be so difficult that some people would choose to stay in limbo.

If you were in a stormy relationship, remember how long it finally took you to get out? There was a point when you weren't very close anymore, but you stayed anyway. Gradually you grew away from each other and if you used to share your thoughts and dreams, you noticed you weren't doing that anymore. You were talking to someone else about your problems, and the conversations between you and your ex-love sounded like letters to your family with whom you have nothing in common anymore. Everything was superficial and you talked about the weather— or the neighbors. Sometimes you shouted about yourself in fights, but that was the only time you really shared how you felt. And, that wasn't really all you felt—only what you were afraid of.

Funny how you'd forgotten that. You've been so busy missing your lost love and feeling like a failure, that you'd forgotten how empty and cold your relationship really was.

How long did it last after that? The idea of leaving scared you so much that you probably stayed there a lot longer than you should have—for your own sanity.

But, finally the relationship got painful enough, and leaving became less frightening to you. So, you gulped what little pride you could find and ended it. You should have done it sooner, but it took a lot of courage, especially when you are not absolutely sure that the choice is the best of all possible choices and you secretly wonder if you deserve anything better. There are a lot of risks in sticking your neck out and saying: "this is what I'm going to do." And then doing it.

Why did your relationship die in the first place? Who knows? Maybe it was a relationship that was doomed from its beginning. Or, maybe, you grew out of it—or, there was too much pressure placed on it from the rest of the world.

STANDING UP FOR WHAT YOU WANT MAY MEAN WALKING OUT!

Some couples stay in a relationship that is dissatisfying and panic when it's ended because they've decided, for whatever reason, that it is what they should settle for. Life, they've concluded really isn't all that fair or necessarily happy, no matter what they're read in popular stories where people live happily ever after.

Having a close, satisfying, refreshing intimate relationship is a fantasy for most. The cynicism expressed by couples who leave a theater seeing such a relationship on stage can be heard on almost any night.

The secret fears that many of us have about not being good enough helps convince us to settle for less than what we want in an intimate relationship.

> Doug and Janice T., a couple in their late twenties, have lived in a small rural community outside of Portland since they were married four years ago. Their relationship is not particularly happy, but both agree that it could be worse. Each leads a separate life. Doug, an aircraft engineer, works in the city and commutes sixty miles each day. On the weekends he often goes fishing or hunting. Janice is a nurse at a local hospital and does a number of things with her co-workers outside of work. She'd like to be with Doug more but understands that he wants his own private life. Periodically, they've argued about Doug's lack of commitment or attention to Janice. Doug says: "That's the way I am. If you want something different, you'll have to go somewhere else." Janice figures that maybe she's too demanding anyway. The kind of love she wants probably only happens in the movies.

If you were in this kind of relationship you probably remember the unhappiness you felt. The longer you stayed in it, the less you felt you deserved something better, and the more undeserving you felt. But, if you began seeing your good points, along with your frailties, you may finally have decided that you deserve something more or better, resulting in the demise of the relationship.

> Another year passed and their relationship continued as before. Doug was off in the woods most of the time and Janice

continued to reach out to her co-workers for emotional support and sharing. She began noticing that some of her friends were closer to their mates than she and Doug. So, it just didn't happen in fairy tales. She began comparing herself to other women at work who had the kind of relationship that she wanted. As far as she could tell, she was just as attractive, intelligent and considerate as they were. "Maybe," she began thinking, "I don't have to settle for less than what I want. I can't get it with Doug; I've tried." She made a decision and told Doug she was leaving. "I've decided," she announced, "that I really want and deserve a better relationship than what we have. And, I'm going to get one."

The failure in this relationship is in its inception, not in its death. For Janice, or anyone, to sell herself short and settle for less than what she really wants or deserves is absurd. The relationship had no future and its death was necessary for Janice to enjoy life.

Making the decisions that you do not have to settle for something less than what you want and that you deserve a caring, sharing, mutually accepting relationship with an intimate does not mean you've failed or that you're a failure. They do, instead, initiate a very significant change and a greater possibility for growth.

At the beginning of this chapter, I shared the idea that although most people who end an intimate relationship feel they have failed, this is, in fact, contrary to much of our reality.

A relationship, we have seen, can be terminated for a number of healthy reasons. In fact, Margaret Mead suggests that we are no longer in a culture that is compatible with permanency in intimate relationships. It is her belief that the idea of "til death do us part" came from a society where life was not that long, nor were people exposed to so many different alternative mates throughout their lives.

According to Norman Scheresky and Marya Mannes, co-authors of *Uncoupling: The Art of Coming Apart*, there is a lot of information which shows that intimate relationships are lightly entered but hesitantly left. "Intimate relationships fail," they say, "because they are entered into when we are least likely to exercise sound judgment about priorities. Inflamed by passion, consumed by hope and giddy with love, we enter into an intimate relationship without even the questionable objectivity we display in choosing a new car."

Experiments and Exercises

If you judge the ending of your relationship as a personal failure, when you are feeling good about yourself, ask and answer the following questions:

*On what "facts" do I base my judgment?

*Do I have any "facts" to support the opposite point of view?

*If my best friend was in my position, would I be more understanding and less judgmental?

*What would my friend need to hear to help with the feeling:
(a) of sadness?
(b) that he/she had done something "wrong"?
(c) that the ending meant failure?

*Which of my hurt feelings and fears am I confusing with feelings of shame, guilt or resentment?

*What would I be doing about my current situation if I wasn't wasting time judging myself or my ex-mate so harshly?

List the parts of your life in which you are competent:

1.
2.
3.
4.
5.

Place a time limit on how long you will ignore your accomplishments and give yourself permission to feel like a failure (ashamed, guilty, resentful, sorry for yourself) before you begin growing again. The rest of the week? a month? a year? five years? when? Be specific!

The following exercise is repeated at the end of the book so that you may compare your progress and emotional growth. Jot down the first words that come into your thoughts as you read the sentences.

1. If I were to use three words to describe myself, they would be _____, _____, and _____.

2. If I were to use three words to describe my ex-mate, they would be _____, _____, and _____.

3. When I look at my past, the word that comes to mind is _____.

4. When I look at my present, the word that comes to mind is _____.

5. When I look to the future, the word that comes to mind is _____.

6. My three greatest fears are _____, _____, and _____.

7. My three greatest strengths are _____, _____, and _____.

8. The one quality I would like to develop in me is _____.

9. Right now I feel I can look forward to _____.

2: Exploding The "Togetherness Myth"

One of the reasons you may be feeling a lot of extra pain, now that you're single again, is that somewhere down the line you may have bought the ever popular "Togetherness Myth." The one that says "you're nobody 'til somebody loves you," or "together you can be happy, fulfilled and maybe even conquer the world."

Sure, being together *can* feel better than being single, and, it is comforting to share your thoughts and feelings with someone you love. But, it does not necessarily follow that being together means happiness and inner peace. Or even comfort and mutual respect.

When you're in love, the "Togetherness Myth" is romantic, but, romanticism is as fanciful and fictitious as its dictionary definition. And, when you're saying good-bye to an ex-love, it's time to give up the fiction and look at some of the facts.

Join with me now as we begin looking at some of the realities that explode the "Togetherness Myth."

19

"TWO AGAINST THE WORLD" IS NEUROTIC.

The song "You and Me Against the World" romanticizes a neurotic relationship in which two people are bound together by their mutual mistrust of the rest of us. In view of their attitude, the fact that they got together in the first place is a mystery. But, together they are and ready to fight or avoid everyone else in the world.

Look at how this "game" is played and notice its neurotic foundation:

Rule 1: To play "You and Me Against the World" (Y.M.A.W.), each player must have a basic disbelief in his own value as a person because each believes that, given a chance, "people" will hurt or reject him.

Note: To qualify as a potential Y.M.A.W. player a person must:

1. Never accept/believe compliments or praise.
2. Pay attention to the parts of him that aren't perfect (too skinny or fat, nose too big, chin too small, etc.).
3. Always feel he should do better. And, do everything for himself because he can't depend on others.
4. Believe that no one could ever really care for him.
5. Have few friends. (One is *ideal*.)
6. Encourage others to gossip about acquaintances and use that to justify why no one should be trusted.
7. Have as a motto: "Do Unto Others Before They Do Unto You."
8. Never tell anyone how he feels—remember the motto.
9. Always look at the "bad" in others and the world.

Rule 2: Two potential Y.M.A.W. players must meet, "fall in love" and agree to mistrust all others for the duration of the game.

Rule 3: Both players should spend all of their time (outside of work) with each other. It is preferable that they work at the same job—or live on a farm together.

Rule 4: If the players decide to have friends, it should probably be one other "couple" who share in their mistrust of the world. Naturally they must be mutual friends. Probably it's best if they're relatives.

Rule 5: It's a good idea *not* to have children. (The players wouldn't want them to grow up in this kind of world.) If, however, they waiver and decide to parent, the children must be taught not to trust anyone—except, maybe, the family.

There are other rules, of course. But these are the basic ones which most people who play the game abide by.

You can look around for yourself and probably see a "hermit couple" in your own community. It's even possible that you grew out of a relationship like this.

Healthy adults don't play the game. At least, not for very long. They know they need more than one relationship. Sure, an intimate relationship is of primary importance. But we all need friends and family too. If you're a healthy adult you don't fight the world, you recognize that you're part of it. And, you encourage most people to be your friends, not your enemies.

THERE IS MORE TO A PERSON THAN BEING HALF A PAIR.

Intellectually, you must agree that "there is more to me than being half a marriage." Yet as silly as it may sound, we romanticize that neither value nor identity appear until after becoming the other half of a pair. How often have you heard—or even said—"this is my other half" or "meet my better half" to reinforce that belief?

Most of us are guilty of thinking in this fashion—at least to some degree. I remember even as a child I never thought of my favorite aunt without automatically listing her husband in my mind. I saw them as a unit. It wasn't just Aunt Mary or Uncle John, it was Aunt Mary and Uncle John. After he died there was much more to Aunt Mary than being Uncle John's widow. And, in order for her to live again and feel like a whole person, she had to find those other parts of her identity—mother, business

woman, friend, relative, amateur golfer, sexy single lady again
—and build on them.

And, just as Aunt Mary has to give up the myth that she is
nobody without Uncle John, so everyone who says good-bye to
an old love must be able to see themselves as separate individuals.
Not just half a pair.

Begin to think about who you really are. I am a woman, marriage counselor, part-time writer, amateur skier, lover, friend,
daughter, aunt, niece, American, Protestant, philosopher and
fool. All of these parts (and more) make up my identity.

They make me "ME". And when one of them changes, I still
continue to be a valuable, unique, person. In spite of the "Togetherness Myth," I am somebody special—even out of a love
relationship. And, so is everyone else.

There really is more to me or you than being half of a pair!

A HAPPY PAIR MAY NOT MEAN TWO HAPPY INDIVIDUALS.

The "Togetherness Myth" tries to make you believe that a
happy pair means two happy individuals. If you are happy with
HIM or HER, then you'll be happy. I know that there are times
when two happy individuals can make a happy pair—but the
opposite just ain't necessarily so!

There are a number of happy pairs made up of insecure, unhappy individuals. The sado-masochistic units: he beats her,
she knows he loves her because of it. The parent/child partner-
ships: she knows what's best for him and he obeys her. There
are others, of course. But I think I've made my point.

Whenever I hear the statement, "You two are so lovely together, you must be very happy," I smile. What that observer
doesn't know is that I am "happy together" only because I am
also happy separately. As an individual, I must feel good about
me to be able to feel good about anyone else—including him.

When someone says: "I should be happy—my marriage is
good," that person needs help to break out of the "Togetherness Myth" nonsense and see himself as an individual: as a

separate person with his own needs, wants and desires, as well as his own ability to make himself happy or unhappy.

If all this sounds fatalistic, it was written, nevertheless, by a very romantic soul who still watches old movies on television where the hero and heroine meet and fall passionately in love. Then, surmounting all tragedies with their love, they go off in the sunset to cure the lepers in Africa. Neither one of them needs or wants anything but each other. And, as they fade off into the sunset, the audience just knows that Africa will be a bit brighter because of their love. But—

ROMANTIC LOVE BURNS OUT QUICKLY.

And, if the audience were around to watch the next scenes, they'd be very disillusioned to see that the fiery passions have been transformed into cold routine. He works all day in the leper colony. She's at home with the kids. He comes home tired. She's exhausted. By the time dinner is over, the dishes are washed, the kids are in bed and the mosquito nets pulled down, it's time to sleep.

There isn't much fire in their love anymore. In fact, there's nary a spark. The trouble is that most of us romantics will never know such mundane facts: the movie always ends at the embrace scene.

So, part of the "Togetherness Myth" is created on the silver screen—and, in our hopes. We may see that our parents don't have a Cary Grant-Ingrid Bergman love affair, but we somehow build the fantasy that ours will be the way it is in the movies.

What a shocker when we discover for ourselves how quickly the passionate flames are doused if and when we stay with our Cary or Ingrid beyond the embrace scene. And, for many people, this reality can produce an added sense of guilt or failure; they have failed to achieve their fantasy goal of a lasting, fiery love.

But, love is a feeling that is learned. We can be instantly infatuated by someone or sexually aroused. But, love is a matter of learning to risk, care, trust and mutually respect each other.

So, if you buy the movie version of love with the smoldering desires and dazed enchantment, remember that they rarely show the lovers with a full-time job, bills that come due, house that gets dirty, yard that needs mowing or kids who get sick. Two people do need more than flame and fantasy for the foundation of a shared, real life together.

BEING TOGETHER CAN BE LONELIER THAN BEING ALONE.

It is easy to blindly accept the idea that if you "have" someone, you will not be lonely. But the truth is that being "together" with someone has little to do with whether a person feels lonely.

> "I can't talk to my husband. He doesn't know how I feel. Or care—or even listen. I'm so lonely I could die. At night, when I reach over to touch him, I can feel his body, but I still feel alone. What would I ever do if he left me? I'm so lonely now, with him. I think I would die of loneliness by myself."

That statement is not unusual. I've heard it, with some variation, repeated over and over again as a common theme for many intimates. Being together has not made people less lonely.

And ironically, sometimes being alone can be less lonely than being together. I remember a comment made by one of my clients, Callie:

> "Sure, I'm lonely now. But, I'm not as lonely, if you can believe this, than when I was married. Then, there were all those people in the house, but I couldn't reach them. My husband. The kids. They seemed so close—yet, so far away. I guess I just withdrew from everyone, after a while. Now that I'm alone, I'm forced to reach out to people. And, although it's not easy, and sometimes I slip back, I'm actually less lonely now than I've been in years."

Callie was 46 years old when she made that statement and for over half of her life (25 years) she'd been married. A year after the marriage was over, she was well into the healing process.

Callie isn't the only one to describe this sensation of feeling less lonely without a mate than with one:

"I felt isolated."

"There was no one to turn to."

"I thought there was something wrong with me because I felt lonely."

"I wondered why other people seemed so close and we weren't."

"I planned most of my activities without my wife, because she never wanted to go anywhere."

"Thank God I had my children."

"I don't know what I would have done without a hobby."

The explanation for this phenomenon is quite simple. When there is someone else "with" you, you expect to share, love and care about each other. It is natural to expect that you will not feel lonely. But when you live with someone and discover—as many people do—that these expectations are not met, you may feel even lonelier. The pain is even deeper if loneliness triggers frustration at not being part of a close intimate relationship. So, if you've bought the "Togetherness Myth," you may damn yourself for feeling lonely when you are not physically alone. But, the fact is that unless two people work at developing intimacy and a feeling of closeness, being together can be lonelier than being alone.

And often when the individuals are alone, they expect to feel lonely. So, they learn to accept a certain amount of it and develop plans to combat the rest, like reaching out to meet new people or learning to enjoy their own company at times.

TOGETHER AND SHARING ARE NOT SYNONYMOUS.

Another part of the "Togetherness Myth" that can increase an intimate's frustration and loneliness in a relationship is believing that being together means sharing. According to this belief, when you are part of a pair, you have someone with whom to share all of your good times, bad times, troubles, happiness, feelings and experiences.

Only, sometimes, when you think you're going together, you discover that your partner has taken a different route. Troubles are shared with your friends or relatives or kept to yourself. Happy times begin to mean going bowling with the guys, having lunch with the women, drinking with your co-workers or working on your hobby alone in the garage. For many intimates, sharing means they live in the same house together and share their anger at each other. Sometimes it doesn't even mean that. Thousands of married couples live separately during the week and only see each other on week-ends.

It is in the movies, poetry and song that being together means sharing your life. It is part of the "Togetherness Myth" and in the theme for the happily-ever-after group. In real life, being together means sharing only when each partner works hard to include the other in his life. Talking with and listening to your mate's attitudes and feelings does not come automatically or magically with being together, as the myth might imply. I know that doesn't make sharing quite as romantic and it pokes another hole in our balloon, but when we become realistic about how to develop a sharing relationship, it becomes much more possible to attain.

ONE CAN'T MAKE THE OTHER HAPPY.

No matter how much you love someone, you cannot make him or her happy if the sorrow comes from within. Sure, you can cheer someone up temporarily, and be there to wipe away the tears, but you cannot stop someone else from always feeling hurt and crying—if it's against his or her nature.

The "Togetherness Myth" would have you believe that one person can make another happy if only there's enough love. But, the fact of the matter is that you are the only one that can make you feel happy and enjoy being alive. Someone else can help, but only if you choose to believe that he can help you and decide that you really do want to enjoy living.

Lyrical phrases like "when you're in love the whole world is beautiful" are inspiring. And the poets who write of love which changes a pauper to a prince are romantic—but fictional. In reality, people believe what they want to believe, and what fits their own self-image. If an individual feels he or she has the ability to feel good and makes the decision that something or someone else will heighten that happiness, then, whatever the person has decided will do it—like love, or making money, or having a nice house or being a good mother—will fulfill those expectations. Otherwise, forget it. No amount of love, being together, success or money can make someone happy who has decided, for whatever reason, that he or she will never be happy.

I stress this because many intimates labor unsuccessfully under the myth that they can make their unhappy love feel cheerful if only they love strong enough, or are the "right" person. And, ex-intimates hurt themselves when they feel that they will never be happy again because they have lost the love that brings sunshine into their lives.

Someone can give you an invitation to feel happy (or sad). It is in your power to decide whether to accept that invitation.

HAVING SOMEONE DOES NOT MEAN YOU'RE LOVABLE.

People in love rarely question whether they're lovable. People out of love worry they're not and take as proof the fact that they are alone.

Everyone has a fear of being exposed as an unlovable person. And, sometimes, when we lose an old love, we assume the reason for that loss is because we've been discovered; our fear has allegedly become a reality.

It's silly when you think about it, isn't it? That any of us should be so wrapped up in our fears of being unlovable, that any rejection would be seen as "proof" we're no good.

In spite of the fact that most of us can look around and see many pairs that are built and held together for neurotic or social reasons, we still force ourselves to forget the facts and believe blindly in the fiction that being together proves you've lovable.

The point is that people get together for a whole raft of reasons. Some of which are, perhaps, just as sensible and "right" as others, such as, "it's time to get married and you're the kind of mate I want." So, therefore, being part of a pair is no more a measure of one's lovableness than it is proof of one's happiness or self-confidence.

If you read over what's been said in this chapter and look at the examples from your own experience, you will quickly see the "Togetherness Myth" as a fable—not a fact. We want to believe that "love cures all"—or "together down the highway of life will be magical." Sure, being together can be warm and wonderful and much better than being alone, but it can also be cold, routine, drab and lonely. It takes hard work, not magical pixie dust to develop intimacy. Remember the times in your own relationship when being together meant arguing, loneliness and feelings of being used or misunderstood?

At the end of an intimate relationship you need to explode the "Togetherness Myth" for yourself and look back on it with more realism and less romanticism. It's natural to paint a rosy picture of the past for yourself if the present looks bleak. But believing in the "Togetherness Myth" when it wasn't true for you, can only help to keep you sad and perpetually frustrated.

Experiments and Exercises

How would you rate your own belief in the "Togetherness Myth"?

---

see it   see it
as *Fact*   as *Fantasy*

Where would you rate yourself *before* you met your ex-mate?

---

saw it   saw it
as *Fact*   as *Fantasy*

If there is any difference, what do you think causes it?

Most people want to believe in the "Togetherness Myth" when
they are alone and feeling "down". How does this "fit" with
your own pattern? When do you want to believe that it's true?
What does that tell you?

List the "parts" of you that have nothing to do with being part
of a pair:

1.
2.
3.
4.
5.

This exercise is designed to help you explode the "Togetherness
Myth" for yourself. Do it when you feel strong, not "down" and
have some uninterrupted time for yourself.

   *Imagine yourself as a movie camera reviewing old scenes
from your past. Reflect on a time in your relationship when
you were together but *not* happy. What was going on? Could
you share your feelings with your ex-love? What happened when
you tried? Try to re-experience that scene (and your feelings)
now. When you feel "finished", take some time to reflect.

Use this space to list what you've discovered from the above.

1.
2.
3.
4.
5.

List what you *could* in fact count on your ex-mate to provide for you.

1.
2.
3.
4.
5.

List what you wished he/she would provide for you but did not.

1.
2.
3.
4.
5.

After looking at your relationship realistically, how would you evaluate your belief in the "Togetherness Myth" now?

---

see it   see it
as *Fact*   as *Fantasy*

If you felt like half a pair, what can you do to make yourself "whole"?

1.
2.
3.
4.
5.

3: Fallout From Dissolution

Intimate relationships don't always end with a bang; sometimes they just fizzle out. But even when the relationship has been dead for years, you may *still* be hit by some of the fallout of dissolution.

A friend of mine was telling me:

> "Here I am, six weeks after *I've* kicked Bob out of the house, feeling like one of the walking wounded! I don't eat. I have trouble sleeping, I'm worried and confused. I can't make even the simplest decisions anymore—like how to rearrange the furniture or what to eat tonight.
>
> "It doesn't make any sense," she announced. "Our relationship was over a long time ago. Yet, when I'm alone, I find myself wondering what Bob's doing and dialing part of his telephone number before I hang up.
>
> "What's with me? How can I miss someone I didn't even love anymore? Or was I wrong about that too? I just don't know anymore—it's hard to believe that I used to think I was strong!"

My friend's feelings and doubts are not unusual. In fact, almost everyone who goes through a dissolution experiences some sort of "buyer's remorse" for the first three to six months: a period of doubt and confusion about what they've bought in saying good-bye to a part of their past.

And, although every human being is different, there are some common side effects in ending an intimate relationship that many may be able to identify with. I've labeled these feelings, patterns and realities the "fallout from dissolution." They are as present in the ending of a love affair as fallout material from the explosion of a bomb. (Even when the love affair died through lack of interest.)

Looking at this fallout will help you to understand that they are a natural part of the grief process and nothing to fear or avoid.

LOSS OF SELF-ESTEEM.

Whether you experience a minor nagging of self-doubt or a loud voice shouting "I'm a loser!", it's almost impossible to avoid a blow to your self-esteem when the relationship is over. And, to some extent, that can be healthy if it motivates constructive self-exploration.

For example, it's important for my friend, Helen, to look back on her own behavior and attitudes in her relationship with Bob. Vehemently insisting that she has been victimized by Bob and that she, personally, had no part in the demise of their love, might keep her stuck in the same pattern. (Like the lady who just divorced her fourth alcoholic husband!) So, anything you can learn *now* about your part in the break-up will be most helpful to you—for the next time around. It's almost as if the natural instinct to question yourself after it's over is a way of trying to improve or grow emotionally so that your next relationship will be stronger. Therefore, do some self-examination. Look at your part in creating the distance. Maybe you chose the wrong partner at the beginning, or maybe didn't grow with your partner but away from him or her.

Helen discovered, in looking back, that from the very beginning Bob had told her he was afraid to have permanent intimacy.

> "I remember when we first started dating, Bob told me he usually got bored with a love after a couple of years. It's funny, I heard him—but I didn't believe him. Know what I mean? But I think I did act on the fear that he'd leave unconsciously. I smothered him by asking him to meet my every need. I was jealous of his friends. The tighter I hung on, the more he wanted to be free. Next time I fall in love, I think I'll do it with at least one eye open. Learn to give my man more comforting and less smothering."

Whatever the insight you discover, learn from it and use it! Avoid beating yourself with feelings of self-doubt, inadequacy and blame. They can become overwhelming and immobilize you in self-condemnation and depression. Before Helen could learn from the past, she found herself sinking deeper and deeper into a depression. Piled with self-doubt and condemnation, she tore apart everything she did with criticism. She was so busy beating herself down, she had little energy left over to pull herself up.

> "I feel so empty and abandoned now. And when I look at next year—or the years after, it looks just as bleak. I feel like somehow I deserve to be alone. Even though I kicked Bob out of the house, he had really left me before then. He's living with someone else now. You know, I was so afraid that he'd get tired of me and find someone else, I drove him away. If only I'd been different. But, it's too late now—I'm alone."

But Helen discovered, as many ex-intimates do, that she wasn't *that* awful nor did she remain alone forever. Once she was able to feel sadness over her loss and then look at her relationship with Bob less judgmentally and more realistically, she began feeling better.

LOSS OF IDENTITY AND LIVING STRUCTURE.

Loss of identity and living structure may not always be a feeling or fear. It can be a reality.

A father without his children loses the role of teacher, disciplinarian, friend, referee and part time football coach. At least on a day to day basis. He and his children must learn, if they are to adjust at all, how to substitute an "always there" relationship for a "sometimes near."

For the last six years, Ed and Marsha's marriage was glued together by their love for their sons, John, age 14, and 12 year old Mike. Ed owned his own hardware store and could make a lot of "free" time to be with his boys. He was a scout leader, little league manager, score keeper for the junior high football team and president of the local P.T.A.. As concerned parents, they decided a marriage held together just for "the kids" was unhealthy. And so, when they divorced, Marsha and the boys moved near her family: two hundred miles away.

Ed's visiting rights consisted of one week-end a month and every other holiday. His role as a full-time father and active member of the community disappeared. And, although he saw John and Mike on "visiting" days, his life felt pretty empty. He missed his role as teacher, coach and concerned citizen for children's rights.

Finally, after floundering for several months, one of his friends suggested he join Big Brothers. "A guy like you needs kids—and there are a lot of boys around who need a man."

At first Ed said no. It wouldn't be like fathering his own sons. But then he decided to try it. He felt he had nothing to lose.

As a matter of fact, Ed found by joining Big Brothers that he gained a lot. He got back part of his identity as a leader and teacher of boys. It wasn't the same but it was a whole lot better than nothing.

Then there are times when a "sometimes near" relationship is an improvement for both father and child. With less time and tension, both can put more effort into building their relationship.

> Mark was 35 when he and Marie divorced. They had been married for ten years and were the parents of three children: Mark, Jr., age 8, Danny, age 6, and 3 year old Karen. Since the birth of their first child, Mark had spent most of his time and energy making money as an insurance agent to "give the kids the things they need to feel secure." When their marriage dissolved, Marie took the kids and Mark gave child support.

> Then with the family absent, he discovered that there is more to child support than money. His children were no longer the hassle they were before. He didn't see them breaking toys or ripping their Levi's he'd spent so much money to buy.

> What he did see was that they needed his emotional support and understanding as much or more than his money to feel safe. And, he wanted a relationship with them. So, with the tensions of the marriage gone and less time to take his children for granted, Mark put more effort into the hours he had with them. End result: Mark's relationship with his three offspring was better after the divorce than during his marriage.

There are other identities that are lost or changed in saying good-bye. A housewife with no husband is a housekeeper. A wife and mother changes to a working single mother. A lover without his mate becomes an ex-love. A friend and companion turns to an enemy. A partner becomes an acquaintance. The list goes on and on—

And, with each of these changes, there is an "identity crisis" followed by an adjustment. A period of time when the ex-intimate needs to begin looking at him or herself as an individual again, rather than part of a pair. A time to decide, once again, who am I now and what do I want to be or do? It's never very easy.

But for some it's more difficult than others. A woman who saw her major role as Mrs. has trouble viewing herself as a Ms. And, the longer she was the "better" or "other" half of a pair, the harder it may be for her to feel "whole" on her own.

For example, Mrs. Jones who was married for 25 years will probably have a harder time adjusting to her new role as an ex-intimate than Mary Smith who had a love affair with Cory Johnson for six weeks. But both Mrs. Jones and Mary Smith will have the same shift in perspective with regard to how they see themselves: including the pleasure of discovering they are, indeed, "whole" people.

If you're going through an identity crisis of your own right now, find some comfort in the fact that you've gone through others in your life (going from grade school to high school, adolescence to adulthood, your first job to the second one, etc.) and remember with each change you were able to grow!

The other day I was talking about loss of identity and living structure with one of my co-workers. Six months earlier she had divorced her husband of seven years and moved from a charming old house in the country back to an apartment by herself in the city.

"It must have been awfully hard for you," I said, "to give up that home with it's beautiful yard for a dinky apartment."

"Hard?" she smiled, "It was the best thing that ever happened to me. That house was so old—and big. I spend most of my spare time working on it.

"You know I used to feel like I should always be working or accomplishing something. With that house, I had plenty to reinforce my 'work horse' image.

"I'd always been taught that you have fun, after you've finished your work. And there was always plenty of work with that house. And little time for fun.

"When I moved into my apartment, I discovered I had lots of free time. Nothing needed to be repaired or repainted.

At first it was hard to adjust. But, let me tell you, I love it! I'm finally learning after thirty years to take time and enjoy life, rather than work your way through it.

"I can't tell you what a change that's been for me," she bubbled. "I've become a lot less up-tight or critical of me and other people. I'm really a lot healthier and happier than I've ever been.

"When you write your book, Trudy, make sure you tell the readers not to be afraid of giving up some of their old self-images. It could be a blessing in disguise."

LOSS OF AMBITION; INDECISION.

But even when the changes become a blessing in disguise, during the transition period it is natural to feel some loss of ambition and indecision.

Like my friend, Helen, who had trouble "even making the simplest decisions on how to rearrange the furniture or what to eat tonight." And, major decisions? Like, should I move? What do we do with the kids? Now that I'm free, what am I "free" to do?

Those can be real stumpers! For anyone. Even people who are still in an intimate relationship and have someone to support them with their decisions. It's funny, most people don't notice until they're alone how often they depend on others to help them with choices.

But an ex-intimate may need to make some major changes with very little emotional support or "cheering on" from a fan club. No wonder it's natural in an ending to give up your ambition or decision making power—for a while.

It's hard to know which comes first: indecision or loss of ambition. If you have trouble making decisions (and all of us do), it's easy to give up. On the other hand, if you give up after you've said good-bye, making decisions doesn't seem worthwhile or possible. Either way, it's a self-defeating cycle.

When you feel good about yourself, and your past choices,

it's easier to have ambition and quickly decide what to do next. But when you feel as Helen did, "like one of the walking wounded," your desire to zip through and conquer the challenges of single life is temporarily lost.

Ex-intimates who find themselves in a stupor about what to do now may find it helpful to stop running around in circles or standing in a daze and Sit Down. With a pencil and paper in hand, write down questions that need to be answered and choices that have to be made now and sometime in the future. List "Current decisions I've decided to make" on one sheet of paper and "Decisions I would like to make later" on another.

Avoid asking vague, unanswerable questions like "what's the meaning of life?" or self-defeating ones like "has my life been worthwhile?" Your list may include anything from "where do I want to live?" to "what should I have for dinner?" Some decisions will be easier than others.

Include on your list some decisions that are relatively easy for you. By making these and owning your ability to do that, it will help build up your confidence. When you list the choices you have for major decisions, like where to live, try to give yourself at least three options. Then write down the pros and cons of each. Once you have listed all of the alternatives (with their good and bad points), pick the one you *lean* towards. Try to get out of the "bag" of waiting until you can make the perfect decision. Many of your choices right now may be between alternatives you don't exactly like anyway.

If you make a mistake, don't be too harsh on yourself. Take comfort in the fact that few decisions are absolutely irreversible. As my co-worker said,

> "Once I was forced to make decisions on my own, I discovered that I really was a worthwhile person. And I began looking at what I wanted to do because I actually felt I had options for the first time in my life. It's terrific to discover that I have freedom of choice rather than the burden of decisions."

BITTERNESS.

It's hard to look at what you really want to do if you're seething with bitterness. It takes a lot of energy to be bitter and disagreeable. And, you can lose a lot of friends in the process. Still, it is part of the "fallout of dissolution" and perfectly natural to feel to some extent.

But, please be careful with how much bitterness you hold on to. You can get stuck.

> Betty had been married for sixteen years when her husband left her for another woman. Betty blamed everyone for the divorce, except herself. Her daughter was a hassle, her husband was a baby and the "other woman" was a fool. She was glad when her daughter moved in with them. They deserved each other. Her only hope as far as they were concerned was that she'd live to see the day when they'd all be sorry.
>
> In the meantime, she planned to get everything she could from her husband. "That Bastard will pay!"
>
> She spent most of her free time (out of the lawyer's office) trying to get her friends to take sides. Only most of them avoided her. (One referred her to therapy).

It's easy to understand that Betty's bitterness was masking her hurt. And that she needed to grieve her loss and gain support and understanding to feel better. But it was very hard for Betty to ask for any comforting or give it to herself. Her bitterness was self-consuming and making it harder and harder for her to trust people.

In therapy, she learned how to let herself feel the hurt without being overwhelmed, to understand her own part in the demise of her marriage and how to trust and have respect for people again. Herself included.

So, when you find yourself getting bitter, go ahead and feel the sorrow beneath and learn that you can trust yourself and others for support. Don't become another Betty Bitterness. Even if you have a right to be bitter, you may want to ask yourself if it's worth it to be so disagreeable.

SELF-PITY.

If you feel bitterness long enough, pretty soon you'll begin feeling sorry for yourself. Or is it the other way around? In any event, self-pity is just as much a part of the "fallout" as bitterness, and, often hits around the same time.

Total stranger passing by: What are you doing down there?

Little person in a hole: I'm feeling sorry for myself.

Total stranger: How come?

Little person: Because I fell into this hole.

Total stranger: Oh? Well, can I throw you a rope to help you climb out?

Little person: No thanks. It probably wouldn't do any good anyway. Even if I did get out no one would care. And I'd probably just fall in another one anyway.

Total stranger: Well, okay. I'll be back later if you change your mind.

Little person: I knew he'd leave me.

Poor little person. Once he fell in the hole of depression after saying good-bye, he stayed there so long feeling sorry for himself;

Little person: It's awfully dark down here. Too bad I'm stuck. I don't deserve it. I wonder what everyone else is doing? No one probably even misses me. I knew this would happen. I guess I'll go to sleep.

Total stranger: Hi! I'm back.

Little person: Big deal.

Total stranger: Don't you want to get out yet?

Little person: Well, maybe—it is empty and dark down here.

Total stranger: I can still throw you that rope if you'd like to climb out. But you'd better make up your mind quickly, I'm leaving soon.

Little person: (First to himself) If the stranger leaves, I may be stuck here forever. (And then, shouting out loud) Stranger! Throw me your rope—I want *out* of this hole!

Hurray little person! It took some guts to grab the stranger's rope and pull yourself up again. There's nothing wrong with licking your wounds when you've been hurt, but it is very easy to get wrapped up in self-pity. Especially when you've said good-bye to an ex-love. Part of the healing process is to give yourself sympathy occasionally. Growing beyond that may take some time and conscious effort on your part.

PHYSIOLOGICAL CHANGES.

All parts of us—mind, body and feelings—can be affected by the death of an intimate relationship because they are so closely linked.

Several years ago a friend of mine developed diabetes after the death of her father. Although she must have had a predisposition towards that disease, her grief was so strong that it affected the metabolism in her body. The doctor explained to her that diabetes triggered off by emotional trauma was rare, but not unknown. Few people develop diabetes over the loss of an intimate relationship, but many do experience temporary physical upsets.

According to Dr. Aaron T. Beck, author of *Depression: Causes and Treatment*, there are several common physiological changes that may occur when a person is depressed. Among these are:

1. Changes in appetite and subsequent weight loss or gain. Some people lose or gain as much as fifty pounds.

2. Loss in energy levels. A normally active person may suddenly discover he has no energy or tires easily. Feelings of being "run down" or "too weak to move" are common.

3. Excessive energy or hyperactivity may occur. A normally calm individual can suddenly develop great bounds of energy—to the extent that he may become restless and fidgity after short periods of time.

4. Difficulty in concentration and shortening of attention span. Reading a paragraph in a magazine and then remembering what it said can be an impossible feat for the first days or weeks.

5. Frequent headaches or a feeling of tightness in the head may occur. Many people complain of feeling "like there is a tight band around my head."

6. Upset stomach or nausea and vomiting. Although this is usually a temporary complaint, there are cases recorded in psychiatric literature where this sympton lasts for years.

7. Menstrual disturbances are often seen, with amenorrhea (absence or suppression) being the most common. Excessive cramping may also occur.

8. Changes in intestinal functioning may occur with subsequent constipation or diarrhea.

9. Resistance to viral and baterial infections may go down. People who are normally healthy may find themselves in bed with a common cold or the flu bug.

So, not only may you feel like one of the walking wounded during this crisis period, but your body may actually react as if you had been through a war.

Cures for these symptons take time. It's important to remember that many of these physical upsets are natural and to be expected. The first few days and nights are comparable to a time of acute illness. Your reflexes may be slow and your attention span brief, as your mind darts from the past to the present to the frightening future. Gradually the fog will lift and the pressure will cease as you begin to see your way more clearly.

Treat your physical symptoms as they occur. Even though you may need to force yourself, continue to eat well-balanced meals. And avoid excessive use of alcoholic beverages. If the symptoms persist, go to your family physician for treatment.

CHANGES IN SLEEPING PATTERNS.

When you lose a person close to you, you may need to sleep for a while to find the guts to start again, or you may spend your nights trying to figure out the past, plan for the future, and worry about your inability to sleep.

Human beings are the most flexible animals in the world. And, within a short period of time, most ex-intimates discover they are either tired of sleeping their life away and get on with the business of living, or they get tired of stalking in the night and begin to sleep again.

Either way, it's important to remember that sleeping patterns may change during the first few nights or weeks after you've said good-bye. But they should return to normal.

CHANGES IN SEXUAL PATTERNS.

The scale for "normal" sexual patterns of the ex-intimates varies from complete celibacy to promiscuity. During the time of ending and while you're going through the grief process, almost anything is normal.

Adults who are normally active sexually may find that they have lost their drive or interest in sex. As one man confided to me, "Women don't arouse me anymore. Sex got so bad during the last few months of our relationship, that I'm beginning to wonder if I'll ever be 'turned on' again." Gradually he did gain back his sexual drive and interest again. But, it did take time. First the wounds to his pride and self-image had to begin healing.

Loss of sexual drive and interest is most often seen in the partner who was left behind. The one who feels rejected is most apt to be depressed and see himself as a failure. And, from that view point, it is natural to shy away from encounters (especially sexual) which will once again place the individual in a position where he may be hurt.

Depression and loss of Libido, according to Dr. Beck, may go hand in hand. And time spent going through the process of both grief and re-building self-confidence seems to be the only "cure".

On the opposite end of the scale, many ex-intimates find that their sexual drive becomes increasingly heightened. Men and women who normally see themselves as "home bodies" may find they are haunting the bars at night looking for one night stands. Although the sexual behavior is different, the core issues of feeling empty, alone and inadequate are similar. A man or woman who becomes sexually promiscuous after the loss of an intimate relationship is, in his/her own way, dealing with the grief process.

Heightened sexual activity can be an attempt to substitute sexual intercourse for feelings of intimacy. It can also be an angry statement (a way of getting even) with members of the opposite sex. Or as a way of proving to oneself that others still do find the individual sexually attractive. Whatever the underlying reasons, it is not unusual during the grief period for an ex-intimate to be more sexually active.

Although it might seem unusual, many ex-intimates continue to have sexual intercourse with each other long after they have parted. One man I met continued to go to bed solely with his ex-wife ten years after their divorce. This is highly unusual. But it is pretty common for ex-intimates to continue gaining sexual support and comfort from each other for several weeks or months after their relationship is over, thus making it much more difficult for either partner to bury their relationship and go on. But, it does seem to be part of the natural ending process for some ex-intimates. Especially those who have been together a long time.

Masturbation is another sexual behavior that may again (or

for the first time) become more prominent during the grief period. And, although there are no accurate statistics in this area, it is my guess that many ex-intimates do at times quite naturally seek gratification through their own bodies. I have talked with a number of ex-intimates who tell me that when they lost their sexual partners, they began meeting their own needs through masturbation. Some shared that this was their only source of sexual gratification for awhile, others said that they did this in conjunction with seeking sexual comfort/sharing from others.

So, during the time of ending, and while you're going through the grief process, almost any change in sexual behavior is natural. You need not be overly concerned or worried about your changing sexual patterns; it is part of the "fallout of dissolution."

The important issue with regard to sexual patterns is how you feel about it yourself. If your behavior makes you feel guilty or even more like a failure, and understanding that it can be a natural, normal process does not help, then try to alter it. In time, as your wounds heal, your sexual patterns, desire and interest will probably return to status quo. Or, if you did not enjoy sex in your previous relationship, you may pleasantly discover, with your next love, you do. One lady who was married for thirty-five years and, now divorced and remarried, has happily found that she is finally enjoying sex.

FINANCIAL PRESSURES.

Bob loves Carol, but can't afford to marry her because of the alimony and child support he pays Alice, his first wife.

What to do? Get a husband for Alice. That will get Bob off the hook.

Bob finds Ted, a recent divorcee and introduces him to Alice. Ted and Alice fall in love. But, Ted can't marry Alice because he's paying alimony and child support to his ex-wife, Gertrude.

Obviously, in order for Bob and Carol, Ted and Alice to live happily ever after, they have to do something about Gertrude.

That would get Ted off the hook to marry Alice, which would free Bob to marry Carol.

Solution? Find a husband for Gertrude that could financially afford to take care of her.

Sound crazy? Not really. It's a variation of the comedy plot of a movie "The American Way of Divorce." And, it can also be a not so comic plot for many real life divorcees. Money is tight. And the rising costs of living makes taking care of two separate households very difficult.

Today, many husbands and wives find they both have to work just to keep up with high prices. And, when they divorce, some couples are really in financial trouble, especially if they have children. Lawyers charge money. Moving costs. Living separately eats up cash.

It's hard to avoid the "fallout" of living poorer. In fact, you can probably count on extra financial pressures after you've said good-bye.

LOSS OF FRIENDS AND FAMILIAR SURROUNDINGS.

Another "fallout" that you can probably count on when you say good-bye to an ex-love is the loss of friends and familiar surroundings.

As my co-worker who moved from a country house into a city apartment told me:

> "I really miss some of the friends we had together. On Sunday afternoons we'd gotten into the habit of doing something with two other couples. A barbecue or picnic or maybe just lounging around. I really like them—but, I haven't seen them very much since then. We really don't have very much in common anymore. And, I can't tell whether they're awkward or I am, but the few times we've been together since then have been very strained."

The amount of this "fallout" varies with each ex-intimate. The ex-mate who stays in the same house or neighborhood obviously loses less of his familiar surroundings than the one who moves across town or to another area. Likewise, the ex-intimate who has friends outside of the relationship will have less change or loss of friends than the person who was totally dependent on the intimate relationship to provide outside friends.

The longer an individual has been in an intimate relationship, the greater chance that his friends are her friends, too. The couple that divorced after twenty-six years of marriage probably has more mutual friends than the couple who lived together for only six months. In any case, when it's over, your friends will be affected by the ending. And some of them you may abruptly or gradually lose.

According to Dr. Arthur A. Miller's article in *Divorce and After*, there are a number of different reactions that friends may have to a divorce, or, I might add, to the ending of a non-married relationship as well. Included in this list are:

— anxiety because of their own marriage.
— shame.
— preoccupation with the divorce.
— desire for a sexual relationship with one of the divorcees.
— pleasure about divorcee's suffering.
— feelings of superiority or surprise.
— experience of emotional loss and grief.
— conflict over allegiances.
— disillusionment about friendship.
— crisis about personal identity.
— preoccupation and curiosity about the settlement.

As a wounded ex-intimate, it may be hard to understand how some of your friends can desert you in your hour of need. But, remember that the ending of your relationship has kicked off painful or awkward feeling in your friends as well. And, some of these are often handled by their saying good-bye. You may also discover, as did my co-worker, that you no longer live in the same world as your friends from a former life. And so, as part of the "fallout of dissolution," you may leave some of your old friends behind—just as you did when you left home.

So there you have the ten most common instances of "fallout from dissolution." You may not experience them all, but it's important to remember that most are self-limiting. Usually, they come and go with a great deal of frequency during the first few days or weeks. Then, gradually by the second month, they subside.

Everyone is different and the intensity and duration for most "fallout" varies with: the length of the relationship; the ex-intimate's own feelings of insecurity before and during the relationship; and the number of roles or identities tied up in the relationship.

But, whatever the length or intensity, it is important to allow yourself to experience the feelings and grow through them. They are part of the grief process. If you totally avoid or deny them during the mourning phase, you may be stuck with them the rest of your life; thereby becoming unable to say good-bye to your old life and go on to the new.

Experiments and Exercises

Below is a list of the "fallout of dissolution". Everyone will experience some or all of these during the grief process. Place a (√) next to those which you have experienced mildly; an (x) next to those which you have experienced strongly; and a (0) by those which you have not experienced as part of good-bye.

__ self-doubt, lowering of self-esteem.
__ change or loss of specific role identities.
__ change or loss of living structure (home).
__ loss of ambition.
__ trouble making decisions.
__ bitterness.
__ self-pity.

— change in appetite/weight loss or gain.
— loss in energy level (feeling "tired").
— excessive energy level (feeling fidgity).
— short attention span.
— difficulty in concentrating.
— headaches.
— upset stomach, nausea.
— menstrual disturbance.
— diarrhea or constipation.
— lowered resistance to flu and cold "bugs".
— change in sleeping patterns.
— change in sexual patterns.
— financial pressures.
— loss of friends.
— loss of familiar surroundings (home town).

Now look at those you have marked:
   *Which ones do you feel will improve with "time"?
   *Which ones will need some effort and change on your part?
   *Are there some which you have already resolved or learned to handle effectively? How did you do that?
   *Pick one you feel would be the easiest to work through and plan how to change it.

As you read through the book, periodically return to this list and re-evaluate your progress. Change the "fallouts" you want to work on as you grow or replan your "attack" on those which need more work.

4: Alone and Free: This is the Time to Decide to Live!

Who knows which one of you really made the decision to bury your love? The one who first shouted "I want out!" or the first one who turned away in bed? In any event, love between two people doesn't usually die a quick and violent death; rather, it is eaten away slowly by the lack of kindness, respect, and consideration in a retreat further away from each other.

And, by the time it's over (whether it's a matter of thirty years or just a few short months), you may be sharing very few of your thoughts and feelings with each other or yourself. So when you finally walk out or he asks you to leave, it may not feel *real* but rather like the scenes that you're viewing (the packing and moving out) are happening to someone else. Many people describe this phenomenon as a sensation of being an actor in a movie: playing a part but not feeling the words.

This shock effect is a self-preservation technique your body uses to help you through the exit scenes, so that you can function when underneath it all you may feel like folding. It lasts

50

anywhere from a few hours to a week, depending on how much time you need to go through the mechanics of physically separating and relocating yourself. And, when you have done all that, then it may hit like a ton of bricks that you are ALONE.

What follows after that is fairly predictable (with slight variations) but still very agonizing at times.

Couples who end a relationship are individuals who want more from a mate than just living together. But when the first impact of good-bye hits you and living alone becomes your reality, it is easy to forget what you wanted, especially during those first few days or weeks. Remember, now that you're up to your neck in alligators, that your original goal was to clean the swamp.

And while you'll feel everything from "Yippee I'm Free" to "Golly I'm Scared," this is the time to decide to live!

INITIAL REACTION OFTEN RELIEF.

There isn't just sadness in saying good-bye to an old love affair. There's freedom from fighting and fencing with someone and relief from feeling "on guard", especially if the relationship has been a particularly stressful one.

It's common to hear the spouse of an alcoholic or an abusive mate talk about his or her sense of relief when the chains have finally been cut. A patient of mine who had been married to an alcoholic for fifteen years speaks of her freedom from worry and anger when she finally left her husband.

> "I'd forgotten what it was like to take a deep breath and relax. I was always so tense—never knowing when Jake would lose his next job, or come home soused. Anything was reason for him to get drunk—he celebrated good times with scotch and drowned the bad times with beer. I never knew whether to comfort like a mother or nag like a fish wife. I think I did both. Thank God, I'm out of that!"

The sense of relief is a natural part of any ending even when the relationship hasn't been "all bad" or self-destructive. The decision has finally been made. And, the internal battles of "Should I go or should I stay?" are ended.

As Geri confided:

"After a week of mechanically going through the routine of moving, the first thing I felt was relief. A kind of peace within. And a freedom. My ball and chain had been cut and I was free to do what I wanted—when I wanted. I felt like dancing! There was no one to nag at my every mood or action anymore. The fighting had stopped and the war inside me seemed settled. It was nice not to struggle with me—or with Steve."

Geri and Steve's love had died a gradual and agonizing death. The first year was beautiful, like love from a story book. But then it began to sour. And at the end of five years, there was no longer magic between them—just a cold war. Both had careers (she's a nurse and he's an insurance agent) and often the stresses at work were taken out on each other at home. Work all day, be pleasant to strangers, come home at night and labor or just die from exhaustion. Spend the weekends on the house or recouping from the week. They began to lose sight of their love and blame each other for their internal unhappiness. Steve yelled at Geri, she turned away in bed. He accused her of coldness, she stiffened even more. So, before the age of thirty, both Steve and Geri had decided to part. No wonder they felt relieved when the marriage was over. A war, even a cold one, is draining.

There is little reason to give you any advice through this stage. It's a phase to enjoy and in time you will be able to happily develop an awareness that you are free. Free to make your own choices. All things (within reality, of course) are up to you. If you want to eat artichoke hearts for breakfast, lunch and dinner—do it. Arrange all the furniture in the center of the room if you'd like. Cover your home with flowers. Watch T.V. or try your hand at painting. You can have your home as neat or as sloppy as you want. Nothing can hold you down—enjoy this relief and worry only about yourself. Feel free to make your own mistakes and your own successes. And you will know that you're a separate person with the right to live as you see fit—not as someone else would like you to do.

SECOND PHASE: DEPRESSION AND OVERWHELMED WITH LOSS.

And just about the time you've settled in to feeling good, patting yourself on the back for saying good-bye, or telling yourself you don't feel as bad as you thought you would, it suddenly hits. My God, I'm alone!

The house is empty and so am I. You can hear your heart beating and feel the ache. Disconnected and hollow are the words most often used to describe the depression in this second phase. The sadness of not belonging or feeling obligated to someone close can lie heavy in your body. Moving is a chore and lying still impossible. And the more you've invested in your old life, the larger the loss and the greater the pain.

For this is the time that the impact of loss will hit you the hardest. What you thought of as your world will seem gone. And in its place will be the emptiness you feel so keenly now.

As Geri related:

"During those first few days, I cried myself to sleep, when I slept at all. Thank God I had a job to go to. I woke up tired, dragged to work, often looking like death warmed over. By the end of the day, I was ready to go home and drop. I was miserable with people or by myself.

"I couldn't concentrate on anything. My mind kept flashing on Steve. I so desperately wanted him back, but knew he was gone. I felt trapped. Everywhere I looked there was nothing. I'd lost all my friends and happiness. What I had left meant nothing. If only I could go back—back to the

beginning and start over again, or make it up to him somehow. But I didn't have the energy to do anything—I just
hurt."

Almost nothing you do will relieve the pain you feel so intensely the first few days or weeks. At least, not for very long.
It's like a fever that has to run its course in order to break. You
will need to feel some of the pain in order to let it go.

Geri's statement that she's lost everything and is helpless to
regain it is a natural evaluation for an ex-intimate to make in this
second phase. For that is how it seems: your old love is gone,
mutual friends seem to avoid you and the image of yourself as
part of a pair is erased. The sadness and loss may pierce so deeply
that you feel like dying. All that seems left is your loneliness
and pain.

> *Please briefly state your problem*: "Going through a
> divorce, I'm depressed and feel like killing myself. I can't
> find a reason to live. I need help."

Although the words vary on the admissions forms at the
mental health clinic where I work, the theme remains the same.
Someone's going through an ending and is immobilized by
depression and loss. The only way out he/she can see is to die.
The most intense part of this depression usually lasts no more
than a few days or weeks at the longest. After that, there may
be periodic feelings of severe depression and loss but usually
the natural survival instincts in your own soul will keep you
from ever feeling so desperate again.

TENDENCY TO DECIDE TO GIVE UP: WITHDRAW/ISOLATE SELF.

Part of the healing process, ironically, involves withdrawing
from people, isolating yourself for awhile and, in general, giving
up on life. It shouldn't last very long and for many people it is

just a matter of several hours or an occasional couple of days. But this is the time to lick your wounds after you've been hurt, examine your needs, goals and wants and find a reason to go back out in the world again.

"I can't say how long it lasted or how often it came back. All I know is that during the first three months of my divorce, there were times when my only contact with people was when I was at work. Otherwise, I stayed in my apartment and did nothing. Just laid around and listened to music. I remember coming to the conclusion that I'd done everything I'd ever wanted to do and that anything now would just be a repeat. I could get over Steve, probably. And no doubt find someone else to love—but then what? I examined my life and took note of all my successes and failures. My parents wanted me to be a nurse and so did I. Well, I'd done that and am very good at it. I've traveled around the country and seen almost everything I wanted to. I have all the material possessions I want. I've had a lot of good friends in my life—many of them are lost or forgotten now. But I could do everything all over again, if I wanted. So what's the reason to keep trying?

"Even the thought of giving up didn't bother me. I remember thinking that it was odd for me—such a goal directed person—to quit trying. But that's what I did."

The process that Geri talks about is normal for many ex-intimates. If you've been hurt deeply by the loss of your mate and have decided that you don't want to keep going through your life making the same mistakes and living the same hang-ups, you need to take the time to stop. And, maybe even give up on living for awhile. At least the part of living that has you out in the world interacting with new people again.

Like anything, of course, you can go too far on giving up and isolating yourself. But, within moderation, it is a very healthy process.

Geri ended up finding for herself some reasons to live.

"I discovered first of all that I'm very goal directed and that actually part of the reason for my unhappiness with Steve was that we really weren't going anywhere. Just working to survive. I found that most of my goals had been handed to me by someone else—my parents, the nursing instructors, or Steve. What kept me feeling so lost during the divorce and also contributed to my unhappiness in our marriage was other people handing me expectations to meet. And my trying to meet them—while really resenting them. Now I have no one to rebel against, or feel obligated to please. And, I'm finding it very healthy for me. I'm actually becoming a much less uptight person because of it. Now my reasons for living are much more simple: to continue being a separate person and enjoying others for their own specialness. It's hard to describe this feeling I have. It's like I don't have to play games with people anymore to get their approval. I make my own goals and please myself."

Without the time of isolation and withdrawal from life, it is difficult for an ex-intimate to reach such a deep understanding of himself and to find, just as Geri did, his own personal reasons for living.

Such reflection can give you emotional strength, so do not be afraid of isolation periodically or of questioning your goals —but, don't overdo it and remain stuck there.

TENDENCY TO LIVE IN THE PAST.

"It seemed to me that I became obsessed by the thought of Steve and my memories of him—especially at the beginning. Suddenly I loved him more than ever and thought about what we used to do together, where we went, what fun we had. Every tune on the radio reminded me of the past and all that I'd lost. I'd wake up in the middle of the night, dreaming about yesterday. It was like I couldn't keep my thoughts on today or tomorrow. Like some unseen force kept pulling me back."

This sensation of being pulled back to the memories of yesterday almost against your will is consistently brought up by ex-intimates.

> "Last Christmas we went skiing, that was a lot of fun. I remember——."

> "I still keep a bottle of scotch around, Brad loves it."

> "Whenever I date a new girl, I remember what it was like with Marge."

> "I haven't changed anything in the house since George left."

> "I remember the night we first heard that."

> "Sometimes I go through our old photo albums and just reminisce."

> "I still have our old house key on my chain."

> "If I'm not busy my mind wanders back."

> "I've even caught myself talking to Carol when I'm alone."

> "I keep his picture in my wallet."

The healthy side of this natural phenomenon is that it protects you. It gives you a chance to go through the mourning process and piece by piece say good-bye to the past.

> "I found I did not dwell very long or often on any one situation or event. It was like my mind was going through a sorting process—'the time we repainted the living room—forget it Geri, you've already said good-bye to that.' Some of the memories were harder to bury than others. A few I've still kept. But, it's nice to know I have control over that now—at first I didn't feel like I did."

Pleasant memories may also act as a reminder that you can have a loving relationship. Especially if your present situation casts some doubt.

"I had a fight with my new boyfriend the other night and I almost immediately began doubting whether I even had the ability to love. Then I remembered my relationship with Steve and felt better. In a strange way, it gave me comfort and strength to know from the past that I am capable of loving."

Unpleasant memories can be used to help an ex-intimate feel better about saying good-bye. Like the divorcee whose ex-husband is an alcoholic. "Anytime I get lonely or scared I remember how much worse it could be with Jake."

And, both pleasant and unpleasant memories are brought up by ex-intimates as a protective device against falling in love again too soon—before all the wounds have healed. This is a natural defense and a part of the healing process every ex-intimate needs.

"Sometimes I wonder if I need the memory of Steve and our past to keep my heart from falling for someone my head knows isn't right."

If you find yourself asking a similar question, the answer is probably "yes". You'll need time to get over an old love affair and learn from the mistakes that were made. And, pulling in the past to make space in the present will give you that time.

But be careful you don't take too much time dwelling in your past. Even though a little bit of it can be healthy—too much daydreaming can be dangerous. Filling up your present with past memories can be like filling a stove full of smoke rather than fire. It's cloudy and full, but the room is still empty and cold. Reminiscing should gradually be replaced by new experiences from your present.

HOW TO "PICK YOURSELF UP."

Like most other ex-intimates, somewhere along the grieving process you'll fall flat on your face. Maybe more than once. You'll trip over discouragement and disappointment or slip

on hurt feelings and whamo! You're down on your knees or
flat on your back again. And when that happens, especially the
first time, you'll have to make a decision not to give up on living.
It may take some time for you to come to that choice—an hour
or a month. It doesn't always come easily. And, sometimes you
don't even notice at first that you've given up. But, sooner or
later it will hit you and the decision will come. So, whether you
pull on the strings of your hopes for the future or push yourself up with the anger from falling, look inside your world for
a reason not to give up.

As one woman related:

> "There was a point in time when I knew that I'd given up
> on living. I mechanically worked, came home to my dog
> and avoided any other contact with feelings or life. After
> several days of this hollow existence, it hit me one night
> while I was walking that the oak tree near my apartment was
> gigantic. I hadn't noticed it in a long time and thought that
> was strange because I've always loved nature. It's hard to
> describe, but suddenly I knew how small and insignificant
> the loss of one person really was in my life. He was as big as
> I wanted to make him—and so was that tree. There is so
> much more to living than being a robot, and without even
> noticing I had gypped myself out of several days in my life."

Whatever you discover in the world that's worth living for,
begin gathering your strength. Take the time to brush yourself
off, renew some faith in yourself, reaffirm your goals, and learn
from the fall before you start all over again.

HOW TO "BRUSH YOURSELF OFF."

As an ex-intimate, you will be up and down emotionally like
a yo-yo through the first few days or weeks after you've said
good-bye. The process gets easier and you will find that the
yo-yo effect will level off after a while, but still it's important
to take some time after you've picked yourself up from one of

your falls to look at what happened, clear out the cobwebs and replan your goals.

The first part of brushing yourself off is to look at what parts of you were injured by the fall:

1. What got damaged: my pride? self-confidence?

2. Do I look worse physically than before?

3. Was I betrayed by a friend—or slapped by a stranger?

4. Which wounds will take time to heal?

5. What will help me to feel better?

After you've answered the above questions, begin to look at what caused you to fall. Sometimes, especially in the beginning phases of the grief process, ex-intimates are extremely vulnerable and overly sensitive to any scene or remark that may even feel slightly negative. If an old friend tells you he's busy or someone doesn't answer her phone, it's possible to overreact and decide you're alone in the world and no one cares. Take a look at your self-image and extreme sensitivity and do some reality testing in this area. Accept the fact that the whole world does not center around you (even if you feel like the whole world has crumbled in on you) and that your friends or strangers you meet sometimes react because of their own needs. A friend can really be busy but still care. The lady at the supermarket doesn't crowd in front of you because you're unimportant; she does it because she's in a hurry—and rude.

So look through the past twenty-four hours' events and see what caused you to trip. Then, try to understand it, putting your own wounded pride and lack of self-confidence in perspective.

By now you should know what areas of you have been injured and what caused you to fall. The next thing you can check is whether there is a way to avoid tripping over the same kind of problem again or diminishing the depth of your fall the next time you slip.

"I was feeling lonely, so I called my old girlfriend—but

she was busy. Then I felt even lonelier and stupid besides.
Next time I'm lonely, I won't call her—I'll call someone
else that I'm pretty sure will be available, maybe I'll think
of three or four people before I start calling."

"I was passed over for a promotion at work and when I talked
to my boss, he said I didn't deserve it, anyway. I think he was
right. I need to get more involved in business—I've been
letting work slide."

Once you've discovered what started your fall, in the "brushing yourself off" process you may develop new goals and direc-
tions for living. Like meeting new friends so that you have more
than one person to call for a Saturday night date, or a Wednesday
card game. Or going back to school to sharpen up your employment skills. Or learning to be a little less sensitive and not overreacting to every little comment you hear.

HOW TO START LIVING AGAIN.

After you've taken a deep breath, look around at the parts of
the world you want to enjoy again, maybe for the first time. Like
taking a big bite out of a fresh crisp red apple and letting the
juice run down your chin. Or allowing the warmth in a small
child's eyes to touch you. It's rediscovering that the world is a
pretty nice place after all, and glowing over your decision to
participate in its life again.

Knowing that your attitude and mood affect your perception
of everything, look at the parts of your world you will need to
repair or replace, like your own self-esteem or self-confidence.
In spite of all the rationalizations and reality testing in the world,
it's hard to leave an intimate relationship without suffering a
number of blows to your pride.

Building that confidence back up again—or maybe for the
first time in your life—is a gradual process, but one that is worth
the time and effort it takes. Now begin looking at what you have
left in your world with a healthier attitude. You may have
already spent several hours bemoaning your fate and staring

blankly at what you don't have anymore. But this time, look at it differently. Look at what you have left that you want to keep: your health, some of your old friends, children and family perhaps, a house or material goods, an occupation, fun hobbies and special talents. At first it may be hard to find very much. Most of us have the habit of taking for granted the positives like good health, a sense of humor, friends that we love, etc.. But now it is important to look at all of your assets, so practice that skill.

Once your list has been made with the things that you'll keep, head up a column of "New Goals". Some will be short range and some will take time, but write them all down. On the first draft of your list, let your imagination go wild.

For example:

New Goals:

1. Join a belly dancing class.
2. Start a boarding home for single millionaires.
3. Write favorite movie star and tell him/her you're available.
4.
5.
6.
7.

MAKE SURE YOU INCLUDE:

8. Finding new love interests.
9. Building up employment skills.
10. Creating new friendships.
11. Developing dormant and obvious talents.

If you have trouble coming up with ideas, look through magazines and books or check with some friends. When your list is complete, go back through the ideas and decide how long each project will take, plus the steps inbetween to accomplish your goal. If you decide, for example, that you would like to become a real estate salesman, check out the professional requirements and skills needed to do that, including availability of training and employment in your area.

Finally, it's time to decide which goals you will choose. Be careful not to set your ambitions so high that you fail. Put yourself in situations where you'll meet someone. But, on the other hand, never underestimate yourself or the heights you can reach.

THE OTHER SIDE OF SCARY IS EXCITEMENT!

As you went through your list of "New Goals", you may have noticed the ones that were scary were also exciting. The idea of quitting a safe secure job to start a small business of your own can be exciting, but still very frightening. The two feelings are closely connected. Sometimes the fear is of failure or embarrassment: "I'd like to do that but what if I fail?" And, sometimes, the fear comes from stepping out of a normal secure routine, like moving away from your home.

The degrees of excitement vary with the amount of risk and change in routine that's involved. A teenager who moves away from his parents' house into an apartment down the street, but comes home for meals, will be less excited about his freedom than the boy who moves completely on his own to a new town. The one that stays near home is in reality less on his own two feet and taking fewer risks than the one who is away from his family completely.

Part of the good-bye process is leaving security and routine and saying hello to change and unknown. So it is natural for anyone in a transitional phase, including an ex-intimate, to feel afraid and excited, at times simultaneously.

As Geri related:

> "When I finally decided to leave Steve, I began thinking about all the different things I could do—go back to college, save some money and go traveling. There were all kinds of ideas. But during the first few months, I traded actually doing some of those things for being afraid to try anything

new. But when I finally did begin taking some classes and short weekend trips to new places by myself, I not only enjoyed myself, but began feeling excited again."

The process is slow and at first, if you're feeling numb or depressed, doing something new like meeting new friends, moving into a new neighborhood, or changing back to single status again may just scare you or leave you depressed. But after a while you will begin feeling the excitement that creeps in along with the fears.

When an ex-intimate doesn't allow himself to feel the excitement of change, it may mean he's overloaded with feelings of failure and insecurity. Some of these feelings are a natural fall-out from saying good-bye to an old love and a life style of being part of a pair. Others may come from a basic sense of insecurity that was there before or during the "marriage" as well.

Many of these fears will lessen with time and with doing some things to help you feel a little more secure and less disconnected: like establishing your own new home, gaining support from friends and building up your deflated ego. And as you begin feeling a little less shaky about being single again, you will find, just as Geri did, that there will be times when you actually enjoy and are even excited about your new single status.

There's no doubt about it, the journey from leaving an ex-love and being part of a pair to enjoying single status and starting anew can be a painful and agonizing trip. And, in order to successfully reach your destination, you will need to bury the parts of your identity which have died. There is sadness in saying good-bye to these familiar pieces of your old existence, but to become a growing individual, you must let go of some of the old dead life styles and develop new, more functional ones for today and tomorrow.

Experiments and Exercises.

This exercise will help you "get in touch with" and nurture your sense of relief over good-bye. Choose a time when you will not be interrupted or distracted by noise. Wear something comfortable and choose a comfortable body position.

*Go back through your memory of the last few days as if you were a movie camera and re-experience a time when you felt an inner calmness or sense of relief. Remember the scene: what had just happened—where you were—who was present. Try to re-experience the relief you felt then. Some people find it helpful to verbally state and repeat: "I'm relieved that it's over" until they finally feel the words in their bodies. Deep breathing exercises often help you learn to flow with your relief—practice taking slow, rhythmic, deep breaths.

During the next two days notice those times when you feel relieved and allow yourself to flow with that feeling.

Set aside some time each day (30 minutes or so) for the next month to enjoy your relief and calmness. As you continue practicing, you will find it easier to develop awareness of this feeling in you and will be able to recall it upon your command.

Emptiness can be controlled as easily as your sense of relief, but requires experiencing your loss. Instead of running from sadness, pick a time when you decide that you feel "good" enough to allow yourself to feel your loss. Then, close your eyes and give yourself permission to feel your emptiness. (Sometimes repeating "I feel empty inside" helps your awareness). Go slowly and experience your pain in small doses. Cry when you feel like crying. If you get scared, pull yourself out. Some people find it helpful to tell themselves: "It's going to be okay _____, you're just feeling your hurt right now." As you repeat this phrase—or something similar—you will begin closing off your awareness of the emptiness in you.

After this exercise, take some time to reflect and ask:

*What did I learn from this about my *own* control over feeling empty?

*What can I do to fill up some of my emptiness? Would calling a friend help? How about developing some new goals? Taking the responsibility to begin loving someone new?

In this chapter we talked about some of the energy guzzling techniques ex-intimates use. Go through this list and (✓) those you currently use.

__ living in the past.

__ bemoaning your fate.

__ cutting down your self-esteem.

__ wishing it hadn't happened and hoping it'll change.

__ waiting by the telephone for ex-love to call.

__ checking up on ex-mate.

__ trying to get friends to "take sides".

__ pumping friends for information about ex-mate.

__ staying too busy to allow self-awareness.

__ skipping meals.

__ not getting enough sleep.

__ frantically searching for a new love.

Go back through the list, and pay attention to those "energy guzzlers" you have already stopped.

Now pick one you have checked which you feel would be easiest to "give up" and make a concerted effort to stop this for a week. Then constructively evaluate your progress.

From time to time go back through this list and work on one or two of these "guzzlers" until you no longer waste your time on any of them.

Use this space to jot down examples of when you got your feelings hurt or felt disappointed *but* were successful in getting over your hurt. Note how you did it—techniques or an attitude that was successful for you. Refer to this "resource" when you feel hurt the next time.

5: How to Build Your Own Backbone

Building up your own self-confidence and ability to feel good again isn't really as difficult as you may fear. It requires some effort at first, especially if you're in the habit of cutting yourself down or finding other people to do it for you. But with some concentration and a little bit of faith on your part, you can begin rebuilding your own backbone: that part of your body that protects your heart and your feelings from too much abuse.

By the time most ex-intimates have finally said good-bye they are, at best, discouraged about their own self worth and value as a friend and lover. So, don't ,be discouraged when you feel like giving up and decide that resigning is what you'll do for awhile. Floundering is also part of saying good-bye to the past and hello to the future. But, to get beyond the floundering stage, you'll need to develop and use your own backbone.

GETTING YOURSELF IN PROPER PERSPECTIVE.

When the reality that the partnership is over finally hits you, it is not unusual to feel a loss of identity and self-esteem. Especially if the relationship was long or a trust has been broken. Ex-intimates often walk in a daze not knowing who they are and questioning every part of their being. "Who am I really?" "I hate myself—I'm awful." We have already talked about many of the reasons for this: individuals viewing themselves as part of a pair rather than as separate people; the belief that togetherness is winning and single again is losing; and the erosion of self-esteem caused by a lack of respect and kindness in the latter part of a "marriage".

To build your confidence back up, begin looking at yourself realistically rather than so judgmentally. No one can begin feeling better if he decides he is basically worthless and deserves to be left alone. So, one of the first tasks at hand in building your backbone is to look at who you really are without immediately condemning what you see.

To help you view your behavior with more understanding, add your own examples to the following list:

Judgement	*Reality*
1. I was too quiet.	1. Sometimes I don't talk.
2. I should have been more understanding.	2. I am someone who withdraws when I get scared or shout when my feelings get hurt.
3. I never do anything right.	3. Right now I'm discouraged.
4. All I do is sit and feel sorry for myself.	4. Sometimes I feel sad.
5. I demanded too much.	5.
6. I'll never love again.	6.
7.	7.
8.	8.

Now, take some time to reflect on the above. What can you learn from this? During the next 48 hours pay attention to how often you weaken your own backbone with self-criticism. Then, practice the art of self-acceptance.

Although you will no doubt spend a number of hours evaluating why the relationship ended, it is a good idea to do this when you begin feeling better about yourself. That way you can do something about changing the parts of you that may need improvement for the next intimate relationship. The automatic tendency to look at your mistakes in your old relationship when you're feeling low anyway, will only overwhelm you. Therefore, set aside changing the faults that you find for another day.

Also, when you begin looking at who you are, avoid making comparisons with others or with who you'd like to be. To decide that you'd like to be better than you are or like someone else when you're feeling crummy about yourself anyway, will only make you more dissatisfied.

So, at the beginning when your confidence and self-esteem are low, quit reinforcing the self-condemnation. Then, you'll discover the increasing strength of your courage and pride, both of which you'll need for growth during the mourning phase and to initiate change of those parts of you that you've decided could be improved.

HOW TO GIVE UP YOUR EX-LOVE'S TOTAL PERCEPTION OF YOU.

No one lives in a vacuum of course, and we gain much of our image of who we are and how we fit into the world from those around us. The closer someone is, the more important that person's opinion becomes. It begins as children when our parents tell us by their words and actions what they think. If they tell us we're worthwhile, we believe it and if they tell us we're bad and will always get in trouble, we see ourselves in that light. If a parent tells a child he can't be trusted, he begins believing that. He may even begin looking for examples in his own life of when he did something dishonest like cheating on a test for fear of failure as proof of his parents' opinion that he cannot be trusted, rather than as an example of his own need for success. Then he begins to do dishonest things deliberately as a self-fulfilling prophecy. (The act of becoming exactly what he feared that he would.) Eventually he and everyone around him is firmly convinced that basically he is dishonest and cannot be trusted.

But children are not born "good" or "bad"; they are molded into their parents' fears or views of what they'll be like. I suspect that most of us, as adults, already know how easy it is to believe our parents' perception of us and the world, and how difficult it is to make up our own minds while seeing their opinions as the results of a similar process. As a matter of fact, many people never give up their parents' ideas and marry someone just like their mother or father.

In any event, it's obvious to most of us that we human beings often believe other people's opinion of us and sometimes accept it as our own. This is just as true for ex-intimates as it is for children with parents. By the time you finally say good-bye, you may believe a number of negative things about yourself which are not necessarily true. Especially if you felt unsure of yourself before the relationship began, or the "marriage" lasted a number of years, or the relationship was self-destructive in that both of you focused on each other's fears and weaknesses. Giving up your ex-love's negative perception of you will be hard, but necessary, to build up your own self-esteem and to see yourself as you really are.

Letting go of your ex-love's image of yourself requires several steps. First of all, it is necessary for you to see him or her as a human being with frailties, not a god without faults. As long as a child gives his parents magical powers, he cannot see them or what they say about him as anything other than divine truth. This is also true for ex-intimates.

Once you have taken your ex-love out of the god category, begin looking at all of the things he or she has said about you. Include the positive along with the negative and your list may look something like this:

Good	*Bad*
1. warm, loving	1. too dependent on others to feel good.

Good	Bad
2. outgoing, makes friends easily.	2. superficial.
3. good sense of humor.	3. dishonest.
4. easy going.	4. irresponsible.
5. good looking	5. too concerned about appearance.

NOW ADD SOME OF
YOUR OWN

6.	6.
7.	7.
8.	8.
9.	9.

When your list is completed you may discover that most are value judgments rather than facts and that some of the things that were seen as "good" in one situation may also be seen as "bad" in another light. In any event, many of these images you will automatically discard as not valid because you do not believe that they are true. Keep the positive ones and build on them. The negative ones that you retain will no doubt be those which you fear are accurate. If you decide that they are parts of you which you believe to be true, own them. Then make a decision whether you can change them or not. Some will be possible to change, others you will have to learn to live with or may decide that you want to keep.

The important thing to remember in building your own backbone is that all of your ex-love's viewpoints of you (or anybody else's for that matter) cannot be totally accurate or unbiased. Someone can say certain things about you which you decide are true, but that does not mean everything he or she says is gospel or would be true if you had a different kind of partner. For example, a woman may not be a nag if the man follows through on his responsibilities. Or, a man may not be unfaithful if his partner is loving and warm.

With practice you should be able to separate your ex-love's

perception of you from your own feelings about yourself. As time progresses and you find yourself saying "she told me this was true" or "he always said I was like that," see if you can't stop yourself and look at whether the statement is really true or just your own fear, coupled with his or her opinion that it's a fact.

DEVELOPING YOUR OWN SELF-PERCEPTION.

If you have followed the advice in the first part of this chapter, that is avoiding both self-condemnation as well as total acceptance of your ex-love's judgment of you, then you are already in the process of developing your own self-image and rebuilding your backbone.

Now, self-image is a useful tool because it indicates not only how you see yourself but your feelings about what you see as well. It includes all of the different facts and roles of your existence: sex, age, nationality, religion, occupation, lover, friend, relative, plus your opinion tempered with everyone else's on how well you do with each one.

Begin to list down the different parts of you that you know and across from each how you feel about them. For example, a man might list:

Parts of me	My feelings about each
Male, Caucasian	Okay
Late forties	A little scared of getting old.
Insurance man	Okay, but sometimes I worry about the money—takes a lot of energy to make sales.
Italian, Catholic	I'm a little too traditional and old fashioned. My head's filled with a lot of "shoulds".
Physical appearance	Not bad; worry a lot about my hairline and weight—feel fat.
Divorced	It's wrong, I feel ashamed; it's against my religion.

Father: 2 sons	I should be with them now; they need a man.
Intelligence	I'd like to be smarter; wish I'd gone to college.
Fears	Afraid of failure; getting in over my head; getting hurt.
Personality	Pleasant, kind to those I love usually. Dependable; sometimes short tempered.

Use this space provided to create your own "word" self-portrait.

Parts of me	*My feelings about each*
1.	1.
2.	2.
3.	3.
4.	4.
5.	5.
6.	6.
7.	7.
8.	8.
9.	9.

As your list expands, review it for self-condemnation. One of the ideals you may have to give up is your wish to be perfect or absolutely satisfied with all parts of you and everything that you do. And what you might substitute is a compassionate self-acceptance that doesn't deteriorate into complacency but is receptive to growth and change.

In fact, you may also discover that your self-image varies from day to day. When things seem to be going well, you will feel better about yourself. When you're scared or feel rejected, it is natural to be more critical of yourself and therefore weaken your self-esteem.

In order to get a more accurate picture of who you are and how you really feel about yourself, it's a good idea to make up two lists creating your own "word" self-portraits. Fill out one when you're feeling good and the other when you're sad. In this way, you will be able to see how your own perception of yourself varies with your mood and outside situations.

When you fill out the above lists make sure you include *all* of the different factors that make you a unique individual. Many ex-intimates discover that they have gotten so wrapped up in their role as an ex-lover or a divorcee that they have forgotten all the other parts of them.

CHECK OUT FEEDBACK FROM ALL FRIENDS AND ACQUAINTANCES.

Once you have a fairly clear picture of how you see yourself and feel reasonably comfortable with your image, look around you and begin noticing how others perceive you. How do people usually react to you? Of course there are exceptions, but, in general, do they treat you with respect or are you usually stepped on by others? Do people ask you for your opinion or are you usually given someone else's?

Now, get a little more specific and list the names of your co-workers, friends and family members and jot down how you think they treat you. Use the following format:

Name	*How he/she treats me*
1.	1.
2.	2.
3.	3.
4.	4.
5.	5.
6.	6.

Now take some time to reflect on the above. What can you learn from this? Do they treat others this way or only you? Make sure when you look at this information that you look at it with a fair amount of objectivity. Don't wait until you're feeling crummy to see if everyone else sees you that way too.

Ask those you are close to how they see you in specific instances, i.e.: "Do you see me as quiet or outgoing?"; "Can you tell that I'm a warm and caring person?"; "I have the feeling I'm over my head in this project, what's your opinion?" Use a little common sense and don't ask someone you're having a quarrel with or when a person is obviously involved in his or her own worries or fears. At first your friends may be caught off guard by your questions, but explain you are gathering information for your own interest to see how others view you. Tell them you're serious and you really do want to learn something about yourself and you think they can help you.

Although asking someone specifically how they view certain parts of you may be scary, the reality is we unconsciously make decisions about how people see us without finding out for sure how they feel. We assume a number of things about people's judgement of ourselves, and much of that is inaccurate. Usually we assume a much more critical stance than our friends would take. And, in building your own backbone, it is important to find out as objectively as possible how other people see you.

MATCHING INNER AND OTHER DIRECTED PERCEPTIONS.

After you've gained some information about how others see you either by directly asking them or through your own assumptions, study it. Choose a time when you think you can look at the comments somewhat objectively.

The first thing you will find is that each person views you in a slightly different light. This is true because no two people see anything in exactly the same way, and, groups of individuals will see you in different roles. For example, an elementary school teacher will be viewed in a different role by his students than he will by his colleagues, family or members of his bowling team. While his ten year old students may see him as a formidable figure, his mother may still view him as her little boy. In spite of these factors, you will find a consensus of opinion on how you generally come across in each role. Most students, for instance, will see their fifth grade teacher in a certain way.

The next step in building your backbone is to match your own ideas of how you come across with other peoples' general viewpoints. The teacher, for example, might list the following:

How I See Myself As:	*How Others See Me:*
A teacher: Pretty good; sometimes boring.	*My students*: Good; makes learning fun.
A colleague: Okay, but too quiet.	*My colleagues*: Bright, respected, dependable.
A son: Good, but not loving enough.	*My friends*: Fun to be with, trust him.
A bowler: Average.	*My bowling team*: Good bowler, fun, a leader.

Notice that the teacher sees himself much more negatively than others do, even when his overall perception is favorable. With the exception of his image as a friend, in every other role he has focused more on his frailties than others have. This is a common human characteristic—to pay more attention to the parts of us that still aren't exactly the way we want them.

Following the above example, use this space to list and compare your self-perception with the opinions of others.

How I see myself as:	*How others see me:*
1.	1.
2.	2.
3.	3.
4.	4.
5.	5.

How I see myself as: *How others see me:*

6.   6.

7.   7.

Now take some time to reflect. What can you learn from this?

The purpose of matching other peoples' viewpoints with your own is to help you see a broader, more objective picture of yourself. In doing this, you will strengthen your self-esteem and therefore, your backbone.

HOW TO DEVELOP A PRIORITY LIST.

In looking over your image and others' of you, you may come up with areas that you feel need to be improved. It is important not to be overwhelmed with all the things you feel you should change. Because of the common tendency to follow patterns of looking at everything at once, being too critical and then getting overwhelmed, I suggest that you develop a priority list. A list of areas you feel could be improved—those things about yourself that you would like to change. For example, you might jot down: broadening your sense of humor, strengthening your ability to follow through on tasks you usually give up on, or learning to spend time alone creatively. Whatever you find that you would like to improve or change to feel happier and better about yourself, list here:

Things I could change

1.
2.
3.
4.
5.

Choose one item from the above list and begin finding ways you can change it. Let's say, for example, that the first thing you decide to change is your tendency to take things too seriously. Begin reflecting on all the ways in your daily living that small, really unimportant scenes in your life become major catastrophes. The toast gets burned, someone darts into your parking space, you're ten minutes late for an appointment, someone doesn't call and ask you out for dinner and you hoped he would. Your response is really your own choice: you can make these very significant events in your day, or see them as unimportant. Why not try placing them in the realm of events which are disappointing but not catastrophic? Then, practice responding to them in that manner. Learn how to scrape off black toast and cover it with jelly. Learn how to put your car in reverse out of simple expedience rather than explosive frustration, and go look for another parking space. Practice the art of apologizing when you can't make an appointment on time. Find ways to spend your free time creatively by yourself without depending upon someone else's beckoning.

It will take a lot of time and effort to change a personality trait such as taking things too seriously. And you will no doubt find, especially in the first few tries, that it's more automatic to revert to your old practice than to strengthen your new skill. Expect a certain amount of failure. If in just one out of ten attempts you are able to change your habit of taking scenes too seriously, that is an improvement.

Do things on a day by day basis and one at a time. That way you will be more effective, because the greater the number of things you try to change at once the less you will accomplish. And give yourself credit for each success—no matter how minor it might appear to be—because you are attempting one of the most difficult, and yet most rewarding, tasks: self-determined growth.

HOW TO BUILD ON STRENGTHS.

So far in this chapter we've spent a great deal of time talking about weaknesses and very little space on the parts of you that you already like. The first step in building on your strengths is to recognize that they exist. Use the space provided to jot down the things you enjoy about yourself: the physical parts of you that are attractive, your health if it's good, the skills and talents you have that you're proud of and all the neat qualities about you that help make you special. Write them all down— this is no time to be modest or shy, you're the only one that will see the list and it should be as complete as possible to be useful.

Things I like about me:

1.
2.
3.
4.
5.
6.
7.
8.
9.
10.

Once your list is complete, go through it and pat yourself on the back for each item. I know that may sound silly, but don't forget that you compliment others for their positive qualities. (If you don't, they feel unappreciated.) So, don't neglect yourself with praise. Go ahead and give yourself some applause. And do that each time you notice in your daily living that you've done something well again.

When you've discovered your strengths, begin to use them more often. Wear the clothes you look best in. If you're a good cook, bake something for a friend or treat yourself to a gourmet meal. If you like the part of you that helps people, volunteer or get a job helping out at a hospital, children's home or convalescent facility. If you appreciate nature, spend extra time at the park, down by the river or out in the country. If you enjoy a sense of humor, read, write or tell comical stories.

Learn to put yourself in situations where you know you will do well. Nothing builds up your confidence more quickly than doing something well and giving yourself a pat on the back for your own success.

HOW TO CORRAL AND TAME FRAILTIES.

Learning to corral and tame your frailties involves five major steps: recognizing what they are, putting them in proper perspective, understanding and forgiving yourself, changing the frailties that you can and learning to live with the rest.

For our purposes I will define a frailty as a piece of behavior that gets you in trouble with yourself or other people. The parts of you that are most often criticized by yourself or others. Included as frailties are: drinking excessively, overeating, a quick temper, hiding from people, lying, failing to follow through on responsibilities, putting off decisions, getting others to make them for you, or, at the other extreme, expecting too much from yourself or being too critical. Almost any behavior or trait that you have which you see as a "fault" can be included in this category.

So, the first step is to recognize which ones you have. You will find some of these on your priority list of things you would like to improve. To show step by step how you might conquer a frailty, let us say that one of your faults is a quick temper.

After you've identified that this is a problem for you, the first thing you need to do is look at how often you lose your temper and what happens when you do. Do you fly off the handle everytime someone says something that you don't like or anytime you don't get your way? Or are there times when you feel like exploding, but control it? Look back over the last week and see how many times you actually exploded versus the times you did not. This will give you an idea of just how big and uncontrollable the problem is for you. Now look at what you do when you lose your temper. Do you physically strike out or explode verbally? How often do you stomp away from a fight? There are a number of ways that people lose their tempers and it is important for you to understand specifically what you do when you've lost yours and whether that varies. Once you have answered these questions, you will have not only an understanding of the specific problem, but will no doubt recognize that you do not, in fact, have an uncontrollable temper nor is it your total personality. This is an important realization because it sheds some reality on the fear you may have that your temper always controls you and that there is nothing you can do about any part of it.

The third step in taming a frailty is to understand and forgive yourself for owning this "fault". Developing an understanding requires finding out why you do what you do. In the case of a quick temper, look back over each incident during the last week and try to figure out what you were fighting for. You may discover that you were fighting for someone to recognize your opinion as valid, or see you as someone to respect and not use or put down. If this is the case it should be easy to forgive yourself. All of us want to feel that we're valuable, and damning yourself for having human needs will not make them go away. You will find that most faults, when you understand why you use them, are easy to forgive because they are usually defense mechanisims we use to protect ourselves from pain.

Once you have developed an understanding and forgiveness for the frailties you own, the next step is to see in what ways you can change them. Even though a quick temper, for example, may be understandable, it can get you in more trouble than it's worth. In fact, some of your frailties may actually compound the problem and make it worse. So that the more often you fly off the handle, for example, the more frequently you are given a lack of respect by others. Therefore, recognize the value in changing a piece of behavior that gets you in trouble, like learning to control your temper. If you don't think it's worth your effort to change it—you won't.

Learning to change a frailty is a matter of finding out what value the behavior has for you and then finding alternative ways of attaining the same goal. If, for example, you found yourself shouting at your boss last Wednesday because he questioned a decision you made, you may want to look at what you can do to feel better about yourself as an employee. There are other ways to gain respect from your boss besides shouting at him for questioning you. Or maybe you threw down a ceramic pot you were making because it didn't turn out the way you wanted. Perhaps a better idea would be to learn to walk away from tasks that are frustrating until you can calm down or figure out exactly how to do it. Or, if the goal in ceramics is to create something which thereby helps you feel worthwhile, it's a good idea to find something that's more suited to your talents. The point is that once you find what the goals in your behavior are, it is possible to gain the same goals by altering your behavior.

There will be times when, no matter how hard you try, you will continue to own the same frailties. Some of them you will be able to tame but not get rid of entirely. You will have to learn to live with these. In the case of a quick temper, you learn to live with this by knowing that you have one and trying as much as possible to keep yourself out of situations where you'll lose control of it.

Try these suggestions faithfully for a week or two on one of your frailties. You will begin to notice that you have the ability and power to change or improve almost any "fault" you own.

HOW TO PROTECT YOUR VULNERABLE SPOTS.

Learning to protect your vulnerable spots is a worthwhile skill for anyone and especially for ex-intimates who may feel extremely fragile at times. Vulnerable spots are the wounds in your self-esteem, pride or identity which have been reopened or were created by the ending of an intimate relationship.

The first step in protecting your vulnerable spots is to recognize that there are certain scenes which will cause additional pain to your pride—at least until the wounds are healed. Seeing your ex-love with someone new, hearing your children call someone else "Mommy" or "Daddy", listening to your old love songs, seeing the old house that used to be yours, going back to your favorite places alone or, oddly enough, trying to love someone new too quickly.

The best way to protect yourself from these additional blows to your pride is to avoid as many of them as you can. Do not purposely place yourself in any of these scenes before the wounds begin to heal. Those that you cannot avoid, face with an understanding friend or relative, if that's possible. Take someone with you for moral support when you have to go back to your old house and pick up your furniture. Don't go alone to your favorite old haunts unless you have decided for yourself that you want to feel extra pain again.

Finally, there will be times when you can neither avoid a scene or take someone with you to cushion the impact. When those times occur, prepare yourself by doing something that helps you feel worthwhile. Make sure that you at least feel like you look good for the scene. And, after it's over, go visit a friend or treat yourself to a special favor. For example, plan beforehand what you will do after you see your in-laws for the first time. That way you can go automatically from the painful scene to a pleasurable one.

Gradually, as the wounds begin to heal, you will no longer need to protect them from additional blows. As time goes by and your backbone strengthens, you will discover that less and less from your past causes pain in your present.

HOW TO DEVELOP YOUR DORMANT TALENTS.

A hobby, even if it's training and walking your dog, gives you a chance to focus your energy and attention outside of yourself. Additionally, it can act as a diversion when you're feeling down, a vehicle for the expression of pent-up feelings and frustrations and be productive or creative—thus, giving you an ego-building end product.

So, take the time to develop a hobby or go back to an old one. If you are already aware of some of your hidden or slightly apparent talents, begin to develop them. Dust off the old paint brushes, crochet hooks or wood carving tools and get busy making something again. If you've never had a hobby before, go to an arts and crafts store for ideas or leaf through the leisure time magazines at the supermarket. Many department stores, local "Y's", adult education centers, craft centers, local colleges and high schools offer classes in leisure time fun activities.

Initially you may be hesitant to try something new, figuring that you don't have the time or assuming that either you probably won't do well or you'll get bored. But as you begin actually doing something new (whether it's making grandfather clocks, casting jewelry or tinkering on your car), you'll discover that you are enjoying it and will begin taking pride in those dormant talents you didn't even know existed.

HOW TO USE ANGER TO GET YOU MOVING.

In spite of the fears you may have about anger or maybe losing your temper, anger (when properly used) can be a very helpful energy source. It is the energy your pride calls on to help you stand up for yourself and meet new challenges. It is the strength in your backbone that keeps you straight when you would otherwise collapse. It is, in fact, such a valuable source of power for helping us feel better and attaining new goals that all of Chapter 12 is devoted to it. For the purposes of this chapter, however let's look at some ways you can recognize and use your anger to help your strengthened backbone walk away from people who stomp on your feelings or try to poke holes in your self-esteem.

By now you have no doubt discovered that you really are neither as bad or as helpless to change your sadness as you sometimes fear, and in fact, have a great deal of power even over the parts of you that aren't exactly the way you want them yet. With that knowledge, you may begin feeling a surge of energy, a flash in your gut, or a voice in your head that periodically tells you it's time to quit feeling bad and start living again. Even *you* are getting tired of cutting yourself down or letting other people do it for you. Gradually this feeling will come back again, even louder and stronger, until you finally decide on a conscious level to do something about it. Each time you do something to build up your self-esteem, it will grow stronger until finally your need to punish yourself for losing your ex-love or for being alone in the world will be defeated by your self-confidence and desire to feel better.

All of this takes time. Your feelings will come and go. One hour you may be deep in self-pity, wallowing in sorrow and loneliness, and the next you may briefly decide that you need to get out of your house and go to the park or visit a friend. Use your energy to do that. Don't just sit there until the idea is buried with self-doubt again.

Every time you stop demoralizing yourself, shake off a nagging self-doubt, or walk away from someone who's cutting you down, your anger has been the energy that helps you. It acts as a defense mechanism to protect your self-confidence from unfair blows. The voice in your head that tells you to try something new or fix yourself up will need your anger to get you moving. Ambition, some say, is merely the direction that anger takes in the spirit of revenge.

Experiments and Exercises

Below is a list of ways people build their self-esteem. Check (√) those you are currently aware of using and put an (x) beside those you decide to try in addition.

__ take care of my health.
__ keep physically active.
__ keep myself well groomed and physically attractive.
__ wear clothing I feel good in.
__ compliment myself when I do something well.
__ treat myself as I would my best friend.
__ take pride in my traits and strengths I enjoy.
__ stand up for my "rights".
__ understand and accept myself for making mistakes.
__ refuse to condemn myself for frailties.
__ do one thing a day that makes me feel good about me.
__ entertain friends at my house occasionally.

__ help other people.
__ allow others to help me.
__ develop my talents.
__ increase my job skills.
__ develop my interest in the community.
__ enjoy a hobby.
__ use my anger as motivation and ambition.

Now look at those you have marked:

   *What can you learn from this?

   *Pick one or two items to begin practicing this week.

As you read through the book, periodically review this check list to evaluate how constructively you are trying to build up your self-esteem. When you find yourself "slacking off", take the responsibility to invest more energy in you.

Use this space to list ways you have lowered your self-esteem in the last 48 hours. (For example, agreeing to someone's criticism of you without looking at whether it was factual.)

   1.
   2.
   3.
   4.
   5.

Now take some time to reflect on the above list:

   *What can you learn from this?

   *In the next two days try to be aware of how you make yourself feel bad about you.

   *What can you do about this?

Use this space to draw a picture of how your ex-mate sees you. Does he/she see you as happy or sad? Bright or dull? What colors would he/she use—warm? cool? earthy? natural? What parts of you does he/she emphasize—your mind? eyes? ears? mouth? back? hands? genitals? legs? what? Does he/she see your total body or just part of it? Does he/she see you on a pedestal? level with others? underneath everyone? Are you standing up straight or bent over?

Use this space to draw pictures of how other significant people in your life see you (your parents, children, co-workers, friends, etc.) Use the same format as the above.

Use this space to draw a *self*-portrait in the same manner as you have done with the others.

After you have finished these portraits take some time to reflect:

*What can you learn from these drawings?

*Is there a pattern in them?

*Are the "other" portraits consistent with how you see yourself? How do they differ?

Increasing self-confidence and self-reliance is often a matter of becoming aware of your own inner strengths. Before going to sleep each night practice saying one of the following (or any other you may think of) until you feel it in your body.

"I am courage."
"I am a loving being."
"I am pride."
"I am creativity."
"I am important."
"I am peace."
"I am optimism."
"I am safety."

The following exercises will help you develop body awareness and/or learn to relax. Choose a time and place that is physically comfortable for you—where you will *not* be distracted. You may need to practice these exercises several times before you can actually allow yourself to experience them. Practice them when you genuinely want to and *don't* push yourself to relax. Set aside 30 minutes or so to experience any of the following:

For relaxation:

*By focusing your attention on the automatic process of breathing, you can achieve a blissful state of deep relaxation and detached body awareness.

1. Become aware of how you breathe. Allow yourself to inhale and exhale as you normally would. You may discover that you breathe smoothly or hesitantly, deeply or shallowly, rhythmically or erratically. Don't change how you breathe. Just become aware of it.

2. Now notice if you inhale and exhale smoothly with balance and rhythm. Try to smooth the irregularities in the flow without strain or force.

3. Notice how deeply you breathe. Try to gradually increase the depth of your breathing.

4. Now concentrate on the rate at which you are breathing. See if you can gradually slow down your breathing.

Continue this experiment for a few minutes to establish a pattern of smooth, deep, slow breathing. Then, just flow with your calmness.

1. Sit on the floor and curl up into a ball. Then contract—tightening all the muscles in your body. Scrunch up your face, squeeze closed your toes, fingers, arms, legs, thighs, etc.. Hold this position until it becomes absolutely unbearable. Keep tightening all the muscles that loosen.

*You can relax with relative ease by physically tightening and releasing all muscles in your body.

2. Now release and instantly do the reverse: stretch on the floor as much as you can. Arch your back. Spread your toes and fingers. Pull apart your elbows, shoulders, ankles, knees. Stretch your face. Open your eyes and mouth wide. Stick out your tongue. Hold for a minute or two.

3. Then release and breathe deeply and slowly. A great wave of peace is almost certain to come over you.

Releasing tension:

*Emotional tension in the form of body tightness/pressure houses itself in many parts of the body: temples, jaw, back of the neck, shoulders, arms, legs, knees, etc.. To release your own internal tightness, focus your attention on your body. Become aware of any internal stiffness or pressures. When you discover your tense or pressured "spot" concentrate on that area and gradually increase the tension until it is as "tight" as you can make it (as you did in the tighten and release exercise). Then hold that tightness until it becomes unbearable. After a minute or two release the pressure. Then take a few minutes to breathe slowly and deeply. Many people find that with practice, they are able to permanently let go of their internal tightness.

Anxiety:

*Anxiety is often experienced physiologically as a "shakiness" which many people attempt to control by trying *not* to shake. To effectively release your anxiety, try the following:

Become aware of where your anxiety lies in you—hands shaking, nervous 'tic', butterflies in stomach, arms or legs shaking. Once you are aware of your shakiness, concentrate on it and exaggerate it. Try to let yourself go until you are shaking all over and meanwhile try to give up all your rigidity. When you're through you are likely to feel refreshed and relaxed. Take a few minutes to breathe slowly and deeply.

6: Gaining Strength Outside Yourself

Some of the special qualities about a person who has loved before are his or her need and ability to care about others, trust in the value of relationships, and a basic belief in the intrinsic value of life. It may be difficult to see these qualities as helpful, especially if you're feeling demoralized by your loss or sabotaged by your heart. Initially, many ex-intimates damn their vulnerability and vow they will never care about anyone or anything again. "If only I hadn't loved and trusted so much, I wouldn't be hurting now" is a common feeling to have, as is the desire to die or give up on ever feeling good again. But, in spite of this pain and emptiness (or maybe because of it), ex-intimates will discover they almost instinctively begin searching for someone or something outside of themselves for additional emotional support to make them feel better again. They turn to everything from liquor to religion, with people in between.

HOW TO GET POSITIVE FEEDBACK AND SUPPORT FROM OLD FRIENDS, FAMILY AND ACQUAINTANCES.

One of the reasons that saying good-bye to an old love is so painful is that we usually say good-bye to some of our old friends and acquaintances in the process. But, in spite of losing some friends, there will be those whose friendships you will keep and cherish all the more.

Old friends, family and acquaintances are a valuable source of emotional strength during the grief process and especially in the first few weeks, if you know how to gain their support. They can help you soothe your shattered pride and fill up some of the emptiness by letting you know that you are still lovable and worthwhile—and not totally alone in the world. They do this by their words and actions, and just by being "friends". Some will call immediately or eventually take the initiative to contact you. Others, because of their uncertainty about how you feel, will wait for you to make the first move.

It's important for you to decide what kind of relationship you want with your friends now. This may be easier for you to decide with the friends that you know separately than those who are mutual friends with your ex-love. People that you know from work, school or other outside interests and those whom you knew before your "marriage" began will probably be the easiest to maintain or nurture. They will no doubt automatically offer you support and encouragement because they have little or no connection with your ex-love, and, therefore, feel no pressure to "take sides" or get the two of you back together again. You are their friend and since you are hurting, they will want to reach out. You will need to do little to encourage their support other than maintain your usual charm and accept their concern. Listen to the positive feedback they give you and give yourself permission to believe it. Do not abuse their support by constantly complaining about your plight or expecting them to take total responsibility for helping you feel better again. Also, beware of pushing your old friends away by burdening them with your expressions of bitterness or self-pity.

Mutual friends that see you as part of a pair may have trouble viewing you as a separate person. They will no doubt feel the need to take sides or support one of you by attacking the other. Although this may initially feel good if you are the one they support, you will find in the long run that their opinion about whether you're the "good guy" or not will actually do very little to build up your self-esteem or fill up your emptiness. With mutual friends it will be important for you to clearly define to yourself and to them exactly what kind of relationship you want, and then see whether that's possible. You may say, for example: "Even though John (or Jill) and I have ended, I would still like to have a relationship with you—maybe have dinner together or see a show occassionally. How does that sound to you?" It will be important to let your friends know directly that you do not want them to take sides. The break-up of your "marriage" will affect your mutual friends and it may not be possible for the friendships to continue. Perhaps you might wait for some time to pass before you decide to maintain or resume their friendships—especially, other couples. After all, the first few times you see another "pair" that the two of you used to enjoy together, you might discover that many of the memories of your ex-love will painfully surge forward again.

Relatives, like your other friends, can be extremely supportive and offer a great deal of protection to your shattered ego or your feelings of being disconnected from the world. Your own relatives, with a few exceptions, will no doubt stand by your side, even if they do not approve of the "divorce". In fact, many ex-intimates actually move in with their relatives during the first few weeks of the grief process and can count on their family for financial and emotional support. As with your friends, it's important not to abuse your family and to use your own backbone plus any strength they may offer to help you feel better again. You can quickly wear out your welcome by taking their friendship for granted.

Relatives of your ex-love are another matter. Do not be surprised or feel personally assaulted when relatives of your ex-love, who used to be warm and caring to you, suddenly turn cold and rejecting. Unless there is a definite reason to maintain a relationship with his/her family, such as children, it's better to sever the relationships—at least until the wounds are healed and both of you have started a new life.

HOW TO GET EGO-BUILDING FEEDBACK FROM NEW FRIENDS.

One of the scary but really worthwhile adventures of saying good-bye to your past and your ex-love is the opportunity to meet, develop and enjoy new friends and relationships. With the change in your status and maybe even your environment, plus the loss of many old friends, making new friends will almost be a necessity. And, just the act of making new friends will give your ego a boost by proving to yourself in practice that people like you.

But, obviously before you can make new friendships, you will first have to be in a position where you can meet new people. If you move to another neighborhood or get a new job, the opportunity is there. Apartments are filled with a number of ex-intimates in a similar position. Choose an apartment rather than a house in the country for meeting new people. If you stay in your neighborhood and continue with your old job, look for leisure time or growth activity settings as a place to meet new folk: classes in night school or college, volunteer organizations, political parties, singles clubs, churches and last, but most tricky, night clubs and bars. All of these can provide the settings.

Once you are physically in situations where new people are present, give up fighting for emotional support in a loud demanding voice. Practice a smile and an attitude which will signal to others that you are worth the energy to meet. Give up feeling sorry for yourself or complaining constantly to new friends about the "raw deal" you got from your ex-love. Few people are in-

stantly attracted to pessimists or complainers and your new
friends aren't going to know that your total personality isn't
gloomy if you don't let them see the positive parts of you too.
As an ex-intimate, you have the advantage of caring about others
and believing in the value of relationships, or you would never
have gotten involved with your ex-love. Use this strength in
developing new friendships. Let the caring side of you show.
Learning how to be interested in others and practicing that skill
is a marvelous way to not only make new friends but also get
outside of yourself and your worries.

A relationship (new or old) should be developed with people
you like for mutual enjoyment rather than from a desire on your
part to meet someone new to abuse or drain. And with a mutually
satisfying bond, you will automatically gain a great deal of emotional strength as well as pleasant company to enjoy leisure time
activities with.

HOW TO MAKE YOURSELF LOOK BETTER.

Attracting new friends or retaining the old ones may not be too
easy if you feel unattractive. So, if you feel like hiding rather
than gathering the courage to step out in the world of new people,
it might be a good idea to refurbish your physical appearance.
Actually, it's a good idea to improve your appearance even if
you don't feel like hiding because a new beginning justifiably
demands it! With the exception of major overhauls, like gaining or loosing excessive amounts of weights, there are things
that most of us can do rather quickly to help make us look better.

Begin by taking an inventory of yourself and your wardrobe.
Start at the top with your hair and end with your ankles. Take
note of your good points as well as the parts of you which could
use some improvement. Think about changing the style of your
hair, going on a diet and toning up your muscles by getting in
some physical activities. Go to a hairstyler, join a physical fit-
ness program, or leaf through some magazines for ideas about

accentuating the positives parts of your appearance and deem-phasizing the negative ones.

Now for your wardrobe. Add a little flair! Brighter colors make you look livelier, dull colors can make you look washed out or drab. Keep looking around and trying on clothes until you find something that helps you look absolutely smashing!

HOW TO GAIN FEEDBACK AT WORK.

An occupation can be an invaluable resource for gaining additional strength and emotional support. It is especially valu-able for ex-intimates who often feel useless or a failure at the end of a love relationship and have a tendency to withdraw into themselves. Many ex-intimates acclaim the value of working as a resource that saved them from despair. "If it wasn't for my job, I think I would have gone crazy or killed myself" is a com-mon statement to hear. It gives you a routine to follow, a place to go during the day and a feeling of still being connected to the world.

If you don't have a job, think about getting one. In spite of whatever fears you may have about not being qualified, you will find if you put enough energy into actually becoming employed, that it can be an invaluable resource for helping you to feel better again. There are all kinds of employment and training agencies available to help you, and day care centers for your kids.

If you already have a job and find it emotionally satisfying, keep it for awhile and utilize whatever ego building support it may offer. Try not to change jobs immediately after you've said good-bye to your ex-love if you can possibly help it. You will find that the stability of a known routine will be helpful emotionally during the first few days or weeks. This is not to suggest that you remain stagnant professionally. The ending of an intimate relationship often acts as a catalyst for people to examine their lifetime goals. And, many ex-intimates change or develop careers after they've grown through the grief process. One lady I know went back to college and subsequently became an elementary school teacher—after twenty-four years of marriage. Another woman, age twenty-five, with two little children and eight years of a self-destructive marriage, enrolled in nursing school and became a registered nurse. A forty-five year old man was kicked out of a twenty-one year marriage and subsequently changed professions from an office manager in a large computer business to opening his own insurance agency.

To continue getting positive feedback from your current job or the new one you take, make sure that you work in a manner which will merit others' approval and praise. Keep yourself physically attractive, be punctual for appointments, put some added effort into improving your occupational skills and follow the suggestions for gaining support from your friends in relating to your co-workers. Avoid the sometimes natural tendency of allowing everything to fall apart, including your job, while you wallow in feelings of self-pity and rejection. At first you may need to concentrate on doing your job well. But, you will find that the energy is well spent for the rewards you will earn.

GETTING THE MOST OUT OF INSPIRATIONAL LITERATURE.

Many people who are down gain a tremendous amount of emotional strength and guidance by reading and applying inspirational literature to their own lives. Inspirational literature can include everything from sagas of people who overcome handicaps and the power of positive thinking to philosophical writings by nineteenth century transcendentalists like Henry Davis Thoreau and Ralph Waldo Emerson who spoke on the merits of individualism and self-reliance. Humanists from the 1970's, such as Dr. Carl Rogers who acclaims the idea of accepting yourself as a person and armchair philosophers like Dr. Jess Lair who authored the book "I Ain't Much Baby, But I'm All I've Got" offer people-oriented ideals which inspire millions.

Perhaps you'll be inspired to look for the beauty in your world and in others, in spite of whatever disillusion or disappointment you may harbor from the death of an intimate relationship. Look beyond the phoniness in others or yourself for the parts that are honest and real. And, nurture those. Set aside your broken dreams of love everlasting with your ex-love and begin replacing them with dreams for the future you can build on today. Be realistic and cautious in selecting your dreams or planning for your future, but always strive to be happy. Each day of your life, take the time to see the beauty in yourself and the world.

GAINING STRENGTH FROM OTHERS IN A SIMILAR SITUATION.

Getting together with people who have similar problems and sharing ideas about how to feel better or developing mutual problem-solving techniques can be a tremendous source of strength. Anyone who has ever confronted a problem or felt hurt and confused, isolated or scared can tell you what a relief it is just to share his feelings with someone else who "knows what it's like to feel that way." Ex-intimates often gain a great deal of emotional strength and practical support from others who are in the same psychological "boat".

It's hard to feel alone in the world if the person you're talking to knows exactly what it's like to feel a failure at love—or be rejected—or walk out of a relationship and feel guilty. A bond develops and a strength comes from actually knowing someone else in real life who looks "okay", but is also living alone again. It's easier to talk with someone who has "gone through the same thing." You don't have to feel foolish or embarrassed—or feel the need to justify your actions. Some things you don't have to painfully divulge all at once. You say, somewhat hesitantly, to the man you've just met, "I'm divorced," and automatically you can see in his eyes that he knows some of what you may be feeling. There's a sense of relief that settles in your body when he replies, "So am I," thereby lifting the pressures of self-condemnation and the fear about how your listener may judge you. You can then begin talking about what it's like for you to be single again. And, maybe later, he'll share a couple of answers that worked for him when the question of "Will I always be alone?" arose, or perhaps he'll offer his friendship because he feels a kinship with you. Definitely, this is a source of strength! You can gain empathy for your scary feelings, companionship when you're alone but don't want to be, courage from watching others in the same predicament feel better, knowledge on how to help your children cope with their feelings about divorce, and a sense of being needed again when you help someone else.

The strength you can gain from other ex-intimates while you're growing through the grief process can be invaluable if, as with any other resource, you know where to look and how to go about getting support, as well as how to filter out the "garbage" (their own cynicism, bitterness or self-destructive behavior, like alcohol abuse). In fact, recognize their possible manifestation of behavior you're trying to avoid and, by helping them gain strength, you'll be getting stronger too.

There are a variety of settings where you can meet other ex-intimates who are already giving and getting additional emotional strength and practical advice on problems that arise from being single again. Singles' clubs and national organizations like Parents without Partners, the Singletons (for adults between the ages of 27-45), and the Junior Officers and Professional Association (for single men and women between the ages of 21-35) are just a few of the groups that are designed specifically for you.

Another resource to help ex-intimates gain strength from each other is through group therapy sessions specifically for the problems of being single again. These sessions are usually led by a mental health professional and are available through community agencies such as the Y.M.C.A. or through private clinics and counselors. The time and cost of these sessions may vary from 1½ hours a week for a specific number of weeks to all day or week-end marathons, with prices ranging anywhere from free to expensive.

Community colleges have begun in the 1970's to offer classes for single adults on living alone. Such subjects as loneliness, human sexuality, housekeeping for men and mechanics for women are just a few of the courses available through night school.

If there are no singles' groups available in your town, start one yourself. Check with community agencies, churches and clubs to see if they will help you begin one. Contact a national organization like Parents without Partners (80 5th Ave., New York, 10011) or Junior Officers and Professional Association (3286 M. St., N.W., Washington D.C., 20007) and begin your own local chapter. This will provide a perfect opportunity to meet others who are single again.

GAINING COURAGE FROM RELIGION, IF YOU'RE RELIGIOUS.

Many people gain courage through their religious beliefs. Their faith that God will provide or see them through a crisis, even the death of an intimate relationship, gives them additional strength during the time when they may feel the most dejected and alone. Those who have had a strong religious background turn to their faith to help them understand and accept the change in their status. Even when a man has forgotten his faith, he may find himself automatically turning to God for additional strength during the mourning phase for his past love.

If you have a personal faith in some sort of divine power, you may find that at times it is helpful to use it for extra courage or strength. In a world that is often seen as godless, there are still a number of people who call on their faith to help them through crises they are unable to understand by themselves or feel helpless to handle without divine power. In spite of the cynicism we may have in our land, people still do ask for God's help to give them additional strength—and many will tell you it helps them to feel stronger.

HOW TO FIND COMPETENT PROFESSIONAL MENTAL HEALTH SUPPORT.

Emotional stress may lessen with the guidance from mental health professionals. To decide whether you can use the additional help of a therapist is a personal choice. Contrary to the comic belief, you do not need to be "crazy" to talk to a "shrink". A counselor can help you understand some of the inter and intrapersonal conflicts you may have about ending, help you work through a depression, and find direction for your present and future life. He or she cannot take away your pain and suffering or give you a magical answer, but may be able to help you discover some answers for yourself. When you find yourself stuck in a painful phase, such as self-pity or bitterness, and no matter what you do, you still cannot get beyond that, you may want to contact a professional in that field for advice and support.

Since there is such a wide variation in theoretical concepts and training that a counselor might have, it's a good idea to ask whomever you see what his or her specific or general approach is in practice.

A psychiatrist, psychologist, clinical social worker or a licensed counselor might treat an individual exactly the same, with the same amount of expertise, in spite of whatever formalized differences each may have had in training. To tell you that one is better or more qualified to help you in therapy would be folly. You can, in general, feel confident that all have had enough formalized training to know how to help you, but your own common sense must tell you that some are more insightful than others because all of them are human.

Another consideration that you should probably look at consciously before you decide on a therapist is your own feelings about the therapist's sex. Some people find it easier to trust someone of their own sex—others rely more automatically on the viewpoint of members of the opposite sex. To a minor degree, your own prejudices about a therapist's sex (or age and race) might affect how much advice you are willing to accept from him/her.

Once you know in general which of the professionals you would like to see and whether any of your personal prejudices would hinder your choices, probably the most effective way to find a competent therapist is through the recommendation of someone you know. A friend, co-worker, relative, minister, doctor or boss may be able to recommend one or several therapists near your home.

It is natural to feel frightened or apprehensive at your first session. For this reason, do not make a decision that therapy won't help or this therapist won't work for you until you've seen him/her at least two or three times. If you feel that therapy might help, but you don't get along with your therapist, it's a good idea to change. People have different personalities and it's time-consuming to work on a personality conflict with your therapist when you need help in coping with your feelings about being single again. So, try another therapist. If you discover with your second—or third—therapist, that you don't like any of them, you might want to look at the possibility that your dismay has more to do with the idea of seeing a mental health professional, or what they are saying to you, rather than with them as individuals. If this is the case, I suggest that you stick with one of them and continue. While there is a certain amount of validity in therapy shopping, no one can help you feel better through therapy if you never get involved in the process.

As you can see from this chapter, there are a number of ways to gain additional strength and emotional support other than relying totally upon yourself. Every time a friend, relative or acquaintance tells you directly or shows you through actions that he thinks you're a beautiful person or someone worth knowing or valuable to him—even in the most minute fashion—your confidence expands, if you give yourself permission to believe it.

Experiments and Exercises

Move quickly through this list and (√) whether you are Likely or Unlikely to do the following:

L   U

1. Invite a friend over for dinner on the spur of the moment.   __ __
2. Plan a week in advance before you invite someone over for an evening's entertainment.   __ __

3. Call up a friend on Sunday afternoon and ask if he/she wants to go to a movie.   — —
4. Sit alone on Sunday because you have nothing to do.   — —
5. Call up a friend just to say "Hi".   — —
6. Start to call someone and then decide maybe you'd be bothering him/her.   — —
7. Invite friends over for a drink after work.   — —
8. Ask a friend if you can come over to his house.   — —
9. Invite yourself to a friend's party.   — —
10. Have a spur of the moment party on Tuesday.   — —
11. Initiate a conversation with a stranger.   — —
12. Drop in on a friend unannounced.   — —
13. Initiate a week-end "vacation" with someone you like, but don't know very well.   — —
14. Send "divorce announcements" to your friends and acquaintances indicating you would still like to be friends.   — —
15. Go to a singles' club by yourself.   — —
16. Share your feelings with other ex-intimates.   — —
17. Ask for guidance from another ex-intimate.   — —
18. Seek professional counseling even though you could handle your feelings by yourself.   — —
19. Tell a friend you're feeling "down" and would like to talk.   — —
20. Talk to a minister about your problems.   — —
21. Seek strength through religion.   — —
22. Ask your family for their support.   — —
23. Move in with a friend or relative.   — —
24. Look for guidance through literature.   — —

Now look at your responses:

*Is there a pattern?
*Are you missing out on some emotionally supportive experiences because of fears?
*Which ones would you like to change?

7: Common Pitfalls and How to Avoid Them

Human beings are strange animals. Sometimes, even when we know we're playing with fire, we do it anyway. We have a fantasy that says: "It can't happen to me. I'm special! And, I'm invincible!" So, in spite of being warned, we blunder into many pitfalls. But, that's okay because that's how we learn. In fact, some people argue that the *only* way an individual learns is by his own experience. But, perhaps, after the second (or third) time you find yourself sliding into the same trap, you'll remember what you've read here and rescue yourself in time.

You might notice that many of the pitfalls mentioned appear to have the same goal: *holding on or going back to the past.* This, of course, makes beginning a new life very hard.

TRYING TO HELP EACH OTHER THROUGH THE CRISIS.

This is a popular trap for nice, kind, intelligent people who are: afraid of getting angry at their ex-love, uncertain about burying their dead relationship, and frightened of beginning a new life. It is natural to feel all of these and to want, at some time or another, support and reassurance that you're a "worthwhile" person.

When you try to help each other through the crisis, you are saying: "I still feel some kind of love, commitment or obligation to you and I'm afraid to let go." Obviously, still needing to hold on makes it very hard to say good-bye.

When you offer to help your ex-love through the depression and loneliness caused by the ending of your relationship, you are saying one of three things:

(a) I still care about you and want you to need me.

(b) I really feel guilty about your pain and it is against my value to hurt you because you are still important to me.

(c) I really feel empty now and you're the person who used to fill that emptiness for me, and I don't believe anyone else will.

Although all of these fears and feelings are very genuine and natural, to act on them when you're feeling so vulnerable can only prolong your pain. To fall into the trap of trying to help each other through the crisis, one or both partners must *still* be dependent on the other to the extent that at least one member acts as an emotional rescuer.

A friend of mine was divorced for three years before she finally quit calling on her ex-husband to wipe away her tears. The sad part about Evelyn depending on Sy all the time was that at the end of the three years, she still had to start over and learn how to find a new love to comfort and support her. Unfortunately by this time, she had wasted three years of her life holding on to Sy who, after the first six months, was involved with someone else.

To save ourselves emotionally we *have* to let go of our past loves and their support in order to gather our strength and eventually develop new loves. Sometimes it takes a few weeks or months to learn that going forward is *much* more exciting than backing up and clinging on to the remaining shreds of an emotional attachment.

So what do you do when you feel you just *have* to talk with your ex-love? Call someone else, or visit a friend, or join a group of other recently single folk. The question you need to ask yourself when you reach for the phone is: "Can I *really* go forward if I keep clutching at yesterday?" The answer is obvious.

And, what do you do if your ex-love keeps clinging to you? Tell him that you can no longer hold him up or be counted on for support. It prolongs the pain for both of you and even though you were once very important to each other, neither can afford to back into the future with an eye on the past.

GETTING BACK TOGETHER WITH EX-LOVE.

> After 30 years of separation, the aged couple gazed lovingly into each other's eyes. And in that moment, they knew what they had always known: that they were meant for each other. And even though the years had dragged slowly by, at that very second they were young again and life was once more worth living. Surely their love was a gift from the gods— who were once again smiling on them. "Thank God we're together again," she sighed, as he held her closely in his arthritic arms!

It really isn't that funny (or romantic) to wait all your life to re-capture that moment when you can once again be in the arms of your lost but not forgotten love. And many recently single folk do try to get back with their "other half" and sadly learn that although the idea of together again is romantic in movies, there are too many roadblocks in real life to make recapturing an old flame that appealing or workable.

To begin with, there are usually lots of arrows flung at each partner during the ending and the exit speeches. And, although each may hope to forgive and forget what was shouted in the past, usually neither can fully trust the other not to be hurtful again.

A friend said:

"I thought that we could forget all the hurt we had caused each other and start anew. But I discovered that we just couldn't do that. Each time we got into a small argument, like any couple does, we made it worse, by pulling in *all* the past hurts—including who had suffered the most during our separation. I guess you can't start anew with someone you've already begun and ended with before."

There is little doubt that you cannot start fresh with an old love. Much of the appeal is that you already know your old love's moods, strengths, weaknesses, habits and favorite foods. You, therefore, save yourself the embarrassing awkwardness of a new relationship. At a time when you may feel fragile and vulnerable, it is quite natural for you to want to protect yourself from any additional hurt a new romance may offer. But to go back to your past love (even if that is possible) may be more painful than moving on.

Another major roadblock that causes rekindled flames to burn out quickly is that there is usually little fuel to keep them glowing. The relationship died and was buried the first time. The same old issues that were there before will still be there when you go back. And, as soon as the honeymoon period is over, they'll return to haunt you.

Remind yourself that going back rarely works out and refuse to kid yourself that it will be different this time. It wasn't before, and, there's little that's changed except you're lonelier now. As W.C. Fields said: "If at first you don't succeed, try again; if you still don't make it—quit! Don't make a fool of yourself."

TRYING TO BE FRIENDS.

George and Alice had been together for seven years when they finally decided to end their relationship. They lived in a middle class "bedroom community" near a northern California city. Alice worked as a teacher and stayed there when George moved out. It was Alice's idea that they separate.

George moved closer to his work as an advertising executive in the city.

He felt pretty lost and empty without Alice and came to a mental health clinic for counseling.

An intelligent, rather mild mannered, sensitive man in his early thirties, George had never loved anyone before he met Alice and still, to some degree, cared for her.

During one of the therapy sessions he was talking about his relationship with Alice and how it ended—five months ago.

"We weren't angry at each other when we parted. We'd fought in the past, but decided, pretty sensibly, that neither of us were "bad" people. We'd just grown apart. I remember when I left, Alice said she'd hoped we could be *friends*.

"I recall as clearly as if it were yesterday, the feeling I had when she said that she wanted us to be friends. It was as if someone had kicked me in the stomach! But in a strange way, I wanted that too—because I didn't want to lost contact with her.

"It suddenly occured to me that I didn't answer with more than a grunt. I wondered if I'd ever get to a point that I didn't love and need her so much. And, if I did, whether I'd choose her as a friend. I knew I would feel too vulnerable for a long time to let myself feel very close to her. I thanked God that we didn't have children! So, having to be friends would be our free choice, rather than a necessity.

"I could never imagine hating this woman, but I really couldn't see myself confiding in her like I do with some of my other friends.

"I guess, I said to myself, that we will be at a point some day in our lives when we will be friends—if that means being pleasant, but stiff, towards each other.

"I felt sadness in the pit of my stomach at the thought that after all she'd meant to me, a friendship with pleasant smiles and 'Hello—how are you?' would be the most we could expect from each other in the future.

"I wondered if it was worth it. I'm still not sure."

George's commentary exposes a lot of internal conflicts that many ex-intimates battle:

1. Why do I really want to be friends with my ex-love?
2. What are the advantages and disadvantages for me?
3. If I'm objective and look at what's *best* for me in my future, will "being friends" really be helpful?
4. Is my ex-love someone I could genuinely enjoy as a friend once I feel better about myself and my future?

Each single-againer has to answer those questions for him/herself. Trying to be friends with your ex-love is altogether possible *if* your wounds are healed and *when* you no longer need the love that your former relationship provided. For George to try and develop a friendship relationship with Alice while he is still feeling the pain and vulnerability of being alone would be silly.

Of course, we've all heard stories about ex-intimates who are the best of friends. A male co-worker of mine takes pride in the fact that he, his present wife and the children from his former marriage, often go on picnics with his ex-wife. I'm sure that's a very cute family portrait, but, I often wonder how the two women feel about it. And why his ex-wife never remarried?

Before you jump into the pitfall of trying to be friends with your ex-love, ask yourself how much it will cost you emotionally to try and hang on to him/her through the guise of friendship. If the cost is holding on to yesterday so that you cannot find someone new today, don't do it.

When you have children or some other outside reason to hold on, work towards the goal of feeling neutral. In general, if you have to *work* at being friends and there are few advantages with lots of disadvantages, avoid the trap altogether. How? See you ex-love *only* when you have to, and reach out to others for friendship and love. No one is really so desperate for friends that they have to remold an old love into a new friend.

SAVING OLD LOVE LETTERS, MEMENTOS, ETC.

Saving old love letters and mementos is about as helpful or productive as saving Confederate money after the Civil War! So don't wait around a hundred years, with your hands full of faded paper! For the love of your own sanity and peace of mind, *don't* save his/her old scribblings—or, anything else that dredges up the dead past. You can't reach out to someone new with your hands (and heart) full of old love letters from your last love.

PULLING IN MEMORIES TO FILL THE EMPTINESS.

"I'm not sure what it means.
Why we cannot shake the old loves from our minds.
It must be that we build on memory
and make them *more* that what they were.
        And is the manufacture
just a safe device for closing up the wall?"
                                —Rod McKuen, *Listen to the Warm*.

In response to that stanza, it is true that part of the reason *all* ex-lovers build on past memories (and selectively gloss over the problems) is to protect themselves from hurt again. But it serves other functions: to help them wallow in self-pity and to stop them from living, growing and loving again. How? By filling the emptiness immediately, and, thereby not making it crucial for the lonely single-againer to risk reaching out and loving someone new.

In fact, many psychologists say that without anxiety and discomfort a person will stagnate or regress. Having a memory close at hand to pull in any time a lonely single-againer may feel empty, limits his/her motivation to find fulfillment anew.

John D. was readmitted to the psychiatric hospital for the twelfth time in seven years—following a suicide attempt. A large, rather apathetic, depressed man in his mid-forties, he lives in a one-room shack, collects disability and stays lonely and "down" most of the time. He's been this way ever since his wife left.

Life has little meaning for John anymore. He spends most of his days reminiscing about the past, feeling sorry for himself and damning his fate. He rarely goes out and has no close friends. Nothing he does compares favorably with what he used to do. And, almost all of his statements start with "I remember when _____ and I used to _____." John is a very lonely man and will, no doubt, die many years from now as depressed and unhappy as he is today. Even John knows his past love is dead, but, he refuses to bury it.

Maybe there's a lesson in his tragedy for those who have loved and lost and feel empty now. Sure, there will be times when all of us harken back to a happier time in our lives. Especially if we're feeling lost and lonely now. But watch yourself. Don't let it become a habit. Whenever you find yourself spending a whole evening reminiscing about the glories of your lost love, remember some of the not so neat things, too.

Handle your nostalgia for what it is: discomfort with today. Then, spend the next evening in your life filling in the emptiness with new memories.

And how did you get the last memories? You found somebody, and you experienced warm and loving events, which means that *you* have the ability to do it! Go out and create new memories again! (And leave the reminiscing to those who aren't as brave as you.)

CHECKING UP ON EX-LOVE.

Checking up on your ex-love is a painful, self-destructive but natural trap for many ex-intimates. Especially for those who were not the first to initiate good-bye and still harbor the fantasy that his/her ex-love will return. Although few ex-intimates spend an entire day tracing the steps of their last love, many *do* drive by his/her old apartment in the evening or just happen to be in the neighborhood on a week-end afternoon. And, sometimes, they make up some of the flimiest excuses to drop in and sleuth, like: "Did I leave my old paperweight here?"

The object of this cops and robbers game is to find out what he/she is doing now. That is, to discover if he/she is as lonely and miserable as our amateur detective. Unfortunately for our detective, he/she probably isn't—or else, he/she would be sleuthing around, too.

So, the only purpose checking up on your ex-love really serves is to cause you more pain. Moreover, it wastes precious time that you *could* be using to enjoy life or find someone new. You'll never meet your new love by staking out your old love's apartment. So, instead of playing detective, get on with the business of living—and, put your old trench coat away. Anytime you find yourself accidently cruising by his/her apartment, quickly make a "U" turn and dash to someone else's door!

TRYING TO GET FRIENDS TO TAKE SIDES/ PUMPING THEM FOR INFORMATION.

"Yes, Madge, I saw him at the party last night. *No*—he wasn't with anyone in particular. I didn't ask him, Madge! You're *absolutely* right! It was his fault. Harry's a Bastard. I'm on *your* side, Madge. *Now* can we go play tennis?"

Madge doesn't know it yet, but she *just* lost a friend. She slid right into two common pitfalls for the recently single: trying to get friends to take sides and pumping them for information about her ex-love. If you need an ally or sympathizer, DON'T USE YOUR FRIENDS. You'll lose them that way.

What are friends for? *Not* to use as a judge or jury to decide whose fault the break-up is. Not mutual friends, anyway. There will be enough friends who fall by the wayside when you separate anyway.

You won't lose all of your mutual friends by pumping them

for information or asking them to take sides. In fact, there will be some who will pump you for all the gory details of the break-up, readily offer their verdict of guilty on your ex-love, and, call you the *minute* they hear any gossip about what he/she's doing! As you might have guessed, these are the same folks who follow fire trucks to watch the buildings burn. When you get tired of talking about him/her and want to get on with the business of living again, you may find these friends dropping by the wayside —or you may want to shove them.

So who can you talk to about him/her in your hour of need? Probably your best bet are friends you don't have in common. Or those who are primarily your friends. That is, if you have separate friends. If you don't, this is a good time to make some. In the meantime, another resource might be an outsider like a mental health counselor or your minister who might help you see that trying to place blame is of little value; and constantly keeping "tabs" on him/her drains energy that you could be using on *you*. In addition, it usually just keeps your wounds open.

Even if you got all of your friends to agree that it was his fault, and he's a bastard for leaving you—or you were absolutely justi-fied in kicking him out—what do you do with that? Draw up an affidavit and have all of your friends sign it? Will that get him back? Or make it easier for you to live with your new status?

What will help is setting aside the issue of who's to blame and admitting to yourself that it really is over. And, in spite of that (or maybe, because of that) you really are a worthwhile person. That's what all the energy you've spent pleading your case is all about anyway. Trying to prove to yourself that others still see you as worthwhile. Maybe now that you know that you're fighting for your self-esteem, you can figure out other ways to win. (For ideas, see chapter 5.)

When you pump your friends for information about your ex-love, you are competing because each time you find out what he's doing now, you quickly make a mental note of how that *compares* with what you're doing. If he seems to be happy, you may find yourself bemoaning your fate or getting angry. Obviously, watching him feel good or damning yourself for *still* being lonely isn't going to help you out. What will? Take your eyes and ears off your ex-mate (quit pumping your friends) and work on getting your own life together.

On the other hand, if you hear that he's still depressed, you may feel guilty because you're not, or relieved that he's miserable. Whatever the feelings, don't waste too much time focusing on what he's doing. It really doesn't have anything to do with you anymore.

WISHING IT HADN'T HAPPENED AND HOPING IT'LL CHANGE.

Ever noticed how little gets done when you sit around and wish something hadn't happened or hope it'll change? Sometimes it's pretty easy to just fall back and feel sorry for yourself and wish this hadn't happened to you. And with all the energy it takes to carry your self-pity around it's hard to have the guts to do much more about your plight than just hope it'll change.

When you're in that pit, what are you hoping for? A miracle? Hoping you were back, living in the good old days, perhaps? Have you forgotten the horrible fights you used to have? Or the put-downs? Or the hurt feelings? Or how little you had in common when you left? Probably you have, or you wouldn't be slumped in your chair wishing it wasn't over.

You really haven't been forgotten down in that pitfall. You're just recovering from a serious injury and, at times, you fall back into feeling sorry for yourself. It's easy to do. And common, too. Not only are you not the only one who has ever fallen in this pit—but, you've probably been here before.

This time put a time limit on how long you're going to wallow in your misery, feel helpless and "pass" on life. A week? Better yet, how about just the rest of the day? You decide, you're the one down there.

It's a natural part of the healing process after the death of an intimate relationship to become depressed and immobilized at times. So you don't really need to panic. Actually, if you're at a

point where you hope your feelings will change, you're beginning to look for ways out of this pit. All you have to do is remember that you can pull yourself out when you've had enough.

And, when you decide that it's time to leave Gloomsville for
awhile, reach out to a friend and tell him how you feel. Just
getting the feelings off your chest helps.

Probably during the first year, you will slide into this "wishing
it hadn't happened and hoping it'll change" pitfall a number
of times. You'll notice, though, as time goes by that you hit it
less often and for briefer periods because you start climbing out
of the hole by reaching out to others or pulling your own
strengths.

BEWARE OF ANNIVERSARY DATES.

You're having an absolutely marvelous time, enjoying the
new exciting you and all of a sudden—ZAP! For no apparent
reason you've gone from the top of the roller coaster down to
the bottom again. As you pick yourself up, you shakily ask
yourself, "What happened? I thought I was getting over HIM
(HER)." *Then*, you look at the calendar and discover that tomorrow *would* have been your anniversary—or his birthday—or any
one of a dozen used-to-be red letter days.

What happened? You have been belted by the *Syndrome:
Anniversary Date* (S.A.D.). And almost every recently single gets
clobbered by this syndrome several times during at least the first
year.

It operates in one of two ways: on or around the date of an
important past event in your life, you may have the same feelings
as those experienced earlier; or, because of loss of a loved one,
you may experience feelings that are the exact opposite (feeling
sad about a past event that was happy).

Examples*

*Feeling sad on the anniversary date of a loved one's death.

*Feeling down on the anniversary date of a divorce.

*Feeling dejected on the anniversary date of your former wedding day.

*Feeling sad and lost around the time of year that you and your ex-love used to go on vacation.

The best protection is an offensive tactic, that is, attacking S.A.D. before it can sneak up and belt you. Go through your calendar for the next month or six weeks and circle the dates that are likely to be troublesome. (Don't go much farther than this because it could be overwhelming—or, in six weeks you may be so busy with your new life that the plans you make now will be outdated.)

Dates that you need to circle are the red letter days you can remember such as: your first date, first time you vowed eternal love, last time you fought, first time you "made up," the day you ended it, vacation times and special "togetherness" holidays.

There will be a certain amount of sadness in remembering these events, but since you really can't forget them anyway, you might as well allow yourself to go through the painful feelings now—just a little bit, anyway.

There are several different things you can do with these special days to not only fill the time, but really enjoy it. Plan a party. Invite a few single friends over for dinner. Go to an art show, play, music festival or antique auction. Plan a short trip. Get involved in a hobby or project. Go to a singles' club dance. BE WITH PEOPLE. DO SOMETHING.

Make it part of your Sunday routine to browse through the entertainment section and make notes on coming events in your town. Fill these special dates on the calendar with your plans. Then, most important, do them. Gradually you will find that the original objective (to attack the S.A.D. by filling up the time with people and activities) has been replaced by a genuine enjoyment for doing more exciting activities and meeting new friends.

If you use this plan of attack, few anniversaries will be able to sneak up and clobber you. There will, however, be times when you've forgotten to plan ahead. When that happens, reach out to someone or some project to help you through it. None of us can avoid feeling some pain and sorrow about the loss of an ex-love, but we can, by turning to other people and events, keep the S.A.D. from immobilizing us.

PANICKING WITH FREE TIME: WEEK-ENDS AND SUCH.

"Well, I make it all right
From Monday morning til Friday night.
But, oh, those lonely weekends!"

Week-ends can be lonely and painful for the recently single. In fact, any free time can be very scary, and so it's quite common to absolutely panic over an upcoming holiday, or, Heaven forbid, a two week vacation.

Whoever said we need *more* three day week-ends? Certainly *not* a recently single. In fact, business men can usually count on their employees who have recently ended an intimate relationship to volunteer for extra work during the evenings, holidays or week-ends.

There's a private club in San Francisco called T.G.I.M. (Thank God It's Monday) comprised of single people who get together on Monday nights to celebrate that they've made it through another week-end.

Armed with anxiety, it is common for the recently single to do one of two things: schedule so many activities that he's hopping from one to another; or, be so panicked that he ends up immobilized and, unable to make any decisions, sits at home all week-end vegetating.

Heddy is a hopper! As a 32 year old single again secretary in a medium sized New York law office, she's constantly running into lots of newly divorced or separated men. Monday morning she begins hunting and planning for the week-ends. She checks through her bosses' appointment books for potential "free" men, looks through the newspapers for upcoming local events, finds out from her friends during the lunch hour if there are any parties planned and usually stops at a bar one or two nights a week to see if she can pick up a date. The routine continues until she has packed her week-end schedule with people and outings.

When she is unable to fill up the week-end, she usually packs up her parakeet and visits a nearby relative. "I just can't stand to be alone on week-ends. When someone at work mentions vacation to me, I panic. Just the work freaks me out."

Vern vegetates on week-ends. As a 43 year old slightly over-weight, recently single insurance man in a small mid-western town, he spends most of the week dreading Friday night to Monday morning. Most everyone he knows is married and unless his friends suggest that he do something with them, he usually spends the week-ends at home alone.

Through the week he can keep busy and, being around people, he sometimes forgets that he's alone and lonely. But on the week-ends, he feels like one of the walking wounded.

On Monday he usually vows he's not going to spend an-other week-end alone, but by Friday night he's usually come up with zero plans. Vern handles his fear of being alone on the week-ends by getting so overloaded with dread and misery that he does nothing.

How can Heddy or Vern learn to enjoy their free time?

First of all, most single-againers say that it takes from 3-9 months to feel good enough about yourself that the prospect of being alone with free time doesn't throw you into a tail-spin. You can speed the process along by planning some activities with people for your week-ends. But, stagger this with some time to be by yourself and get to know and like you again. (You really aren't very good company for you or anyone until you let go of the panic).

Use the time alone to develop some of your hidden or showing talents like: decorating, in-door gardening, cooking, painting, making crafts, reading, playing a musical instrument, or singing in the shower. Take walks—in the country, at the beach, through the city parks and streets. Begin looking at the beauty and comedy around you as you stroll. In your travels, gather in new ideas for things you'd enjoy. Go to an art or craft exhibit. Talk to the craftsman about his wares. Smile at strangers and be friendly. Remember wherever you meet people you have a chance to meet a new friend. Gradually you will find that the pain and panic over the free time will lessen.

FALLING IN LOVE WITH THE FIRST PERSON YOU MEET.

Falling in love with the first person you meet can be just as emotionally destructive as refusing to ever love someone new because it does not allow you the healthy experience of dating again and growing through the grief process. Worse than that, it may set you up for another painful ending. As we have seen from chapter 1, many experts believe the ending of an intimate relationship *begins* at the start. That is, intimates join together blindly because of neurotic needs and fears rather than emotionally mature choices.

Ex-intimates often fantasize about finding someone to sweep them off their feet or take them away from all of their pain from good-bye. Often they desperately search for a "new" love to fill up their emptiness and protect them from hurt, and occasionally they fall in love with the first—or second—or third person they date. But usually this leads to disaster. And a few months later, they are dealing with the death of *two* intimate relationships and are numbed by the overwhelming fear that they cannot "make it" with anyone.

Instead, date and enjoy a number of different individuals. Give yourself the time and experience to grow through good-bye and learn to enjoy being a separate person again before you decide to commit yourself to someone new.

The common theme of most of the pitfalls appears to be: pulling you back to the past. And, the antidote is obvious: pushing yourself to let go of the past and move forward. And that takes the courage and wisdom growing within you now.

Experiments and Exercises.

Below is a list of pitfalls. Check (√) those you have *not* fallen into.

__ trying to help each other through crisis.
__ getting back together with ex-love.
__ trying to be friends.
__ saving old love letters.
__ pulling in memories to fill the emptiness.
__ checking up on ex-love.
__ trying to get friends to take sides or pumping them for information.
__ wishing it hadn't happened and hoping it'll change.
__ getting slugged by S.A.D. (Syndrome: Anniversary Date).
__ panicking with free time.
__ falling in love with the first person you meet.

Now ask youself:

*How do I avoid these?

*What can I learn from my own experience that will help me get out of any I may be stuck in now?

*Are there times when I'm more vulnerable? When? What can I do about it?

*Am I getting anything out of holding on to the past? What?

Go back through the above list and place a big "X" near one pitfall you *do* get stuck in and are willing to give up. Write the following on a piece of paper:

"I'm tired of _____." (Write the pitfall *and* your ex-love's name.) For example: "I'm tired of trying to get back together with _____."

Read what you have written out loud. Repeat this again and again until you can feel the words in your body. (This may take several rehearsals.) Once you have finally acknowledged your own desire to stop hurting yourself, crumple up the paper and throw it in the garbage—or burn it.

Take a few moments to feel your relief. Then, pat yourself on the back for your decision.

Make a commitment to yourself to follow through on your decision to begin feeling better.

8: For the One Who Was Left Behind

Most everyone agrees that when a relationship dies, the first person who says that it's over has an easier time with saying good-bye and burying the past than the one who is left behind. Physically you may or may not have been the one who actually left your apartment or house, but emotionally you were the one who was still in the relationship, or at least felt that you were, when your partner announced he/she was leaving—or had already left. You, who felt committed to or dependent on the relationship or slightly dissatisfied but too frightened to act, will probably suffer the strongest feelings of rejection, hurt feelings or abused pride.

But even if you are the one who was left behind, you can feel better after saying good-bye, as soon as you get a handle on your own feelings of self-doubt and self-pity and gradually learn through the course of your pain how to bury parts of the past and give up your suffering. Your progress may be slow at times because you no doubt have the tendency to criticize yourself more than others, which makes it harder for you to learn how to

122

change. In spite of your fears that you may never feel good about yourself, love anyone else or trust others to love you, you will find that if you really want to give up feeling abandoned and start living again, you can.

HOW TO PUT A LIMIT ON SELF-PITY.

The one who feels left behind at the end of a love affair will be the one who is most likely to engage in self-pity. To some extent, this is natural and nothing to hide from yourself or feel ashamed of. When someone leaves you, you may feel like a victim: abused and abandoned with no control over HIS/HER leaving and less over your future. You may not have people near you to help salve or bandage your wounds—or, if you do, you may push them aside, declaring that only your ex-love can help you feel better again. Because of all this, you may find that you are the only one left to give yourself comfort.

But the problems sneak in when you become so wrapped up in self-pity that it gets in your way of growing and becomes the reason that you cannot reach out to others for support, or be concerned and interested in anything or anyone outside of yourself.

Limiting your self-pity first requires that you recognize it exists in you. In pure form, it may be difficult to spot because it usually travels with the feelings of self-doubt or bitterness. So how can you learn to see the self-pity in you? Anytime you find yourself thinking, feeling or doing any one of the following, you are engaged in feeling sorry for yourself:

 — Bemoaning your fate and not looking at how you can change it.

 — Deciding that your ex-love always used you—"I took care of him and he never did anything for me."

 — Thinking about how other people always have a good time—and you always get left out.

 — Letting the telephone ring because it's probably a wrong number—or just someone wanting to use you.

— Nurturing feelings that you were born to lose—nothing good ever happens and no matter what you do, it ends up in failure.

— Remembering all the bad things that have ever happened in your life and ignoring or minimizing the good ones.

— Reminding yourself that no one has ever felt so alone in his/her life or been so abused.

— Imagining what a good time your ex-love is having now that he/she is gone.

The list could go on and on, but that should give you some clues about the kind of thoughts and feelings you may own that are signals of self-pity. Anytime you become the focal point of the world and its suffering, and you wipe out any possibility that someone else may care or feel the same way, or that you can do something constructive for your pain, you are stuck with feeling sorry for yourself, sometimes feeling bitter, but usually feeling resigned to your fate.

Once you're aware of the self-pity in you, begin looking at what's going on at the time (or just before) you begin feeling that way. Did you hear a depressing song on the radio or see a "couple" that look like they have what you want? Or, maybe, you heard that your ex-love is living with someone new, or dating a friend? Whever the catalyst, see if you can find it. One lady I know told me that during the first six months of her divorce, everytime a week-end drew near and her co-workers talked about their plans, she found herself slugged with a surge of panic, then settling back into feeling sorry for herself because she had nothing to do and no one to be with.

When you discover what scenes set your self-pity in motion, figure out how many times during the day you turn to self-pity and how long you wallow in your suffering before you decide to get out. Once you know this, try to cut it down to one or two times less each day and limit the wallowing by 1/10th. By slowly limiting some of the self-pity you feel, you will be able to recognize for yourself that you do, in fact, have some control over that part of your grief process.

HOW TO FIGHT SELF-PITY AND SELF-DOUBT.

The combination of self-pity and self-doubt can be demoralizing. Self-pity says, "Isn't it awful that this has happened to you—no one else suffers as much", and self-doubt comes along and tells you to "Go ahead and feel sorry for your plight if you'd like to because there's nothing you can do to change it. Anything you try will end up in failure.

Often the ex-intimate who was left behind owns both of these feelings simultaneously—especially during the first few weeks of the ending process because much of his/her pride and self-confidence have been shattered by his/her partner's rejection. This reaction may be magnified if your partner has a new love or you felt insecure before the relationship began. These feelings are also enhanced if you only confided your feelings in the one who left—or looked primarily to your ex-mate for comfort and support. With the ending of the relationship, your only source of nurturing, however unhealthy that might have been, is gone. And so, you are left feeling sorry for yourself; not knowing how to let go of your pain and doubting your ability to do anything constructive for yourself.

In order to fight self-doubt and self-pity you must first recognize that they are more natural at this time in your life than ever before and that they seem to penetrate every aspect of your existence.

As one man related, after his wife of seven years filed for divorce, "I found myself double checking everything I did—even though I know that I'm good at my job. And, I panicked when I had to meet someone new—or even try something different." The woman who shared that her week-ends were filled with self-pity for the first six months after saying good-bye to her ex-husband, discovered that barricading herself up in her apartment with plenty of kleenex and stacks of sad books was her way of handling her self-doubt about being attractive to anyone. She was afraid that if she asked her co-workers to come over for dinner, or go to a movie, they'd turn her down. The thought of being attractive to another man, or having the ability to make new single friends, frightened her too. So, she stayed in her apartment and felt sorry for herself.

How long this self-doubt and self-pity will last varies with a number of factors: the length of your relationship; how insecure you felt before it began; how self-destructive the relationship became; how dependent you were on your ex-love; and how soon you allow others to help pull you out.

The only way to fight these two villains is to begin proving to yourself by your actions and applause from others that you are a worthwhile person. To speed this process along, you will need to give yourself permission to feel more confident and risk making mistakes or being rejected occassionally in order to give yourself the opportunities to be successful. The man who was unsure of himself and afraid to meet anyone new or try anything different minimized his fears by finally corraling his hesitation and actually doing the things he feared. Then with each success, he knew for himself that, in spite of his self-doubt, he really could do his job well, learn new skills and meet strangers successfully. Each success gave him more confidence. The lady who stayed home for six months' worth of week-ends found, when she actually invited people to her house, that they accepted her invitation and many new men she met did find her attractive.

The point is that you can fight self-doubt and self-pity by *doing*. Thinking about how scared you are to try something new and feeling sorry for yourself because you don't have the energy or desire to try anymore will only build up your fears. Doing something about them will help them to vanish quicker.

HOW TO CLEAR YOUR EYES AND LOOK AT WHOM YOU'VE LOST.

During the first few days or weeks after you've said good-bye it is natural to go through a self-purging process, involving self-doubt and self-pity, plus romanticizing the one who initiated the parting. He or she becomes all that you ever wanted or a much better person than you really deserved—out of the "people" category and into an ideal wish for happiness and love ever after.

The lady who spent six months by herself often talked in our singles' group about how wonderful her ex-husband had been to her and how happy she'd be if he came back. The man who was left behind after twenty-one years of marriage would speak of his wife as a strong woman who finally got fed up with his weaknesses. Even many married couples in counseling will speak of their old loves (the ones who left them) as the love of their lives.

It is important, then, not only for your pain during the grief process, but also for your next intimate relationship to take your current ex-love out of the "god" category and place him/her in the realm of a person. No one, including you or your new love can compete with the ideal of perfection.

How do you stop caring for someone who no longer loves you? Decide that you want to enough to do something about it. See differences in your ex-love and new date as just that: differences in people, not proof that your old love was better. (Make sure that you're not suffering from the syndrome of never respecting someone who could care for a person like you.) Remember when comparing your old love to someone new, that you felt more at ease with your ex-love because you knew him or her for a longer period of time than you know the one you've just met.

Look at your ex-love's faults as well as his/her strengths when you gaze lovingly at your past. And see them as the problems that they actually were for you then, rather than trying to minimize or forgive them so quickly right now. If you couldn't tolerate your ex-love flirting with others, or spending more time at work than with you, or drinking too much, or acting irresponsibly or whatever the faults, remember the stress or unhappiness it created for you then and don't whitewash the problems so quickly. Each time you flash on how wonderful he/she was, remember some of his/her imperfections as well.

If you're unhappy or lonesome now, it's easy to minimize the loneliness and hurt in your past. See your idealization of him or her for what it really is—your own desire or need to love someone again. Once you can look at your ex-love realistically, it will be much easier for you to give your love to someone new.

To increase your objectivity in viewing your ex-love, use the space provided to list his/her traits or behavior you did *not* like:

Traits of behavior I did not like

1.
2.
3.
4.
5.

HOW TO DETERMINE WHAT YOU'VE LOST.

Looking at what you have really lost is just as important for your mental health and emotional growth as taking your ex-love off of that pedestal. Initially, you may feel overwhelmed with your loss, as if the rug has been pulled out from under you and there is nothing left in your life worth caring about.

Unlike your partner, you have not had the opportunity for serious forethought in unhooking emotionally from your ex-mate, planning where to live, what to give up or how you'll replace whatever you are losing. So, the loss can feel overwhelming at first. But gradually, as the days and nights pass, the ex-intimate who did not initiate the ending will begin the sometimes painful process of saying good-bye to the past and replacing the objects, ideals and people that have gone.

To help you go through this process in a healthier, more productive way, you will need to determine, somewhat objectively, what you have really lost versus your fears or fantasies of losing everything. This may be a painful process at first, especially if you've decided to feel like an absolute failure. But many ex-intimates discover, upon close examination, that even though they have lost an intimate relationship with a specific person, they have won the freedom to have a healthier, happier relationship with themselves and with someone new.

Begin by looking at what you still have and what you have gained by saying good-bye to your ex-mate. List these below:

What I have left	*What I have won*
1.	1.
2.	2.
3.	3.
4.	4.
5.	5.
6.	6.
7.	7.
8.	8.

Be sure to include things like your job, if you work, some friends and the support from your family, material possessions that you've kept, your children if they are with you, your health, intelligence, talents, personal warmth, *and*, although you may not be aware of it at first, your ability to care about someone and probably love again. Keep all of these factors in mind and add any others you think of from time to time. In the column of what you have won, be sure to include freedom from hassles with someone whom you could not please, nor could he or she please you. Those who were in a self-destructive relationship will find that in saying good-bye, no matter who says it first or how scary it it, they have won the freedom to develop a healthier relationship the next time around. Take for example, the man who, after fifteen years of marriage and twelve of alcohol abuse, finally quit drinking when his wife left him. The people who marry their parent figures often end up becoming adults when Mommy or Daddy finally moves out. So, in looking for what you have won, look at the negatives that were in your former relationship and applaud the fact that you have won your freedom from those.

Now that you are aware of some assets you still have or have won in saying good-bye, begin to look at what you have actually lost. Be careful not to romanticize or overgeneralize. You have not, for example, lost your reason for living, or everything in life that's worth caring for—even though it is typical for you to feel that way at times. You have lost specific people, roles and routines. So, make sure in determining what you are saying good-bye to, that you put down concrete examples. Much of what you have lost, you will want to replace at some future date and it will be much easier to do this if you are specific about what you have lost. The key in making your list is your attitude. You must genuinely want to determine what you have actually lost and not just use this to bemoan your fate or prove to yourself that you are a failure. It may take some time to obtain the objectivity you need to evaluate your losses fairly, but it also takes a genuine desire on your part to look realistically at your current position. This will be easier to do if you can curb your self-doubt, self-pity, and the tendency to glorify your ex-mate while examining your losses with an eye towards replacement.

HOW TO OWN ENDING AS YOUR CHOICE TOO.

> "One of the things that bothers me the most about our divorce is that it was Laurie's idea. Our marriage wasn't all that great, you understand. All it gave me was a housekeeper and an occassional bed partner, but I just stayed there and took it. She at least had the guts to end it—I must not feel very good about myself."

That was part of a statement that Vic, a thirty-four year old insurance salesman made in my office several months ago. He and Laurie had been married for eight years and while neither one of them was acutely miserable, both had gradually settled for a strained, mildly unhappy marital relationship. They had a seven year old son, Scott, who often seemed like the sole reason for staying together.

"This is the first time I have ever lost at anything—and, I don't like it at all. If only I had been the one to come up with the idea of divorce, I might have felt better."

Vic's lament over not being the first to announce that it's over and his resultant loss in pride is not unusual. Many ex-intimates who are in the same position express feelings of embarrassment, hurt pride, low self-esteem, rejection and depression because they were left by their mates. In fact, the majority of those who attempt or commit suicide or spend a long length of time feeling empty and staying alone are those who did not initiate the ending process. Often they view their ex-mates as better than they are: more desirable or emotionally stronger because the ex-mate is either involved with someone new or has the strength to leave an unhappy union without the security of another love affair right away. They see themselves as still committed to the relationship while their ex-mate was someone who needed something better. In some instances, this viewpoint plus anger and a feeling of helplessness can create a sense of being victimized with no control over what happens.

But few love affairs end with one mate still emotionally committed to the relationship and the other one out. Typically what happens is that one person (usually the one that's left behind) deals more indirectly or passively with his/her unhappiness in the relationship and, therefore, convinces him/herself that he/she was committed to stay.

Although Vic recognized that he did not feel the relationship was that good, he chose to deal with his discomfort by passively accepting the coolness and distance which settled over their marriage a long time before he ceased courting Laurie or viewing her as a primary love. His job became more important after Scott was born and gradually he turned to his friends or held the feelings inside that he initially shared with his wife. Laurie was always around and he no longer felt that he had to keep trying to please her. It was easier to take her presence for granted and spend his charm on customers instead of his wife. By taking her out of the category of someone worth pleasing and putting their relationship in the position of something that can take care of itself or let slide, Vic was instrumental in quietly pushing his wife away from him.

And, at many of those times, he was consciously aware of what he was doing. In fact, he could even remember telling himself that Laurie was unhappy and probably if he didn't work harder at showing his love she would leave him. Usually at those times he would find himself thinking: "She's not trying to please me, why should I bend over backwards for her?" or "She doesn't care, why should I?" Sometimes he found himself rationalizing that she expected too much from him, but that excuse didn't hold much water because he knew that if he really thought it was worth the effort, he could do almost anything. It just wasn't worth changing to please her or save the relationship. But, in spite of the years that Vic spent playing mental chess with how much affection, courtesy and respect to show Laurie, when his wife finally announced that their relationship was dead, he felt totally abandoned and shocked by her statement. "She rejected me—I'm not man enough to keep her," he wailed.

With time and professional counseling, however, Vic was able to recognize and own how many times he consciously (but indirectly) rejected Laurie. And, with each awareness, he was able to see that he was not helpless or victimized by Laurie's announcement. In fact, in looking back, he discovered that quietly through the years he had begun rejecting Laurie's affection by tuning her out or deciding that keeping a close relationship with his wife just wasn't worth the time and effort to change his behavior. By owning the choices that he also made to end their marriage, Vic was able to feel more in control of its death, and, therefore, not as helpless or inept in guiding his future.

To facilitate letting go of your feelings of being victimized by your ex-mate or innocent in the mutual decision to kill the relationship, it will be important for you to go back through your memories and recognize the times that you subtly declined to help strengthen the bond or actually weakened it even further. Whose final announcement actually began the burial procedure is really unimportant. Your judgment about whether good-bye was the "right" or "wrong" decision will vary. When you're feeling good about being out of it, it will be the "right" one, when you feel unhappy, it may be viewed as the "wrong" decision. But, either way, the decision to end the relationship was a mutual one. So, you need not wrap yourself up in self-doubt or place your ex-love on a pedestal for having more guts or being more desirable than you.

Going back through the past and owning your choices to end the relationship can be helpful to you. You had and still have just as much control over how close or how lasting an intimate relationship will be as your mate. Owning those choices and a constructive self-examination of when you said no will provide the tools to help guide yourself into a healthier more permanent intimate relationship the next time around.

COMMON SELF-INDUCED TRAPS AND HOW TO AVOID THEM.

Most traps come from feeling inadequate, rejected or abandoned, still being emotionally tied to your ex-mate and dependent on him/her to take care of your needs. If you knew that the relationship was dying and consciously made efforts to unhook from it, while your ex-mate was still present, you will probably not go through all of these traps as intensely or as often.

1. *Viewing your old love affair for what it might have been rather than what it was.* Part of saying good-bye to your old love affair is saying good-bye to your dreams of what it might have been—your fantasy of love ever after. A choice to see the ending as a tragedy and your ex-love as a god or goddess is a painful trap to fall into because any dreams of feeling as good again or maybe even better with someone else are automati-

cally doused. To fall into this trap, you must still feel emotionally connected to your ex-mate and must either be alone or unhappy with someone new to view your old relationship with such warm nostalgia.

Avoiding this trap is a matter of allowing yourself to mourn the death of your old relationship as it was: feeling sad about saying good-bye to the good times, but relieved that you will not continue enacting the bad scenes. Of course, there were times that were good—that's why it began—but there were also the painful, lonely times and that's why it's over now. So, mourn the death of your old love affair as it was, not as it *might* have been.

2. *Remembering the good times and forgetting the bad.* Similar to the trap we just mentioned, this one can also be painful and lead you into a future of emptiness if you stay there too long. Poets say this is a trap for romantics and idealists who find the painful memories too hurtful to recall; mental health professionals declare it's a tool ex-intimates use to punish themselves and remain dissatisfied, your best friend may tell you it's silly and you should stop torturing yourself, your own good sense will tell you that you're not being totally honest. But, in spite of all this knowledge and advice, there will be times when, in looking back over your old love relationship, you'll remember the good times and choose to forget the others.

Since you may do this anyway, despite your good sense, utilize this experience as an awareness that you have the ability to laugh and enjoy someone else and remember that when you are through the grief process, you can do that again—with someone new.

3 & 4. *Holding on to your ex-love by trying to get even or trying to get him/her to come back.* These two traps may sound different but in many ways, they are the same. Both can be harmful to you because the energy you waste on him/her could have been spent on someone much more important to your happiness—you! And, both traps are the results of the same factor: still being hooked on your past and a love that is gone. You are just as

emotionally hooked on someone you love and try to get back as someone you hate and want to see suffer. (But, you may need to try some of your tactics at getting your old love back or at revenge to find that truth out for yourself.)

You will know that you're trying to get your old love back when you find yourself doing any one of the following:

— calling your old love when you have absolutely no reason, just to see how he/she is doing.

— changing some of your habits or attitudes that your ex-love didn't like and then telling him/her you have done so.

— going out of your way to contact or please your ex-love.

— inviting her out to dinner, or having him over for a "home cooked" meal.

Some of these traps can also be a way of getting even with your old love. In fact, many ex-intimates who have been left behind, often speak of their fantasies of getting their old love back and then dropping them, as a way of getting even.

Other tactics which are part of the revenge fantasy are:

— spreading lies or harmful truths about your ex-love amongst mutual friends.

— turning your children or family members against him/her.

— flaunting your new love or success since the "divorce" in front of him/her.

— finding out your ex-love is unhappy, then rubbing it in with unkind remarks.

Both of these traps, whichever form they take, should be avoided if at all possible. It probably isn't worth your tine and effort to try getting your old love back. Spend that time and energy on someone new.

Getting even with your old love for leaving you or being the first to pronounce the relationship dead can be more harmful than helpful. One of the reasons you may feel vengeful is that you are still hurting. But getting back at your ex-love really won't make your wounds heal any faster, or help you feel worth loving again, or learn any faster to trust a new love. Use the anger you feel towards him/her in constructive ways to help yourself feel better again, rather than wasting it on your ex-love.

5. *Still caring about your ex-love more than anyone else.* If you've found no one new to replace your ex-love or have placed him or her up on a pedestal, it's natural to be scared of trying to love again but still need someone to love. The easiest solution for many (at least at the beginning of the grief process) is to idolize their ex-love. "I never knew how much I loved him until he was gone" is a common lament for ex-intimates. But someone who is easier to love at a distance than while he/she is close up cannot be a love you can live with: no matter how lonely you are or scared of your future. And, all of us need to love and be loved by someone who is present and available to touch or to hold in real life—not in our memories.

Caring more about your ex-mate than anyone else is a way of protecting yourself from getting hurt again. Your ex-love cannot possibly hurt you anymore than he/she already has, so there is no risk in still loving him/her. Someone new whom you're willing to trust with your love does have the power to hurt you, however. The problem with this is obvious, of course: in protecting yourself from being hurt too deeply, you also shield yourself from feeling the strength of your love.

It's your decision. Choose wisely. To relinquish the "love at a distance" for your ex-mate, you must deliberately decide to let go and then work to make it really happen.

6. *Spending a lot of emotional energy thinking about your ex-love and his/her new life.* If you're lonely or unhappy, you may find yourself daydreaming about what your ex-love is doing —who he/she is involved with now and whether they are happy

together. Sometimes you will hope that their relationship lasts so that you can finally give yourself permission to bury your old love and other times you will find yourself wishing it would fail so the two of you can get back together again. "Maybe if she's as lonely as I am, she'll come back to me." Your feelings may fluctuate back and forth between these two from day to day.

You need not be terribly concerned about falling into this trap, because you will find that it tends to be self-limiting: that is, gradually it dies out, either because you become aware that it leads nowhere or you decide to get busy and find someone new.

You can speed up the process by finding someone new to day-dream about or filling your boredom with creative projects and personal goals to attain.

WAYS OF REACHING OUT TO OTHERS.

Since you may have a tendency to be more passive or dependent than your ex-mate, it's important for you to remember not to demean yourself unfairly or allow fate to control your destiny. You will need to actively reach out to other people. Your ex-love will look very good to you (no matter how unavailable or de-structive the love) if the choice for your present and future is between him/her and nothing. Even if you feel that you're not ready to replace the old love with someone new, it's important to at least begin developing new friendships and give your empti-ness a chance to be filled by kindness, respect and support from others.

Let people know that you need them. Show them and tell them directly how important they are to you. Take the time to smile and say hello to strangers. Initiate getting together with friends. Spend at least an equal amount of energy building friends for your future as you do trapped in the past. Use the charm that you used on your last love to find someone new, and the insight you've developed about yourself to make the effort to change. If you discover that in your last relationship you were always too scared to risk saying "I need you" or "You're important to

me," gather the strength to say it this time. Don't let the mistrust
of others or your own self-doubt get in the way of accepting and
giving the warmth and the love that all of us have to share with
each other.

At first you may have to force yourself to break out of your
shell and begin sharing your feelings, thoughts or ideas with
others. But, gradually you will find that your awkwardness and
fears will vanish and in its place will be a sense of pride, self-
confidence and the warmth from your friends.

ON THE THOUGHT OF MOVING.

Many ex-intimates who are not the first to initiate the ending
may remain in their former homes or communities. "If you want
a divorce, you move out! I'm staying here." At first it may seem
like a triumph. At least, you kept the family abode or are still in
familiar surroundings. Everything in your life has not changed.
But after a few weeks, you may notice that the comfort of being in
the same scenes is gradually beginning to make you uneasy.
Going to the same grocery store seems different somehow. The
buildings in your neighborhood or trees on your block remind
you of your ex-love, and when you sleep in your old bed alone,
the memories rush back. This time you're alone in that space:
last time you were part of a pair. Sometimes staying in familiar
surroundings or following the same routines will make it impossible to bury the past because it prolongs the mourning process.

And while, practically speaking, it may be easier for you to
remain in the same house or community, if, after a while (say
six months or so), you find yourself just as deeply entrenched in
the home situation as you were when he/she left, you may want
to make a concerted effort to change your environment. You need
not move all the way across country, and it's true that you cannot
run away from your past or the memories, but you can deem-
phasize them. Think about the idea of moving from your home.
If you own it, maybe selling the family homestead will give you
the cash to launch yourself into a brighter future. If you're rent-
ing, isn't it about time you thought of moving into a singles'
apartment or a house on the beach?

If you decide, for whatever reasons, to stay in the same house—or the same community—begin rearranging your house and saying good-bye to the memories that flash back when you look at the old, familiar "scenes". Use different routes to drive to the store. Experiment with shopping at different times of the day, days of the week—or different stores entirely. Change or reorganize as much of your old environment and routine as you can. It will shorten the mourning process and help you feel better after he/she has said good-bye.

Even if you are not the first one to say that it's over, you can learn through the process of ending that being without your ex-mate can be the beginning of a healthier, happier future for you. Sure, there will be times when you feel you've been abandoned and rejected by someone who's better, but, as you begin looking more realistically at whom and what you've lost and owning your choice to end it also, you may find yourself wishing that your partner had announced his/her departure sooner.

Experiments and Exercises

Consider the following when you have uninterrupted time:

*Say in a sentence what you imagine your ex-love thinks of you.

*Is your current self-appraisal related in any way to his/her opinion of you? How is it different?

*If you have "bought" his/her opinion of you, how long do you plan to keep it? What will you have to do when you are ready to give it up?

For those who are filled with self-doubt:

*Ask yourself, "How was I ever convinced that I'm inadequate?"

*Look back in your memory and watch the scenes which influenced this decision. Evaluate them *now* as you would for a friend.

*For the next 48 hours be aware of all the ways you put yourself down. Then, for the following two days stop yourself from judging you so harshly.

List all the things you do well:

1.
2.
3.
4.
5.

*Become aware of those competencies during the new few days. Pat yourself on the back when you do well.

This exercise will help you say good-bye to your ex-love. Do it when you feel strong, not "down" and have some "quiet" time to yourself. Let yourself re-experience those feelings as you can tolerate them. You may need to do this several times until you feel "finished".

*Imagine that you are in a conversation with your ex-love. Share how you felt during the latter part of your relationship and any "unsaid" words you've kept inside. When you have expressed everything you've buried inside, say "Good-bye."

9:   For the One Who Finally Called It *Finis*

Generally ex-intimates who are the first to say good-bye have less trouble going through the grief process and find it easier to begin a new life than their partners. There are a number of reasons for this: their ego-strengths (pride, self-confidence, independence and ability to adjust) are usually stronger; often they are not as dependent on the relationship for emotional or physical survival; in rare cases, they are not committed to a permanent relationship from the onset; and, finally, they are the ones who actively decide that burying the relationship will be better.

In spite of this, however, the ex-intimate who first declares that it's over will often go through just as much grief in mourning the death of an intimate relationship as his/her ex-mate. He/she may also incur special problems in regards to feelings of guilt or responsibility for his/her partner's future adjustment. This is especially true if the relationship is seen as a parent/child involvement and the ex-mate who is leaving is viewed as emotionally stronger and somehow responsible for taking care of the one who is left behind—or asked to leave. The longer a parent/child relationship has existed, the more difficult ending will be.

Deborah, a forty-three year old high school teacher, was married to her husband, Tom, for twenty-six years before she finally filed for divorce. They married after high school graduation and for the next twelve years, Tom worked at five different sales jobs and Deborah took care of their three sons (Tom, Jr., age 11, Mike, age 10, and Brian, age 8). Tom's hours were long and he spent many evenings away from home entertaining his customers. Sometimes he drank excessively at those meetings and, once, during the first twelve years, he was fired for drinking too much. Finances were always a problem, and Deborah decided to get an education so that she could help support the family. Six years later, she had obtained a secondary teaching credential and was hired by the local high school to teach English. Tom, in the meantime, had just lost his fourth sales job in two years for excessive drinking and unreliability.

For the next eight years, Deborah supported the family and Tom continued to drink. Jobs didn't last very long and the weeks between jobs stretched into months. The boys grew up, went away to school or the service, and, finally, on their twenty-fifth wedding anniversary, with all of their sons raised, Tom and Deborah were alone together, again. Several attempts were made throughout the marriage by both Tom and Deborah to save their relationship and get Tom off alcohol. He was in and out of A.A., admitted to a psychiatric hospital on three different occassions and seen by a number of therapists—with no success. Deborah was also involved in therapy and, finally, after several years of indecision about staying in the marriage, decided that she could no longer live with Tom. She filed for divorce.

The ending process that followed was painful to both. Tom continued to drink, using his failure at marriage and "life" as his reasons. Deborah continued to support him, at times, financially; periodically bail him out of trouble; and, in general, become increasingly more depressed about her own situation and guilt ridden by her felt responsibility to Tom.

Nine months after their divorce, I met Deborah in my office. And through the course of therapy, Deborah was finally able to let go of her depression and guilt feelings and learn to feel better about herself and her life than she had felt in years.

This chapter is written for men and women like Deborah who, somehow, through the course of a "marriage", end up parenting their partners and feeling responsible for their ex-mate's survival and happiness.

MOVING IS NO PICNIC EITHER: PROBLEMS ENCOUNTERED BY THOSE WHO LEFT.

As we've already acknowledged, many ex-intimates who are the first to say good-bye can have just as much pain in leaving a relationship as the one who still sees him/herself as committed. If you physically leave and take with you the burdens of financial support for your ex-mate and children, as well as yourself, you may struggle with all of the problems of poverty—plus. Typically, in our society, this happens to the man: "If he wants a divorce, he'll pay through the nose!" vows his dejected spouse. Often the lawyers and judges agree. Sometimes even the man, who feels guilty may concede: "If I can't give my wife and children the love they deserve, at least I should see that they're financially secure." So, one of the problems that often comes up is the financial strain. An ex-intimate may agree to pay more in money just to ease his conscience or avoid a hassle.

Another type of payment an ex-intimate may agree to accept is harder to see but more difficult to avoid: self-blame or the judgement from others that ending the relationship was selfish and "wrong". Anytime it looks to you like your ex-mate is suffering or you are faced with some of the problems of dissolution like loneliness or fear of your future, you may find yourself "paying" for the decision to leave by condemning yourself for your choice.

Deborah spent many hours condemning herself for being too hard on Tom—not understanding and supporting him as much as she felt she should. "When I married Tom, I vowed to stay with him for better or worse, in sickness and in health.

Alcoholism is a sickness and I broke my vows. I deserve to feel unhappy. God knows, I wasn't a perfect wife—and he stayed with me, anyway."

Relatives and friends who are close to your ex-spouse may also judge you harshly at times, especially if your ex-mate openly declares that he/she still wants to continue the relationship but you won't agree. In this type of scene, your ex-spouse is seen as the underdog. And, whether that is accurate or not, many onlookers will automatically be on his/her side and, therefore, against you for saying good-bye.

The payment of self-blame or negative judgments from others can be a high price to pay for your freedom—and one that, beyond constructive self-criticism, will serve no earthly purpose in helping you to feel better again or become a healthier person. Still, it's a problem you may encounter after you've decided to bury the relationship.

Occasionally an ex-intimate who is emotionally unstable will invite you to feel sorry for him and totally responsible for how he/she copes with the ending by threatening to destroy him/herself or using emotional blackmail: "I can only survive if you're part of my life," or "If you come back I'll change—otherwise, I don't know what I'll do." Although this problem is rare, if your ex-mate has convinced him/herself (or you) that he/she is unable to survive without you, I suggest that you seek professional counseling for both of you: to help you unhook and your partner learn how to be independent. Learning how to feel better after you have said good-bye will be difficult enough without the voice of threatening doom hanging over your head.

Another problem that is not quite so treacherous but much more frequent is the problem of having your ex-mate periodically contact you for continued emotional support or occassional questioning regarding your decision to end it. Each time this happens, you will no doubt feel a slight surge of annoyance, mixed with ambivalent feelings about your decision and a small amount of guilt if the choice remains unaltered. In time, your ex-mate will no doubt cease contacting you to continue the relationship and begin turning to someone else. (Incidentally, when he finds someone new you may feel some sadness.) In the meantime, direct, honest communication that you plan to stay with your choice of ending should speed up that process for him/her.

Most special problems that arise for the first one to end the relationship are self-induced traps which are caused by your feelings of ambivalence about ending the relationship, plus guilt and responsibility for the welfare of your ex-mate.

CAUSAL FACTORS OF GUILT.

Guilt is a form of self-punishment or blame that we apply to ourselves when we have done something that we believe is "wrong" or fail to do something that we think of as "right". It is a tool that we use to control our behavior. Anytime your behavior is different than your value system, you will feel guilty. If you have a value that says fidelity is important, infidelity will cause you to feel guilt. If "marriage forever" is part of your value system, divorce will be seen as an act of shame and something to hide.

There is a wide variation within each person's value system and, therefore, different degrees of guilt that each person may experience—depending on what he/she did and how strongly he/she feels about it. For example, while I may have a strong value for maintaining honesty with those I trust or respect, I may have only mild guilt pangs when not being totally honest with a used car salesman. Knowingly harming a person through an act of unkindness may cause me sleepless nights of remorse; accidentally hurting a friend through a casual remark can be mended by an apology. Within my own value system, there are ideals I feel are extremely important to uphold and others which I would like to follow but understand and forgive when I don't.

Each individual gains his sense of values from his religious background, national or cultural heritage, family and friends. Because of all these variables, every human being has a slightly different value system than his neighbor. But there are some general values that most of us growing up in a Judeo-Christian culture have in common, such as: the value of treating others as we would like to be treated ourselves, viewing adultery as something less than honorable or seeing the destruction of human life as a crime. Some people's value systems are so rigid and narrow that even thoughts of going outside their system cause tremendous feelings of guilt. Others have such loose or broad value systems that almost nothing they say or do creates any feelings of remorse. Most of us fall somewhere in between.

Many ex-intimates who initiate good-bye feel pangs of remorse or intense guilt because of any one or a combination of the following:

— divorce is against their value system.

— leaving their family or mate just because of their own dissatisfaction feels "wrong" or "selfish".

— they believe they have a responsibility to take care of their ex-mate.

— their behavior during the relationship was less than honest or went against their value system.

Whatever the specific causal factors of your own guilt feelings, it will be important for you, in diminishing your remorse or absolving the pangs altogether, to first figure out what personal values you specifically have violated by your behavior. In doing this, you may discover that you can let go of some of the guilt just by knowing how you have let yourself down, or by recognizing the need for change within your value system.

HEALTHY WAYS TO DEAL WITH GUILT.

People can do a lot of harmful things to themselves in the name of self-punishment—suicide attempts, excessive drinking, drug abuse, self-condemnation, withdrawal and isolation from friends and family. The best way to deal with guilt is to never do anything that will make you feel bad about yourself. But the reality is that sometimes we human beings let ourselves down—do things we feel ashamed of or wish we hadn't done.

There are two things you can do with your guilt feelings: beat yourself over the head with self-condemnation or learn from your mistakes and, perhaps, modify your value system. Many people vow that they will never let go of their guilt feelings about something they've done because what they did was so horrendous to them. While a certain amount of guilt may be healthy and help curb you from reenacting a behavior that lowers your self-esteem, an extensive amount can become very harmful. You will know for yourself how many pangs of remorse you need to keep buried inside in order not to let yourself down in that manner again. It will be hard for you to accept yourself and learn how to grow or feel better if you judge yourself unworthy because of your past mistakes or a decision you made which is against part of your value system. The man who beats himself for divorcing his wife because of religious beliefs will find that he may be stuck in loneliness for the rest of his life if he decides he cannot go back to his wife, and that he doesn't deserve or have the right to find happiness with someone new.

Letting go of your guilt and learning from your mistakes or altering your value system can be a long and complicated process. A martyr (someone who sacrifices his own needs for the sake of others) will have a more difficult time letting go of his guilt about initiating the dissolution than someone who feels comfortable in taking care of his own wants and desires first. The more your ex-mate or family is suffering from the ending or begging to have you return, the greater your chances of holding on to your guilt—if you feel at all responsible for their welfare.

Vague, generalized guilt feelings can only be handled by vague, generalized regret and self-punishment. The more specific you are about what actually triggers your guilt, the better your chances of releasing it and growing beyond. Therefore, the first step in this process is to figure out specifically what you feel guilty about. Was it how you acted in the relationship, or is it the fact that it ended? One lady felt guilty about ending the relationship because her ex-mate still loved her and wanted their love to continue. Her recognition that she did not love him and subsequent decision to dissolve their relationship were directly opposed to her values that she should feel the same way about people as they feel about her and that she should not, under any circumstances, hurt someone's feelings. Once she learned why she felt guilty, she could begin the process of dealing with her guilt in a healthier manner, rather than generally feeling guilt and remorse and buying a "mean" or "unloving" self-image. One man suffered a great deal of guilt and self-blame for divorcing his wife who was psychiatrically disabled. In spite of the fact that she spent most of her time in hospitals and had for years, the man felt like a villain. His decision to end their relationship was directly opposed to his values of staying with his ex-mate (through sickness or health), wanting to be someone who was loyal and loving no matter what the circumstances, plus feeling responsible for causing her illness or not helping her become healthier. Once he was able to recognize why he felt guilty, he, too, was able to begin the process of dealing with his guilt feelings in ways that were healthy for him as opposed to harmful self-condemnation.

After you have identified specifically why you feel guilty, begin to figure out what it would take to give yourself permission to let go of or lessen your guilt. This is the "making up" or penance phase of the process. This is only necessary for those actions or decisions you feel guilty about *after* you understand specifically what they are. Go through each item that you feel badly about and determine what you need to do to absolve your conscience that is healthy and helpful to you. Would an apology to your ex-mate be helpful—or, perhaps a vow to learn from your mistakes and try not to repeat your behavior? One man who left his wife lessened his guilt about leaving by helping her get some occupational training and then her first job. Another man who felt guilty about leaving his children learned to lessen his guilt by making it a point to be the best part-time father he could. The list of examples for how to absolve your guilt in a healthier manner than beating yourself with remorse is endless. Any kind of "repayment" which will help you obtain self-forgiveness will do but be careful not to include self-sacrifice or self-denial as part of your penance.

The third step is the hardest to do, but the easiest to explain. Once you have decided specifically what you need to do to let go of your guilt or lessen the shame, get busy and do it. No need to punish yourself any longer by procrastinating. If it's saying "I'm sorry" or making an effort to change your behavior for the next time or whatever it is, grab a hold of your courage and get on with it. The sooner you've paid for your feelings of shame or letting yourself down by some actions, the quicker you can give up your feelings of guilt.

The final step is learning to actually forgive yourself. Once you have really gone through the process of constructive self-examination and have learned specifically why you feel guilty, the reasons you had for your behavior or decisions at the time, as well as developed a way of "making up" for the actions that you cannot forgive just through understanding and accepting yourself as a person with faults, it should be a simple matter for you to say to yourself—"I forgive you." It may sound silly to you now, but actually practice saying those words or something similar while looking at yourself in the mirror. Repeat them until they feel right to you. Forgiving yourself for mistakes you have made or broadening your sense of values will help you feel a whole lot better through the grief process. Plus, you might just find you'll be a healthier person for the next time around.

HOW TO GET YOURSELF IN PROPER PERSPECTIVE.

One of the major reasons ex-intimates who are the ones that initiate good-bye feel guilty is because they mistakenly see themselves as *the* ones who are totally responsible for the dissolution. While this may give some people a sense of power and importance, it can also hand them sleepless nights of regret or self-condemnation, if they decide, for whatever reason, that the decision to end was wrong—or much more difficult than they had planned.

But, the death of an intimate relationship and its eventual burial is the hand-work of two people *not* one. If you're an ex-intimate who currently believes that you are solely responsible for the ending of that last love, you may find it quite helpful to get yourself in proper perspective and take a more realistic view of your own power, responsibility and blame, if you must, for the burial of your old love.

To help you more clearly evaluate your control over and responsibility for the demise of your love, take a few moments and answer the following questions for yourself.

1. How much of my decision to announce "it's over" came from my partner's failure to change or compromise with me?

2. How many times before I pulled out did I hear my partner indirectly say he/she didn't care anymore?

3. When it comes right down to it, what are the reasons our love died and how many times was I responsible versus the number of times it was within my ex-mate's control?

4. Why do I need to feel like it was my sole decision, anyway? What would I do differently now if I didn't?

5. If I'm so powerful, why couldn't I have changed the relationship into something more satisfying?

6. What actually killed my commitment to stay with my ex-mate—did I just stop loving and respecting him/her by myself?

7. What good does it do to "blame" one of us more than the other?

By answering these questions or beginning to look at them, you will no doubt discover that the choice, no matter when you consciously made it, was also guided by your ex-mate. There is a strength in finally deciding to bury a relationship that is dead, but do not damn yourself into believing that this strength makes you strong enough to carry the entire burden of dissolution and the subsequent fall-out for both of you.

You have the strength to make your own decision on what you are willing to settle for in an intimate relationship and what you are not. You will need to nurture those strengths to help you feel better now that it's over—do not zap them by carrying the entire blame for the ending whenever it feels that the decision was somehow wrong or scary.

HOW TO EQUALIZE BLAME FOR DISSOLUTION.

Self-blame and negative judgment from others, including your ex-mate, will occur if the dissolution of an intimate relationship is viewed as unfair or somehow "wrong". Because of the nature of ending, the subsequent grief process, and sociological and religious pressures, it will be impossible to escape blame placed on one or both ex-intimates for the death of their "marriage".

There is nothing wrong with an ex-intimate accepting his own responsibility for the decision to end a love affair. In fact, it can be healthy. The problem occurs when one ex-intimate assumes all of the responsibility for ending and, in doing that, discounts the fact that each of them gradually became negligent in nurturing their love for the other. The ex-intimate who initiates good-bye often takes on this burden of "fault" for some of the following reasons:

1. He/she is the first to suggest or announce directly that it's over.

2. Often his/her mate is more passive and dependent, and may beg the partner to stay or reconsider.

3. He/she is the one who is less emotionally commited to the relationship at the time of ending and will, therefore, probably adjust much quicker to a new life.

4. He/she may see their old love as fragile and therefore,

protect him/her from assuming an equal amount of "fault" for the ending. ("It wasn't his fault that he couldn't support the family, he's always been afraid of responsibility.")

Comments like: "I should have been more understanding—or given in more often—or changed my expectations" are common to hear from an ex-intimate who feels badly about the dissolution even though he/she was the one to initiate good-bye. Many ex-intimates who take on most of the blame for the ending do this because of their own self-concept. They see themselves as people who are never satisfied with less than perfection and somehow, maybe because of that, have the ability to destroy or cause harm to those whom they love. Most clients I see who divorce a spouse that's an alcoholic, for example, often blame themselves for their ex-mate's drinking problem. "He wouldn't be an alcoholic if I hadn't nagged him so much—I knew he had a drinking problem and I just made it worse."

To help equalize blame for the end of a love affair, you must not only recognize that both of you were responsible for its demise, but, also, give up judging whether good-bye was the right or wrong decision to make. The fact of the matter is that the relationship is dead and you are now in the process of burying it for yourself.

COMMON SELF-INDUCED TRAPS.

Ex-intimates who initiate good-bye often fall into some of the following self-induced traps because of their own mixed feelings about ending the relationship.

— Feeling guilty each time you have a good time or when you begin feeling better.

— Acting on ambivalence: going back and forth about your decision to end and acting on it.

— Continuing to meet your ex-mate's emotional or sexual needs out of guilt.

— Screaming at your ex-mate to "shape up" and become independent so that you no longer need to feel tied down or guilty.

— Seeing yourself as emotionally stronger or more prepared to cope with the ending and, therefore, not seeking support for yourself from friends and family.

All of these traps are a natural part of the grief process and it may be necessary for you to slide in and out of some of them in order for you to feel better about yourself and finally let go of your dead love affair. Each time you fall into one of these traps, your energy is spent on trying to unhook from the past or absolve your guilt. It's important to remember that some of your energy must be focused on developing a creative future as well. And even though you had the strength to initiate good-bye, you, too, will need to nurture your strengths and gain support from others to grow through the grief process.

UTILIZING STRENGTHS TO HANDLE OBSTACLES COMING UP.

Every ex-intimate, whether the one who initiated good-bye or not, will run into a number of obstacles once he/she is single again. Just learning how to date again can be a frustrating and awkward experience of trial and error at first. If you've been married for twenty years, you may discover that being single again is a lot like being back in your adolescence—only this time with a slightly dumpy body, greying hair, a battered self-image and a somewhat provincial moral code. You will need a great deal of courage, flexibility and determination (plus maybe a good sense of humor) to tackle this challenge all over again—especially on those first few dates.

One lady I know confessed that she spent all afternoon and part of an evening getting ready for her first date.

"I cleaned up the house, shuffled the kids off to grandma's, spent over an hour putting on make-up and combing my hair, then another hour dressing and redressing. Nothing I put on seemed to look exactly the way that I wanted it to— I hadn't realized that my wardrobe consisted mostly of clothes to work around the house, rush to the supermarket or drive the kids to the dentist. I settled for a five year old dress that I bought for a P.T.A. installation and a vow that I had to lose ten pounds and buy some new clothes. All through the day, I was nervous and no amount of telling myself to relax seemed to help. Twice I thought about calling my date and telling him that one of the kids was sick, but decided that I had to start dating again sometime. I'm glad that I did, we really had a good time and now I can look back on that scene with a smile and some pride at how confident I've gotten since then."

The awkwardness of dating isn't confined to just the female gender, of course. Many men also find it nerve-wracking to go back to the business of asking a woman for a date, figuring out where to go, how to be entertaining, whether and when to make sexual advances, as well as how many times he can see one woman before she expects some sort of exclusive relationship. The chances are that both dating partners have had a previous relationship and will, therefore, feel equally awkward and uncomfortable about these issues in dating again.

Dating is just one of the challenges of being single again. Some of the others which will require your strength, determination and ability to roll with the punches are:

— Figuring out what you really want to do with your life now that you have your freedom.

— Constructive insight and change, including the resolution of some old "hang-ups".

— Learning how to take care of everyday tasks that your ex-mate handled such as: cooking, washing, ironing, shopping and housekeeping, if you're a man; or, taking care of mechanical, electrical and maybe even financial matters, if you're a woman—plus, perhaps, learning how to support yourself for the first time.

No wonder ex-intimates sometimes feel lost or overwhelmed with depression and decide to crawl into a hole. Hiding can certainly be mighty tempting at times. Especially in the beginning.

To creatively conquer these obstacles, it is important to use every strength that you have—and—learn to build more. If you spend a lot of time worrying about your ex-mate or punishing yourself for initiating good-bye, you will have little motivation or energy left over for getting yourself ready for dating again or meeting any one of the other challenges of being single again. You have already begun to use your courage, pride and common sense to announce the end of a relationship that was already dead. Now, it is important that you continue to devote your energy to you and building an emotionally healthier future.

Experiments and Exercises.

The ex-intimate who initiates good-bye often gets "hooked" in guilt and resentment. For those who are stuck in these feelings, the following exercise will prove beneficial. As with any of the exercises, choose a setting where you are physically and emotionally comfortable and will not be interrupted by noise. Make sure you feel strong, and not "down".

Close your eyes and look back in your memory for the last scene which gave you an invitation to feel guilty. Remember who was there and what was happening. Allow yourself to feel the guilt and resentment.

*When you are ready, imagine that you are in a dialogue with the person you feel guilt/resentment towards. Share how you honestly feel towards him/her now and make sure you express your resentment tied with your guilt. For example, "I resent you telling me that you want me back because then I feel guilty about not wanting you anymore." Continue repeating this final assertion until you feel that it "fits" for you. (This may take several rehearsals.) When it finally feels right, close the dialogue with an announcement that you are no longer going to feel guilty about that issue anymore.

After this exercise take some time to reflect:

   *What can you learn from this
__ about your relationship with that person?
__ about your relationship with other people?
__ about your relationship with yourself?

During the next 48 hours be aware of when you find yourself feeling obligated or responsible for someone else.

   *What do you get out of it? (Does it help you feel better than everyone else, for example?)

   *Is there some other way you would like to feel?

   *What would you have to do to change it?

List all of the reasons you deserve to take care of your own needs first.
1.
2.
3.
4.
5.

10: Healthy Ways to Mourn

It may seem strange to include a chapter on healthy ways to mourn; after all, isn't this book designed to help you feel *better* after you've said good-bye? Nevertheless, in order to grow through the grief process and really let go of the past, you will need to go through a mourning phase. In fact, part of this chapter will include constructive ways you can help yourself get in touch with your pain, because, paradoxical as it may sound, your mental health demands it. If you cared enough about your ex-love and the life that you had to feel any kind of pleasure, you will need to feel the sadness and grief consciously when it's dead in order to let go of it and really feel good again.

The process of grieving over the death of an intimate relationship, like the grief for the death of a person involves five stages —denial, depression, anger, resignation and acceptance/procedure with your life. It is necessary to go through all of these stages in order to finally reach the fifth which involves going on with your life. There are thousands of people walking around who have never really gone through the grief process and therefore, have never really gotten over an old love affair. These people continue to carry their hurt feelings or anger into their next love relationship or live the rest of their lives all alone.

No one can tell you exactly how long it will take to finally accept that it's over and proceed with your life without carrying a lot of unresolved hurts. It varies for each person. Do not expect yourself to go through the mourning process in a simple 1,2,3 fashion. Human beings and their feelings are more complicated than that and we need the time, plus regressions, to help us really heal. Consequently, there will be times when you go from the first stage of the grief process to the second to the third, then back to the first or the second again. This cycle will repeat itself again and again as long as you need to go through it—until you have finally resolved all the questions and problems that arise in each stage—or learned to finally set them aside.

There is one thing for sure, however, whether you acknowledge your grief to yourself or not—it will be there. If you deny the existence of that pain, you will wipe out your only opportunity to learn how to control the sorrow and let go of the grief. If, for example, you tell yourself that you really don't have a cold, it doesn't change the reality that it exists; it only alters the way you deal with it. Ignore a cold and continue with your daily routine and you may find yourself lying in bed with pneumonia. Ignore your sadness and continue with your regular routine and you may find yourself feeling numb inside and therefore unable to love someone new.

HOW TO GIVE YOURSELF PERMISSION TO GRIEVE.

> "I don't need to learn how to feel sad—that comes naturally. I need to learn how to turn off the pain."

But being able to naturally feel sorrow over the loss of someone or something actually helps you grow through the grief process and learn to feel better. For, without feeling sad, you cannot bury your dead love and constructively seek out new relationship to overcome the loneliness.

We are taught as children not to feel sorrow or any kind of negative feeling. "Don't get angry, it isn't good for you." "Don't feel sad about your dead kitten, we'll get you another one." "If you can't say something nice, don't say anything at all." "Come on soldier, big boys don't cry." By the time we're adults, we not only do not share painful feelings directly with other people, but sometimes do not allow even ourselves to know what we really feel.

The dangers in this "avoidance" are phenomenal:

— By cutting off negative feelings from your awareness, you also diminish your ability to feel the positive ones.

— Unacknowledged hurt festers inside and may turn into anger or a sensation of not being aware of any feelings.

— When you deny your right to be aware of your painful emotions, the emotional hurt can lodge in your body and become physically translated into ulcers, heart attacks, colitis or headaches.

Children rarely have ulcers or tension headaches; parents often do because adults are taught to think out their problems—children quite naturally feel them. An emotionally healthy adult learns how to do both: feel the pain and then learn how to problem solve and adjust. If you are an adult who has somehow forgotten how to let yourself feel, the first thing that you need to do is give yourself permission to grieve over the loss of your ex-love. You really will not fall apart. Remind yourself that you weren't always so afraid of your feelings—even the painful ones—and that you have a right as an ex-intimate who feels sad to directly acknowledge that pain to yourself. There are some things that you just can't think away. Math problems can be solved by logical abstraction; hurt feelings begin healing after you've given yourself permission to acknowledge that the wounds exist.

WAYS OF ALLOWING SELF TO FEEL PAIN.

If you find it difficult to really allow yourself to feel the grief from good-bye, you may find it helpful to consider these suggestions. First, develop an understanding of why feeling your pain is so scary. For some people, it is foreign to take the time to acknowledge their own hurt feelings. They have learned throughout their lives that their own feelings are not as important as other peoples'; discounting themselves has become automatic. If this is the case for you, begin standing up for yourself. Be as concerned about your own feelings as you are about your friends'.

Others shy away from feelings because their experience with grief has been traumatic and second-hand. They have known or heard about someone who became so overwhelmed with hurt, self-pity, depression or anger that they stayed stuck there forever. If you have no real-life practical experience of your own, the fear of falling into the same trap forever can put the skids on your willingness to experience your grief. But you must have faith in your own ability to grow—and let go of your pain when it becomes too intense. With practice you will discover that when you take control of your grief and allow yourself to feel the pain, you also have the strength to shut if off when it becomes overwhelming.

Another quite obvious hesitation in allowing yourself to feel the pain is that it hurts! And most of us don't like to hurt. But the fact of the matter is that the pain is already there from saying good-bye. Your only decision at this point is whether to go ahead and let yourself feel it directly and then learn to release it, or whether to carry it around inside your gut for the rest of your life and gingerly avoid caring about anyone again because of the fears that you can't take any additional hurt.

Once you have a basic understanding of why feeling pain is so terrifying to you, the next step is to see how you currently keep yourself from feeling the grief. Usually people avoid owning their hurt by either keeping so busy that they don't have time to be alone and think, or they rationalize why they shouldn't feel any sorrow. "There's no reason to feel badly, it won't help" or "I don't know why I should feel badly about losing him—he's a bum anyway." When you find out how you avoid owning your grief, you can allow yourself to feel some of the pain by curtailing the techniques you use to deny it exists. Usually this is the easiest way to get in touch with your feelings. Just ask yourself, "How do I feel when I'm not hiding from me?"

If it's been several weeks since you've separated from your ex-love and have not allowed yourself to experience your grief, the first recognition of the hurt inside your body may come out like a flood. One woman shared that the first time she actually sat down and decided to cry over her divorce, she spent the entire week-end in tears.

"The only other things I did that week-end was periodically fix something to eat and occasionally sleep. I've never been so exhausted in my life. Tears just flowed. At first my whole body felt tight, like there was a bomb inside ready to explode. But once I finally began letting the tears and the sadness out, the pressure inside disappeared. I can't even tell you what I cried about or all of the different thoughts that raced through my head. And, just when I thought I was through crying, the tightness would come back in my chest or stomach and I'd start crying again. At one point I remember thinking that I had to quit this and get control of myself, then I remember telling myself that I had nothing else to do, and I deserved a good cry. I haven't cried as intensely or as long since then. I guess the feelings had to come out—I even remember deciding sometime during that week-end, that once I was over this, I had to find some new goals for my life. I'm just beginning to look at that now—I'm not sure yet what I'll do with that, but I know now that I'll make it."

A man related a similar experience, adding that in order for him to finally allow himself to begin feeling grief, he literally had to force himself to look at old family pictures, listen to sad records and remind himself that his marriage was over.

"The last time I remember crying was when I was seven and my grandfather died. My mother said she was surprised because she didn't think I felt that strongly. It's funny, I really don't know why I never shared my feelings very much. Probably it would look funny for a middle aged businessman to burst out in tears when he loses an account. But knowing that I actually do have feelings, makes me feel so much better about me. I've gotten a lot closer to me and my friends since then. Just by being what I've always been but was afraid to admit—a human being with feelings."

The point is that once you allow yourself to feel the pain from your loss, you will discover some very valuable rewards:

— There is a relief in allowing yourself to experience your pain.

— It will hurt and feel scary at times but will never be quite as intense as the first time.

— Allowing yourself to grieve makes space in body for positive feelings.

— Feeling pain will help motivate you to proceed with your life.

GETTING PROPER PERSPECTIVE ON LOSS.

One of the major reasons that an ex-intimate may feel overwhelmed by his/her loss at first is because the death of a love affair, like the death of a person, immediately gets an individual in touch with his/her own mortality and ultimate lack of power. A death or the loss of anything major in your life literally leaves you feeling disconnected from the world that you know and frightened of the future which is initially unknown. People who are emotionally prepared for dissolution or the death of a loved one and what they'll do next with their own lives will suffer less intense feelings of being alone and abandoned than their unprepared counterparts.

When you first get in touch with your grief you may be trying to cope with an overwhelming fact of life that you could not have been aware of at first—your unconscious fear of death. For a while, life may feel like it has no meaning to you. On a conscious level that meaninglessness might derive from the loss of your ex-love, parts of your identity and former life style. On an unconscious level you may be dealing with the death of the YOU that you have known. The longer you have been involved in your last intimate relationship, the harder it is for you to see yourself as a real live person outside of it. That is why you may automatically begin evaluating your life up until the present (or quickly condemning it), find yourself wanting to return to a nurturing family or someone who can give you love and comforting and, then, slowly, begin to decide, as did the lady in my group, that you need to develop new goals for yourself or a reason to make your life meaningful.

Getting your loss in proper perspective in this case means not only looking realistically at whom and what you have lost, but, also, recognizing on a conscious level that you are still alive. There are many crises in our lives (saying good-bye to our childhood, or our children's dependency on us, or a career, or an intimate relationship) that give us an opportunity to look at who we are and what we want to do with our futures. After careful examination, some people decide that they want to continue with their life career, but change parts of their personalities or methods of coping so that they can truly feel good about themselves for the first time. Personal growth and positive change during a divorce is much more rapid than it is during a marriage. People feel more anxiety during a crisis, which becomes the impetus to grow, than they do when they are dissatisfied but safe in their ruts.

Some people decide at the end of a relationship to change professions or maybe develop one for the first time. Businessmen look at their computer-like life style and decide that they want a career that's more meaningful for them. Housewives decide to go back to school and create a career in the business, fashion, mechanical or art world.

When you begin to look realistically at what you have lost, don't forget to pinch yourself and revel in the fact that you are still alive. The grief over your loss will become much more bearable and less overwhelming when you allow yourself to recognize that your life isn't over yet and you still have a lot more time to grow creatively. You might discover that life can become much more precious when you recognize not only its tenuous quality but also your own potential for its control.

TECHNIQUES THAT HELP YOU LET GO OF PAIN.

In order to let go of your emotional pain, you must first allow yourself to experience it totally. The idea of diving into a bad feeling—precisely what you want to be rid of—may sound like needless self-torture. However, becoming vividly aware of a painful emotion helps you come to grips with it. Then you can experience exactly how severe it is in you, how it affects your body and what its dimensions are, and the pain is no longer an overwhelming ogre you must run away from. Now you know the pain and chose to touch it or sense when it has been touched by some person or situation. It is, therefore, yours—to do with as you wish but certainly no longer to be afraid of.

Emotional pain can be caused by feeling scared of your future, feeling abandoned, rejected or worthless, alone in the world with no one to comfort you, or any number of things. If you genuinely want to know for yourself where the sources of your pain are buried, take the responsibility to get in touch with your feelings.

Put on some comfortable clothes, pick a spot in your house which is quiet and begin to relax. See if you can feel in your body where the hurt lies. Is it in your stomach or throat? How about your neck or the muscles in your back? Some people discover they've been swallowing hurt feelings or "garbage" from others for years and, with the ending of an intimate relationship, they swallow a little more just so they could get through the separation scenes. But now is the time to experience that pain. Really feel it and begin releasing out loud the words and the feelings that are knotted up inside of you. Let your words ramble. Say anything that comes to mind. Cry when the tears come. Scream when you're hurting or angry. If you genuinely want to get rid of what's bugging or frightening you, you can when you feel it.

One way to strengthen emotional awareness is to say what you're feeling over and over again until you actually feel the words in your body. One man in my group practiced saying "I'm lonely" over and over again until he finally shouted, "My God, I really am lonely—I'd better do something about it!"

When you're first trying to get in touch with your feelings, avoid the common tendency to block emotion by trying to understand it or think about something else. Many people have trouble experiencing what they feel because their mind is somewhere else. They walk in the country but think about their problems in the city. They begin to feel pain and quickly think themselves out of it because of their fears.

If you find yourself pulling out of a feeling or stopping yourself from experiencing it totally, relax and don't push yourself. You can come back to it some other time because your feelings stay inside of you until you release them. In learning that you can stop yourself from feeling more pain than you think you can handle, you will discover for yourself, once again, that you have control over your feelings.

Once you have actually experienced your painful emotions, you will discover that some have diminished. Allow time for reflection after you have gotten in touch with your feelings. Look back on your experience and see what you have discovered about yourself; the opportunity for insight at this point is bountiful. One lady found that she kept herself in pain by constantly trying to get her ex-husband back. She did this she discovered because her own father had died when she was a young child and she had always felt that he rejected her, but never had the opportunity to resolve it with him. As an adult, she somehow felt that if she could get her ex-husband (who had been harsh and rejecting) to take back his words or tell her he was wrong about leaving her which she couldn't get her father to do, she would feel better about herself. Once she discovered on a conscious level what torture she was putting herself through for unconscious reasons, she could quit repeating the game of giving her husband continued opportunities to reject her.

In your reflection, take the responsibility to understand how you continue adding to your pain in every day life. All of us have the same feelings and fears, and some of us build on them. Some people keep themselves in a position of feeling like a door-mat by always letting other people's needs come first and taking care of everyone but themselves. Some ex-intimates discover that they keep feeling rejected by reaching out to the same people again and again who refuse to meet them half way or are unwilling to accept them. Others discover they continue to feel overwhelmed by life in taking on more problems than they can possibly handle. Some discover they build on their feelings of loneliness by isolating themselves and not allowing their friends or family to comfort them. Look for yourself at your own situation and take the responsibility to find out how you build on your pain—then change some of those patterns.

To summarize, the techniques that will help you let go of your pain are:

— Taking the responsibility to own your painful emotions.

— Experiencing the pain and discovering its size.

— Releasing part of your hurt, just by letting it out.

— Reflecting on your experience and discovering how you continue to build on parts of your pain in every day life.

— Taking the responsibility to change some of the patterns you currently have which are hurtful.

HOW TO REACH OUT TO OTHERS FOR COMFORT/SUPPORT.

Although it is essential for you to dive into some of your painful feelings alone, it is equally important to reach out to others for emotional support and comforting after you've experienced the pain. Close friends or family members can help you feel better during the grief process by offering you their love and concern, an ear to hear how you feel, a hug to help you know that you're not alone in the world and sometimes helpful advice for your problems. Your body will tell you when you need to seek others for comfort and support. In general, it is not a good idea to go for more than two or three days of "bad" feelings alone before you make the following conscious efforts to encourage the friendship and soothing from others:

1. Recognize your own need and the value of gaining emotional support from someone outside of yourself. Own your feelings of isolation, abandonment, lack of self-confidence and hurt, and accept the fact that as long as you stay by yourself and hesitate to call up a friend or a loved one, you will continue to feel isolated—because you are. The minute you allow someone else to experience your world of feelings, you are no longer totally alone or abandoned. And when someone accepts your invitation (no matter how briefly) to hear how you feel, that act, in itself, tells you that you still have value in part of your world.

2. Deliberately determine who in your current life will be able to give you emotional support and comforting and who will refuse or be unable to do so. People you know separately from your ex-mate are probably the most ideal—and, relatives you have always felt close to are another source. Avoid the tendency to eliminate everyone because of your own fear of rejection. Do, however, eliminate some people from your list—at least during the first few weeks—your ex-intimate, his/her best friends and family. Occasionally, reaching out to mutual friends can also be hazardous. All of these people will be affected by the death of your love affair; for some it will mean a threat to their own "mar-

riage"; for others, an event to judge or choose sides. In any case, it is best to give them and yourself some time to feel better before you decide to get back in touch.

3. Take the responsibility to contact others (those· you've decided might help) and ask for their friendship in person, by telephone or through writing a letter. Having the names in your head of a few friends and relatives who could help you feel less isolated and alone is of little value if you don't contact them. People who are near can give you immediate comforting just by their physical presence. Writing a letter expressing your feelings can also be quite helpful.

4. Own your need for someone to listen to you, care and be concerned about you as a valuable person—make a conscious effort not to turn off your friends by getting them to take sides. It's natural, especially if you were not the one to initiate good-bye, to see your ex-intimate as responsible for your pain, or to spend a lot of energy trying to prove you're okay by getting others to judge your ex-mate as the person to blame for the dissolution. The analogy can be made between healing a broken heart and mending a broken leg; at the time that they're broken, the circumstances which led up to the crash are of only secondary value. The primary concern now is getting it mended. When you're feeling abandoned, it's important to reach out to someone who will accept you and care. Later, when you begin feeling better, you can constructively reflect on why the relationship died.

HOW TO BURY THE DEAD.

The whole mourning process is geared towards acceptance and continuation of your life after you have said good-bye to a dead love affair. Obviously, if you refuse to say good-bye emotionally, you will never proceed with your life and learn how to love again. Each time you attempt to rekindle your old relationship with him/her, you are denying the reality that it is over and setting yourself up for a little more heartbreak. Still, it is natural for many ex-intimates to periodically slip back into the denial

phase of mourning and date their old love or attempt trial reconciliations—especially for those who have children. One couple
I know spent two years of their three year marriage saying good-
bye to each other and then making trial reconciliations. Both
partners were afraid to bury their love and feel the pain of good-
bye so that they could proceed with their own separate lives.

Burying a dead love affair involves finally accepting that your
old love is over and no longer attempting to rekindle the sparks
by dating your ex-love, trying for reconciliations or fooling yourself into believing that someday the two of you will be together
again. It is a painful process accomplished with neither speed
nor ease.

Ex-intimates who have children in common may have more
trouble burying their old love than their counterparts who do
not; especially if the parent who does not have custody of the
children visits them often. The reason for this difficulty is that
most ex-intimates still do care to some degree about their ex-mate
and continuing to see an old love makes it difficult to bury that
fondness. Especially, if both partners attempt to be pleasant to
each other "for the children," try to "forgive and forget" the
heartbreak and neither of them has developed a new love relationship yet. The children will no doubt try to get Mommy and
Daddy back together again—so that they don't have to go
through the mourning process themselves. If you find yourself
in this situation, avoid private contact with him/her as much as
you can. Have a friend with you when it's necessary to see your
ex-love.

Burying your dead love affair also requires getting rid of all
the old love trinkets and mementos that were part of your relationship when it was alive. If you're a sentimentalist and have
saved old love tokens, letters and cards from the "good times," go
through your closets and drawers and throw them away. Do this
with any object that you find yourself keeping "just in case we
get back together again." With each article that you toss away,
go through the process of literally saying good-bye to it first and
allow yourself to feel the sadness you may have. It's hard to pre-

tend that your old love is still alive if you actually allow yourself to emotionally bury each dusty memento.

Another way to help you bury your dead love affair is to actually tell yourself out loud again and again that it is dead. As with the heightening of any emotional awareness, sometimes repeating reality to yourself helps your head and gut finally acknowledge the truth.

As much as possible, avoid other people in your life who refuse to believe that the two of you have ended your intimacy. Obviously you cannot do this with your children or close friends and family members, but many of your mutual acquaintances who seem to have a stake in denying that the two of you have decided to go separate paths should be avoided. Especially in the beginning if you are having difficulty accepting it's over yourself. For those in your life that you will continue to see who deny the burial of your old love, you may explain that the relationship has been dead for a while and your "divorce" is merely a part of facing that fact. Sometimes when you tell others this, it helps you to acknowledge it, again, for yourself.

Remember that you are not dealing with the death of a person; you are groping with the death of an intimate relationship. Your ex-mate will still be alive and occasionally look good to you. Each time you say good-bye to an old memento, let someone else know that your old love affair is definitely over and feel it yourself; you are throwing another shovel of dirt over the casket of your old love affair. Soon, you will be able to walk away from the graveyard.

UNHEALTHY MOURNING PRACTICES.

Many ex-intimates go through an unhealthy mourning process because there is not a socially acceptable, clearly defined procedure to help them deal with their grief. When an individual dies there are funeral rites to bury his/her body and clearly defined mourning rituals to help the bereaved deal with their grief. A widower or widow can expect expressions of sorrow over his/her loss, invitations for social activities during the convalescent stage and offers of assistance from the very beginning. A widower will automatically receive help with the cooking, cleaning, shopping, and care of his children, if he needs it. A widow will no doubt receive invitations from the men in her life to work on the house or keep the car mechanically safe, act as a substitute father for the children, help her move, find a job and whatever else she may need —without any "strings".

But with the death of an intimate relationship, there is no automatic support you can count on from others and few, if any, socially acceptable, clearly prescribed mourning rituals. There is no funeral and no specific bereavement process. If you were married, there is a divorce decree and the trips to the lawyers and courts which can be used as official ending rites. But most of these rituals are handled alone or with strangers. You cannot automatically expect anyone to offer any sort of emotional support or assistance in helping you adjust to your loss. In fact, many of your friends and family (including your priest or minister) may actually avoid you or talk about "what's wrong" with you behind your back, now that you've ended an intimate relationship. If you go out with friends for a "good time," you may find some of your loved ones denouncing your behavior, instead of encouraging you to get away from the house. If you're a woman and one of your male friends offers his help, you may find there are sexual "strings" attached—or, you may discover that his wife will discourage your friendship for fear you are "after" him.

Because of these signals and their own mixed feelings, many ex-intimates get the message or decide for themselves that there is something "wrong" with grieving over the death of an intimate relationship, and, in fact, they should not feel any hurt at all, since they are the "villains" that killed their love. When this happens and an ex-intimate hides his grief from him/herself or mixes it up with excessive self-condemnation, he/she may find him/herself handling that pain with emotionally unhealthy mourning practices. Do not be unduly alarmed if you find yourself in them. The key issue is not whether you grieve in an unhealthy fashion, but for how long and to what extreme.

1. *Enshrouding yourself in black and assuming the role of the "bereaved" as your total identity.* This practice is easy to slip into and quite natural for many during the first few weeks or months of the mourning process. Especially for those who were not the ones to initiate good-bye and feel helpless to ever really change their "fate" of being alone. However, ex-intimates who take on as their total identity the role of the "bereaved" for several years later have based their entire adjustment on how to stay unhappy and feel badly about the loss of their old love affair. Absolutely no effort is made to let go of the past, or make themselves attractive to someone new or develop the parts of their own wounded ego that would help them want another intimate relationship. They also make only minimal efforts to develop any other identity or role for themselves.

A little of the "bereaved lover" can go a long way! To avoid staying in this mourning ritual longer than is healthy, it's a good idea to set up some definite length of time to mourn in this fashion while making a conscious effort to build up the other parts of your identity, such as employee, parent, son or daughter, friend, member of the community, etc., even during your bereavement phase. That way when you are ready to begin living again, those parts of your identity will not be lost or forgotten entirely.

2. *Burying yourself in self-pity.* If you decide that your life is over and there's nothing you can do to change it, you may succeed in beating down your natural instincts to reach out to others or continue enjoying your life. There are some similarities between this mourning practice and the one above. It is natural to feel a certain amount of self-pity and to periodically slide down into hours or days of bemoaning your fate—especially during the first few months. However, some people have a natural tendency to withdraw into themselves and refuse to take the responsibility to change their situation. Others spend so much of their energy trying to change their loneliness by getting together again with

a dead love that they do not give themselves the opportunity to gain love and acceptance from someone new.

If, after the first three to six months, you are still as wrapped up in feeling sorry for yourself as you were in the beginning, you'd better own the fact that the next three to six months aren't going to be any different unless you take the responsibility to change your way of dealing with the loss. The longer you wallow, without relief, the harder it is to do anything constructive with your wounded pride, like build up your own self-esteem or gain positive feed-back and comforting from others.

3. *Drowning your sorrow in liquor or drugs.* Unfortunately, one way to gain temporary but immediate relief from painful emotions is to numb yourself with booze or wipe out your concern about your life with drugs. I label this "unfortunate" because both of these escapes routes are easily available to all of us and, although every person who gets hooked on drugs or alcohol as a tool to deal with life may tell you that it really only adds to his/her problems, he/she has discovered a way to gain temporary relief and the motivation to resolve the troubles and obtain permanent relief somehow gets lost. The reality is that you need to feel your pain and anxiety in order to really let go of the hurt. If you develop the skill of "copping out", you will not be able to develop the art of "coping through" the mourning process. Do not encourage the coward in you to escape each time you feel pain.

4. *Giving up your interest in the rest of the world and focusing only on your losses and personal sorrow.* It is natural for a short period of time, as part of the mourning process, to avoid contact or interest in the outside world and focus your thoughts and energy entirely on who/what you have lost and be concerned only with how you feel about the loss. But set up a definite period of time to withdraw from the world and bemoan your loss. Then, at the end of that time, make a conscious effort to resume the business of living again. It's difficult to tell you exactly how long you should give up your interest in the parts of your world that

are still alive. It varies for each individual. But, probably you should not allow yourself to remain "cut off" from your natural interests and sources of pleasure for any longer than a few days at a time. This mourning practice can cease being healthy and slip over into a self-destructive practice, if, after the first three to six months, you are still mourning the loss of your old love by focusing all of your energy and thoughts on its demise and the subsequent effect on you as a person.

5. *Avoiding feelings of grief entirely and throwing yourself totally into your work or the children.* A common practice for many ex-intimates who are afraid of their own emotional pain is to avoid feeling entirely and begin devoting all of their waking hours to a "cause". Men often do this with their business; women sometimes dive head on into the lives of their children. But this practice does not help you grow through the grief process, let go of your hurt feelings and learn to love someone new. In fact, it encourages you to put off most of your grief, until your "cause" is completed or the children are grown. Many ex-intimates who decide to handle their pain in this way find themselves always feeling not quite fulfilled and, years later, overwhelmed with their losses and feeling very useless and empty. Just at the time when they are saying good-bye to their youth and productivity, it becomes apparent that they have no one to share their personal lives with anymore—nor have they had one for a number of years.

Rationalizing that you really don't have the time to "get involved" with someone new because the children need you, or your job requires so much of your energy, can be an excuse for you not to try. You can protect yourself from ever getting hurt again by love, but you also give up your chances of once again (or maybe for the first time) feeling the warmth and happiness that loving someone can provide.

6. *Consciously devising ways to end your own life, so that you can be buried with your dead love relationship.* I really don't know how many ex-intimates actually decide to kill themselves

as a way of dealing with their grief. Although it is said that each of us at one time or another will contemplate suicide, for those who are especially insecure or dependent on their old love affair, the thought of death may become more than just an idea to consider. If you feel so overwhelmed by your loss that you actually begin contemplating taking your own life, you need to contact a local mental health clinic or suicide prevention center immediately. You will find a "crisis line" or "suicide line" listed in your telephone book. Better yet, contact someone before you get to the point where you feel that overwhelmed.

HOW TO STOP GRIEF FROM OVERWHELMING YOU.

Although it is literally impossible to become overwhelmed by grief, there are times when it *feels* as though you will never get over your sorrow, that there will never be light in your life or warmth in your heart again. No wonder people try to avoid feeling their grief at the death of a relationship or desperately try to shorten the mourning phase. Grief hurts—and it's scary! And, sometimes ex-intimates make it worse by overreacting to their fears, overloading their ability to cope with sorrow, or immobilizing themselves.

You can avoid becoming overwhelmed with grief by actually owning your sorrow and refusing to let yourself become a victim of your feelings, as follows:

1. Accept the reality that it is natural to feel sadness about the death of your old relationship. Expect to feel some pain. Don't be afraid of your feelings. Remember that all feelings, including the hurtful ones, are transitory.

2. Don't overload yourself with past hurts/losses. Sometimes ex-intimates immobilize themselves by pulling in their memories and unresolved grief from all of their past losses: the deaths of other relationships, important people in their lives who are gone, good-bye to their own youth or life patterns and ambitions they have given up. Grief over the loss of their old love affair gets mixed up with the pain from other losses.

3. Do take the responsibility to reach out to others for comfort and support.

4. Don't be surprised if you unexpectedly feel sorrow after you have gone for days or even months of feeling good again.

5. Do take the responsibility to build up your own backbone and self-esteem. Build on your strengths and use them to meet the challenges of being single again.

6. Don't overload yourself with excessive amounts of self-condemnation. If you feel that your life is empty and bleak, avoid cutting yourself down with harsh judgments that will only immobilize you and make it more difficult to begin practicing ways of feeling better again.

7. Do take one day at a time. Avoid the natural tendency to try and predict how you will feel a year or two from now—especially when you're feeling hopeless. Stay with today and your immediate future.

8. Avoid the eleven common pitfalls described in Chapter 7. They will prolong your grief or stop you from becoming a healthier person.

9. Don't psych yourself out with your fears. Panic promotes panic. Many people become immobilized by "what ifs"; "What if I fail again?"; "What if I get rejected?"; "What if nothing I try helps me feel better?"; "What is I'm always alone?" It's natural to wonder, but don't do it when you're feeling scared.

10. Do take the responsibility to help yourself feel better. Don't sit and wait for your ex-mate to come back, or a miracle to happen, or use up all of your energy feeling sorry for yourself. Decide what kind of realistic action would help, then do it.

Often saying good-bye to an old love affair is actually a blessing in disguise. It offers ex-intimates the opportunity and the anxiety to actually grow emotionally stronger, resolve old hang-ups and learn to effectively plan a happier, healthier future for themselves. It's important not to let the fears of letting go stop you from becoming free. If you use your courage and the knowledge you have already learned to help you, soon you will feel better. If you do not, there is a very good chance that you will stay stuck in one of the stages of grief—or choose another intimate relationship exactly like the last one—with the same ending.

Experiments and Exercises.

This exercise is designed to help you bury your dead love affair, accept that it's over and proceed with your life. Repeat it whenever you feel that you need to "unhook". Choose a time when you feel "strong" enough to say good-bye and will be uninterrupted. Place a sheet over the "body" of your ex-mate or the relationship. Talk about the relationship or him/her as if this were the funeral. Express all the words and feelings that you have kept inside. Give yourself permission to experience these feelings. Talk as long as you want and when you feel you are finished with the "funeral rites," say good-bye and walk away.

After this exercise, take some time to reflect and answer the following:

   *What can I learn from this experience?

   *What do I want/need to do with my future?

   *How can I begin working towards my new goals?

The five stages of the grief process are listed below. Look at them and ( ) which one you feel you are currently in.

Denial/ Depression/ Anger/ Resignation/ Acceptance and Procedure

Now take some time and ask yourself the following:

   *What can I learn from objectively looking at where I am now? Can I see an end to my grief?

   *Have I developed any constructive insight about myself through this process?

*Am I staying stuck in one stage longer than is emotionally healthy for me?

*If so, list *specifically* what you do now that keeps you there:

1.
2.
3.
4.
5.

*Put a time limit on how long you plan to continue the above behaviors or attitudes before you move on. Ask youself what you will need to do differently when you decide to proceed.

*Pick one that you feel would be the easiest to change and consider doing so.

Estimate a time when you believe you will have completed your grief. 3 months? 6 months? 1 year? 5 years? When?

11: Depression: The Energy Crisis

I call depression the "energy crisis" because most people who are feeling depressed complain of changes in their energy levels. The majority describe themselves as feeling fatigued, "run down" or "too weak to move." Statements such as: "I can barely drag my body out of bed in the morning—and, I go back to bed whenever I get the chance" are common. A few individuals who are depressed experience the exact opposite; those who are normally calm suddenly develop great bounds of energy and are unable to sit still for any length of time without fidgeting in their chairs. Some people fluctuate back and forth—with no energy on one day and excessive amounts on the next.

Much of this redistribution and loss of productive energy comes from some of the side effects of depression itself: loss of appetite, lowering of body resistance to viral and bacterial infections, insomnia or change in sleeping patterns, feelings of being torn apart inside, dissatisfied, desperate and angry (but internalizing the energy from anger).

People who complain of depression often say that they are

tired of feeling badly, but they do not have the energy and/or motivation to change. The conscious decision to do something about their sadness gets shoved back by a heavy sense of helplessness and hopelessness. Anything that could be done to climb out of the pit of depression seems like too much trouble and not worth the effort. For some people in this emotional state, suicide appears to be the only solution. For everyone, the feeling is bleak and scary.

How long depression lasts and how far down you will fall varies with a number of factors, such as your own ego-strengths, sense of insecurity, ability to adjust, dependency needs, religious or philosophical attitude about ending, age at the time of good-bye, readiness for ending including other options available, physical stamina, unconscious commitment to continue the relationship, self-destructiveness of the "marriage" itself, length of the relationship and number of role identities that were tied up in the union. The more independent and self-assured you are as a separate person, the less intense your feelings of depression will be. If you initiated good-bye, you will probably feel less depressed during the mourning phase than your counterpart who still felt committed to the relationship when it was buried. Passive, polite or stubborn people who did not want the relationship to end will stay depressed much longer than those who assert themselves and their feelings with relative ease.

Depression is usually the first painful emotion that ex-intimates feel. Normally it is self-limiting and, in time, will ease. However, many ex-intimates increase their sorrow by unconsciously (or consciously) preventing themselves from adjusting and growing through this crisis, or prolong their depression by fighting it with fear.

It is natural for depression to come and go during the first six months to a year on a relatively sporadic basis. Initially the pain will be more intense and more frequent, then gradually diminish in size and duration. The more effective you become in dealing with your depression, the easier it will be to let go of your sadness.

The theories of feeling better are of little personal value until you take the responsibility to put them in use. It will take a great deal of effort on your part to pull out of depression, requiring energy you may not feel you have anymore. But the more energy you begin mobilizing and asserting to work your way out, the more you will find you have and the stronger you'll feel.

CAUSAL FACTORS OF DEPRESSION.

Depression is caused by internalized anger and a sense of helplessness. It is a reaction to a situation or scene which is unsatisfactory or unpleasant to an individual who decides (for his/her own reasons) that there is nothing he/she can say or do to effect a change. It is often a reaction to a loss which is initially viewed as irreplaceable. The more important the loss, the deeper the depression. If you get angry about something, but do not express it (to the degree that you feel it) and keep the anger inside, you will become depressed. Because depression is a reaction, it is mixed with a number of other feelings such as feeling inadequate, put-down, helpless, abandoned, hopeless, being scared, feeling trapped, insecure, lonely or sad. These painful feelings, and others, if "sat on" will cause you to feel depressed—in addition to whatever else you may feel. If someone says something to you that hurts your feelings and you passively accept it, you will not only have hurt feelings, but also a sense of depression. Likewise, if a man left alone does not know how to care for his children and fears he will be unable to learn, and deals with his uncertainties by doing nothing, so, he will not only feel anxious about his parenting, but also depressed about letting his children down.

Depression is a passive way of dealing with negative feelings and the situation which set these feelings in motion. It requires no action. If you take whatever negative feedback other people may hand you without asserting yourself, you may get depressed immediately afterwards. The man who passively accepts his uncertainty about learning to care for his children and does not take the effort to try, develops a sense of defeat and depression. A woman who refuses to push herself to learn how to drive reinforces her feelings of helplessness and despair.

There is a natural tendency in all of us to desire that life be exactly the way we want it and to try and effect change when it is not. This desire is sometimes manifested as anger, self-assertion, determination, motivation or drive. When an ex-intimate decides to "sit on" this energy and do nothing to change something over which he has no power (like trying to get back an ex-love who has rejected him), he will become depressed.

Ex-intimates often become depressed from any one or several of the following reasons:

— They have accepted the harsh judgments their ex-love has handed them as if they were "truths" such as: being an inadequate lover, parent or "marital" partner.

— They feel rejected by their ex-love and assume rejection means that they are "losers".

— They are frightened of being single-again and are unsure of their ability to adjust and proceed with their lives.

— They are dependent on their ex-love to make them feel like a "whole" person and now that it's over feel helpless about feeling a "total" being on their own.

— They are afraid of ever being loved or loving someone again and immobilize their efforts to try for that goal.

— They get wrapped up in self-pity or becoming a martyr about the loss of their love.

— They are still emotionally tied to their ex-love and are afraid to get angry at him/her for fear of further alienation.

— They have never developed goals outside of the marital relationship.

— They feel responsible for taking care of their ex-love, feel guilty about leaving, but refuse to return.

— They have lost most of their friendship circle in saying good-bye to their ex-love and feel isolated—but fear making new friends.

If you don't like being single again, but feel helpless to change, you will probably slide into the trap of depression. Some will feel this reaction before they actually separate physically; others will experience it after—a few will feel sporadically depressed about the death of their love years before they leave each other.

Scenes that trigger depression once you're alone are unnumerable: being alone at dinner time, fixing meals for one, going to a party by yourself, festive occasions like Christmas, waking up to the sound of silence, hearing your voice echo in the hallway, or listing your mother instead of your ex-mate on the line that says: "in case of emergency, please notify."

People who are afraid of their anger or feel that they do not have the right to assert themselves may automatically deal with disappointment by passively accepting their plight.

HOW TO FIGURE OUT WHY YOU'RE DEPRESSED.

Ex-intimates become depressed during the first part of the mourning phase because they experience a number of mixed (sometimes unpleasant) feelings which they are unprepared to deal with in an active or constructive manner.

To figure out exactly what you are reacting to, you will need to take the responsibility to learn what you feel beneath the depression. During the first few days, it may be difficult for you to sort through your feelings. The sense of depression may feel too overwhelming—and, your mind may dart rapidly from one painful scene to another. Within a short period of time, however, you should be able to begin looking at the feelings beneath your depression.

If you find yourself at a loss, it may be helpful to re-read the first part of this chapter and see which causal factors and underlying feelings appear to be relevant for your own situation. Usually, there are a number of reasons for a depression, with, perhaps, one or two predominant issues underlying the majority of it.

For example:

One lady who was married for twenty-seven years to an alcoholic found that she was extremely depressed after she finally filed for a divorce. Although she had left her husband several times before she finally divorced him, she always returned because she worried about how he would live without someone taking care of him and felt responsible for helping him. Intellectually, she knew that he was responsible for himself, but, in spite of that knowledge, she still felt obligated. Each time he called her or she found out he had lost another job or lurched into trouble again, she would return. When she finally left him permanently, she was moderately depressed for several months. The feelings and fears she reacted to by depression were her sense of obligation, worry and guilt about not taking care of her ex-mate, internalized anger at both of them for being in a position of divorce, a sense of helplessness to change either her own feelings of responsibility or his alcoholic behavior, and a fear of never feeling better again.

A man found that much of his depression after saying goodbye to his love of three years had to do with his desire to continue their relationship because he still cared about her. Part of him hoped that they could reunite, and so he refused to directly get mad at her or use the energy in his anger to find someone new. He ended up feeling very lonely and empty but chose to "sit on" his needs to love again in hopes his old girlfriend would return. Her departure had shattered his self-confidence and, for over six months, he stayed alone every night and on week-ends waiting for his ex-love to telephone or write.

Questions that you can ask yourself which may help you figure out which feelings you are reacting to with depression are:

1. What's going on in my life that I don't like right now?

2. What would I have to do to feel better?

3. Why don't I do that?

The answers won't come easily at first. But, eventually, you will find that gaining this insight will be well worth the effort—for without that knowledge, it will be impossible for you to ever win your battle with depression completely. Treating the symptoms of emotional pain is one thing; finding out what causes it is the start of curing that pain.

HOW TO FIGHT DEPRESSION.

Depression is a self-inflicted pain. No one makes us cope with our hurt feelings or dissatisfaction with passivity and displeasure. People choose this way of reacting because they do not want to risk becoming assertive or angry, don't see any way to constructively deal with their pain, or feel they deserve to settle for less than what they want. A certain amount of depression is inevitable and a natural part of the grief process—or life, for that matter. Do not be afraid of it—or worry too much. With simple depression, sometimes just feeling sad for a while and releasing that pain through your tears will be all that you need to do to let go of your hurt. Disappointment and loss can often be handled just by feeling "bad" for a day or two. And, if you reflect upon your feelings and thoughts during that "sad time" or shortly afterwards, you may gain a great deal of insight and wisdom. Usually, *when you're feeling relatively good about you*, a depression will lift after it has run its natural course through your body.

If you find, however, that depression has become your primary feeling and that it is beginning to get the best of you, you will need to take the responsibility to begin fighting the "blues". Don't wait around for a magical answer or someone to swoop down and take you away from your sadness. Fighting depression requires INSIGHT and ACTION on your part with an eye towards feeling better again.

The INSIGHT you will need to develop consists of:

— Figuring out what you're reacting to from the good-bye. (Like the lady who was married to the alcoholic or the man who was rejected by his girlfriend).

— Understanding why you feel helpless to take care of the feelings beneath your depression in a more constructive manner. (e.g., Placing the responsibility to make you feel better on someone else who won't help you; cutting down your self-esteem so that you don't have confidence in your ability to get your needs met; or deciding that you deserve to stay feeling "blue" as a self-punishment).

— Learning what reinforces the depression in your present situation. (Blundering into the pitfalls, immobilizing yourself with self-doubt, isolating yourself from others at a time when you feel the most dependent.)

The ACTION part of your battle requires that you:

— Mobilize the energy in depression and turn it back into anger, motivation, determination or drive. This may require a change in attitude from "Oh, well, who cares about my plight?" to "I'm tired of feeling down and am ready to do something positive." (You may find it helpful to keep repeating the second phrase out loud to yourself until you can feel that the words are true for you. Anyone who is depressed, does have enough energy inside him/her to get mobilized again.)

— Give up energy wasting double-binds you may be in, like wanting to love again, but keeping your feelings "hooked" on someone who doesn't care about you; wanting to stand up on your own two feet but looking for someone to help you get up; or, wanting to feel that you are a valuable person, but doubting your every action and the motivation behind it.

— Avoid situations which are set-ups for feeling depressed. Look at your own life and notice the scenes which cause you to react with depression. It will vary for each individual but usually they give you an invitation to feel inadequate, put-down, abandoned, hopeless, frightened, trapped, helpless, insecure or lonely. Those you do not really need to be part of, avoid. Take a friend with you to others, if you can.

— Put yourself in situations which help you feel confident. This varies too, but usually involves being around friends and family who love you or doing tasks you do well.

— Reach out to others for positive feedback, encouraging them to be your friends.

— Build up your own backbone and self-confidence by using the advice in Chapter 5 plus any other ideas that you know work for you.

— Force yourself to eat balanced means, get enough sleep and physical exercise. (It's difficult to "fight" anything if your body's worn down.)

— Separate the issues you are unhappy about and deal with them one at a time. Don't overload yourself.

Every time you make a decision to do something about what seems like a bad situation, you will feel the depression lift from your shoulders. If, for example, you are sitting alone on a Sunday afternoon feeling blue and decide "I think I'll go visit a friend," then climb in your car and do it; your mood will lighten. If, on the other hand, you decide that you would like to go visit someone *but* _____ and end up staying alone, the depression may deepen.

Part of fighting depression is to fight the "buts" in your life. "I could go visit a friend, *but* _____

— he may not be home."
— he could be busy with someone else."
— if he wanted to see me, he'd call."
— what good would it do?"

— I have to learn to stay alone.''
— it's almost dinner time.''
— I shouldn't bother him.''
— it's not worth driving all the way over there.''
— what if he's not happy to see me?''
— what will he think?''
— what do I say when he opens the door?''

You can probably add a dozen more of your own "buts" behind that statement and still end up in the same position. The position of staying at home, not visiting a friend, feeling lonely, helpless to change that—and a little more depressed. When you say "I could, *but*_____" to yourself, you are saying "there's a reason for my hesitation." Of course there is—*but*_____

— do you need one?
— when will you give it up?
— how can you take care of that hesitation?
— would it help to check your hesitations out with your friend?
— when will you do it?

HOW TO FIND WAYS TO WIN.

Winning your fight with depression is similar to winning in a sports event. It requires practicing your skills and playing with a league you can win. Any coach will tell you his trainees have a better chance of winning if he uses some common sense when matching his team. A high school football coach, for example, would never expect his team to win a game with the Miami Dolphins or any other big name professional team. If he did, he (and his team) would be very disappointed after the match because their chances of winning are extremely slim.

If you can think about your fight with depression in a similar light and see your head as the "coach" for your emotions and self-esteem, you will quickly see how the analogy can be effectively used to find ways for you to win.

The "coach" part of you needs to use some common sense and convince the rest of you to put into ACTION the INSIGHT you've gained about your fight with depression. If you're depressed because you feel lonely, your "coach" needs to give you a "pep talk" and convince you to practice reaching out to others and giving your kindness to someone who cares about you. If you cope with fears by huddling in the corner, your "coach" can help you figure out how to feel safer and remind you that you can overcome almost anything that is scary by practicing how to protect your vulnerable spots. Fear of getting in a car accident can be lessened by learning how to drive your automobile defensively and making sure it's mechanically sound. Fear of being alone at night can be reduced by making sure you have locked all the doors and windows, sleeping in a room with a telephone nearby and avoiding the game of psyching yourself out with "what ifs."

Just as the high school coach would not expect his team to beat a professional team, the "coach" part of you should not expect you to win in your battle with depression by overwhelming you with expectations. It would be unfair to expect all of your lifetime hang-ups or insecurities to be cured once and for all when you feel like your ego is shattered from saying good-bye. Sure, you may grow through some of your hang-ups while battling depression. Emotional change and growth often take place when you feel the pressure to change—but only when you can see your way clear to do something about it. If you overload yourself with unrealistic goals for success, you will surely give up the fight to feel better before you begin.

A good coach gives the team members immediate rewards, plus a sense that he is pleased when you try. The "coach" part of you should do the same. Reward yourself whenever you take some constructive action to fight your depression. If you dress up to go visit a friend or apply for a job, praise yourself and do something kind for you as a reward. When you "goof up" or do something that deepens your depression, like begging your ex-love to come back, give yourself a "pep talk" and try to avoid making the same mistake again. Forgive yourself and learn from your errors.

No coach has all the answers for developing a winning team. He learns from others in his field. The "coach" part of you can do the same. You are already reading this book for ideas. Another resource is other ex-intimates who have also felt the pain from good-bye or almost anyone *but* your ex-love or people who may have negative feelings towards you. Many may have positive suggestions that you can use too—ask them. You might gain helpful suggestions *and* build a friendship in the process.

THE ART OF FEELING BETTER.

Sometimes it surprises ex-intimates to discover that towards the end of the grief process they feel better about themselves and their world than they have ever felt in their lives. Old hang-ups and insecurities that they carried with them all through their lives have been resolved through constructive insight and behavioral changes learned during the grief process.

> "If someone would have told me a year ago that I would actually feel better today than I could ever remember, I wouldn't have believed it. I take the time now to enjoy life —and I have a sense of achievement and self-confidence that I've never known before. Like I can do almost anything I want. It's fantastic! A feeling mere words can't describe."

That statement was made by a friend of mine who, less than a year ago, divorced her husband of seven years. She divorced him, but he left her for another woman. And, for several months her despair seemed unbearable to her.

If you're struggling with depression right now, it may be difficult for you to even fantasize a day in your future when you, too, will have mastered the art of feeling better. But most ex-intimates do—even the ones who, at the lowest point in their depression, contemplated or attempted suicide.

The art of feeling better is the culmination of a number of skills suggested throughout this book and an ability to see yourself and your world in a positive light. As with any art, it requires that you master (through hard work and long hours) the skills necessary to practice it. Few people are born with a natural talent to do anything specific. Most of us have the potential to paint, write, sing, play an instrument, bake, sew, grow vegetables, drive an automobile or feel good about ourselves and our world. It's just a matter of learning how to do something, then practicing those skills until we can do them with relative ease.

Your attitude and ability to adjust are the primary instruments that need to be perfected to learn the art of feeling better. Each time you successfully win a bout with depression or self-condemnation and fear, you will have a sense of self-confidence and pride. And, you will also have learned for yourself that you are in control of your feelings.

Ironically, those who feel the most pain in good-bye also have the ability to feel the most pleasure when they finally say hello to their new world. A woman who felt totally dependent on her ex-mate for survival can gain a tremendous sense of pride and accomplishment when she discovers through practice that she can not only survive without her ex-mate, but enjoy her achievements and own the choices she makes. A man who always falls in love with a helpless, deliberately inadequate female can learn through his own struggle with good-bye how to built up his ego without the aid of someone he sees as inferior. And, in doing that, he can discover for himself that he really is worthwhile and, maybe, the next time around, he can choose an intimate whom he can not only love, but respect as an "equal."

The Alcoholics Anonymous' prayer suggests an attitude and ability to adjust which most ex-intimates have the opportunity to attain: "God grant me the serenity to accept the things that I can't change . . . the courage to change the things that I can . . . and, the wisdom to know the difference."

PITFALLS THAT REINFORCE DEPRESSION.

Pitfalls that you may stumble into when you're already feeling depressed are traps which will increase your sense of helplessness or discouragement. In Chapter 7, there are several mentioned which may deepen your sense of depression:

— Getting back together with your ex-love.
— Trying to be friends if it isn't necessary.
— Saving old mementos.
— Pulling in memories to fill the emptiness.
— Checking up on your ex-love.
— Pumping mutual friends for information or trying to get them to take sides.
— Wishing it hadn't happened and hoping it'll change.
— Panicking with free time, holidays and anniversary dates.

Others have already been mentioned in this chapter such as immobilizing yourself with fears and self-doubt or internalizing and "sitting on" your own anger. All of these pitfalls can reinforce your depression, keep you in "limbo" and extend the length of your grief. Although it is not necessary to panic when you fall into one of these traps (or the others mentioned in this section), it is important to avoid as many as you can and climb out of those that you don't as quickly as possible. Sometimes acknowledging on a conscious level that you are in the process of deepening your depression, helps to alleviate your feelings of despair. With that in mind, let us look at additional pitfalls which may immobilize your efforts to let go of depression.

1. *Attempting to escape from your hurt by sleeping or numbing your body with alcohol or drugs.* During the first few days of your depression it is natural to feel overwhelmed with painful feelings and see your only salvation as some form of unconsciousness. The trouble is that when you're conscious again, the problems are still there—and you still aren't any closer to constructive solutions than you were before you went to bed or killed that last

glass of wine, In fact, you may feel more discouraged than before. Unfortunately, choosing a passive "do nothing" solution for a painful, realistic problem deepens your sense of helplessness to master your fate. If, after the first week, you find yourself yawning and preparing for bed in the middle of the day, do some physical exercises to get your circulation moving again. Then use the energy you find to constructively fight a piece of your problem. As for numbing yourself with drugs or alcohol, we have enough scientific information to tell you that chemicals *cause* more problems than they solve; they increase a sense of impotence for their users and most are depressants anyway.

2. *Fighting your dependency needs by withdrawing from others during the deeper parts of your depression.* The human being is a dependent animal. We know that we cannot sustain feeling good in a vacuum. Yet, many ex-intimates during the first part of their depression actually heighten their despair, loneliness and self-pity by purposely isolating themselves from any human contact. They see people at work, but avoid any human contact during their "leisure" hours. It is a fact that when you are depressed, you will feel more dependent than at other times in your life. Ignoring your dependency needs will only make you feel worse. If at all possible, keep contact and encourage emotional support from those who still love you. Share your home or apartment with someone else if that's feasible. If you feel that you have no one to turn to for friendship or are hesitant to talk over your feelings with someone, contact a mental health clinic or get in touch with a singles' organization. Getting at least some of your dependency needs met during your depression can save you from prolonging your grief, immobilizing yourself with self-pity, or making mentally unhealthy decisions for your future.

3. *Viewing yourself as a "victim" of fate or a pawn controlled by your ex-love.* This is a trap that many ex-intimates who were not the first to initiate good-bye, or those who see themselves as fragile or inadequate may fall into. The longer you avoid taking responsibility for your life, how you feel and what you do, the easier it is to see yourself as a helpless "victim" of fate—or your

ex-love's whim. The sooner you practice owning the choices you've made—about not nurturing your old love relationship, choosing unwisely to begin with, taking responsibility to help yourself feel better now that it's over—the quicker you can pull yourself out of the "victim" pitfall.

4. *Seeing yourself as better than everyone else because you don't stand up for your rights directly and, therefore, never risk hurting someone by your words.* An ex-intimate who has a life style of being a martyr is probably the one most prone to fall into this trap. His or her anger and self-assertion is not utilized in a constructive manner; it is usually reshaped into self-sacrificing bitterness and depression. If you have the tendency to "turn the other cheek" when hit, rather than slap back, walk away or protect yourself in some other way, it is important for you to learn how to assert yourself and stand up for your rights. There are healthy and constructive ways to deal with your dissatisfaction and anger besides swallowing the pain and attempting to soothe your hurt feelings with a noble sense that you are above mere mortal imperfections. Part of our "humanness" that helps us adjust and grow emotionally is our natural sense of anger when we are disappointed or hurt. Learn to use that natural emotion constructively.

5. *Setting unrealistic goals for yourself when you already feel depressed.* Many mental health experts suggest that one way to alleviate a sense of depression is to set up personal goals. There is nothing more satisfying than successfully completing a goal you have set. And, there are few things more discouraging than to fail at a personal goal. Therefore, it is important to set realistic goals with regard to your current strengths and abilities. Jumping into the collegiate scene full time when you're raising a family and haven't practiced the skills of effective studying for twenty years may be very unrealistic. Signing up for one night class on a subject that interests you and that you feel you can learn is much more realistic. When you're depressed, you will feel less sure of yourself, be more frightened of failure and, at the beginning, maybe even have trouble concentrating. Take those realities into

account as you plan some of your goals. Don't use them as an excuse to sit back and do nothing, but also, accept the fact that you are feeling depressed and, therefore, may not perform tasks with the same amount of self-confidence and ease that you may have before and will later on. Setting goals which can realistically be achieved is mentally healthy; reaching for unrealistic personal goals deepens depression.

6. *Dragging in all the past hurts and disappointments when you're depressed.* I'm not sure why people who are depressed do this, but there seems to be a natural tendency to drag in from memory all of your past hurts when you're feeling "low". Maybe it's because the gut feeling is always the same and therefore generates the memories. In any event, almost every person I talk to who is feeling overwhelmed with depression shares how he/she increases that sense of sadness and discouragement by remembering all of the other times in his/her life that were similar. A certain amount of reflection and constructive "ghost hunting" from your past can be healthy. Too much can be overwhelming. There's a fine line between wallowing in pain and choosing to acknowledge and feel its presence. You are "wallowing" when you make a conscious decision to give into your fears of helplessness and self-pity and thereby refuse to constructively salve your wounds. Acknowledging your pain, feeling the hurt and then initiating constructive action is healthy. You can tell for yourself when your reflection ceases to be useful and crawls into the harmful category. Pull yourself out of the painful memories when you find that you are beginning to feel devastated. The most effective way to do this is to acknowledge what you are doing and force yourself to focus your attention on the current problems you need to resolve.

7. *Using "insight" as a reason for no action.* It may sound strange for a mental health professional to list using insight as a pitfall which reinforces depression. But, even though I am firmly convinced that insight is necessary for lasting emotional growth and change, it must be followed with action. There are some folks who use their intellectual knowledge of themselves

as a "cop out" to avoid change or taking the responsibility to do something constructive about their own problems. Early childhood hang-ups, sociological pressures or theological implications become their reasons for passivity. And, staying stuck there can really give you an invitation to feel helpless and hopeless. If you find yourself understanding that you are punishing yourself unfairly for the dissolution of your love affair because you feel guilty, but, continue to punish yourself anyway—you'd better force yourself to stop looking at "why" and begin looking at "how you can change." Developing insight without putting it to a constructive use is counter-productive.

Experiments and Exercises.

The following is a list of pitfalls which increase depression. Go through it and check (√) those you currently fall into.

__ trying to get back with your ex-love.
__ trying to be "friends" when it isn't necessary.
__ saving old mementos.
__ pulling in memories to fill the emptiness.
__ checking up on your ex-love.
__ pumping mutual friends for information or trying to get them to take sides.
__ wishing it hadn't happened and hoping it'll change.
__ panicking or dreading free time.
__ dreading the future.
__ being too self-critical.
__ holding your anger inside; refusing to stand up for your rights.
__ escaping your hurt by over-sleeping.
__ trying to numb pain with alcohol or drugs.
__ withdrawing from friends and family.
__ viewing yourself as a "victim".
__ being self-sacrificing.
__ setting unrealistic goals for yourself.
__ dragging in all your past hurts and disappointments through memory.

__ using "insight" as a reason for no action.
__ wallowing in self-pity.
__ letting your physical health or appearance slide.
__ giving yourself excuses to do nothing.

Now go back through this list and study those you have checked:

*What can you learn from this?

*Is there a pattern for you with disappointments?

*Are there any you could avoid if you put an effort into doing so?

Pick one which you feel would be the easiest for you to give up or avoid. Then, on a separate piece of paper, develop your "plan of attack":

*What *specific* actions will you need to take? (If the solution requires a number of steps, be sure to write them down).

*Can you do it by yourself or will you need help?

*If you need help, who will you ask?

*Now set a "time frame" including when you will begin and how long you believe it will take to be successful. (You may find it helpful to evaluate your progress every day initially and make revisions in your "plan of attack" occasionally).

As you read through this book, periodically refer back to this list and review your progress. Work on other pitfalls as you decide, utilizing suggestions from the book as well as others you've found helpful.

12: All About Anger

Anger is perhaps one of our most misunderstood feelings or reactions—one that many people try to avoid or deny because it is scary to them. Many people don't want to feel angry because they associate that energy with destructiveness. They see it as either a mood or an attitude that is "wrong" and designed to verbally or physically abuse someone else, or as something that causes more problems than it cures because they have only experienced the "temper tantrum" form of anger. They have not learned how to turn that energy into ambition or drive.

But feeling angry is not "wrong" and it need not be scary, destructive or an end in itself. It is a natural part of the grief process and a phase that ex-intimates must go through in order to proceed with their lives. Anger is a source of energy and a reaction to a situation which has caused painful feelings. We experience anger during the grief process because saying good-bye to an old love affair or hello to an unknown future can be hurtful or frightening and most of us do not like to feel either one. If an ending gives an ex-intimate an invitation to feel inadequate or rejected, he/she is likely to react with anger to protect feeling any other "hurt". A woman who feels she's been treated unfairly or used by her ex-mate may react with anger, or vengeance to get back at her ex-husband, or decide never to "trust" any man again. If a man's ex-wife judged him as "childish", he may try to get her to take back her evaluation of him by forcing her to admit she was wrong, or take out his anger on other women so that no female will ever "hurt" him again.

The degree of anger you may feel during the mourning phase will vary with how frightened or hurt you are and how adept at dissipating that pain. The less intense your hurt feelings and fears, the milder your reaction of anger will be. The greater your ability to adjust, the easier it will be for you to turn that energy into motivation or drive.

You really do *not* have a choice about whether you experience anger or not. The fact that you have feelings and that some of them may be injured because of the death of your old love affair is enough to cause you some sense of anger. You do have a choice over how you deal with those feelings, however. You can direct them towards yourself and try to "get even" by self-condemnation or guilt (which usually get you back into depression). You can explode in physical or verbal outbursts towards anyone and everything—or just your ex-mate. You can quietly seethe inside and devise ways to "get back" at your old love. Or you can use the energy from anger to help you let go of the past and plan for your future constructively.

Anger can be an effective tool to help you create emotional distance from your ex-mate or it can keep you emotionally tied —depending on how you use it. If the woman who feels used by her ex-mate applies her energy to "getting even" with him, rather than helping her "unhook" emotionally and go on with her life, he can continue to be the most important man in her life years after their divorce. The same alternatives are available for the man whose ex-wife judged him as "childish"; he can either spend the rest of his life trying to get her to take back her opinion or decide to use his energy to build-up his self-esteem, realistically evaluate her opinion, and find a new love who will view him more kindly.

There are several alternatives you may choose in order to deal with your anger from good-bye. On some occasions you may choose to control your anger and utilize its energy to help you grow, and, at other times, you may find yourself screaming at your ex-love just like a child. Your methods of coping will vary depending on your mood, so don't get too worried if you don't always use your anger exactly the way you would like. The important thing is to learn how to release it and utilize the energy to move forward. Holding on to your anger or reinforcing it will keep you stuck in the middle of the grief process. Attempting to skip this phase will keep you emotionally tied to a love that is dead.

CAUSAL FACTORS OF ANGER.

Many things cause us to feel angry because it is natural for all of us to want our lives to go exactly the way we want them. When it doesn't—when we fail at a goal, someone hurts our feelings, or gives us an invitation to feel something painful or scary—we will likely react with some sense of depression, or anger, or both. While depression is a reaction which says: "Oh well, what's the use—I'm too tired to fight"; anger is our sense of frustration, asserting: "This is not the way I want it *and* something should be done!"

Anger, as an attempt to control our own lives, is an emotion which all of us experience. During the grief process it is more pronounced. There are several reasons for this. First of all, all ex-intimates experience loss when they say good-bye; not only the loss an an intimate relationship, but the loss of familiar surroundings, mutual friends, self-image connected with that person, routine, and, probably, the sexual relationship with a familiar partner. Until those "empty spots" are refilled, it is natural to feel some form of frustration. Even replacing those "empty spots" or learning how to live without your ex-mate can create some sort of anger. It isn't easy to find a new love, live in a new area, make new friends or even learn to take over tasks that your ex-love used to perform. A man who has never cooked for himself or learned how to do household chores like shopping, cleaning house and maintaining a wardrobe may feel a mild sense of irritation each time he opens a can or has to eat at a local "greasy spoon" because he's tired of T.V. dinners. A woman who has never managed her own finances before can become livid with rage when the checkbook seems to be fighting with her desire to have it "balance".

Calling it "quits", no matter how wise or emotionally healthy, will give each ex-intimate an invitation to feel like a failure. And, there is nothing more aggravating than feeling inadequate. The first person who pronounces the relationship dead usually feels less like a failure than his/her partner. The one who assumes the most responsibility for its demise will no doubt accept a greater sense of failure than the one who feels "innocent". Ex-intimates who believe that togetherness is "good" and singleness is "bad" will experience more intense feelings (including anger) over good-bye than will others. Those who *always* accept an invitation to feel inadequate, will greedily grab at the chance, then roar with their low self-esteem. Whatever the degree—mild, moderate or severe—all ex-intimates will feel some sense of inadequacy and failure at the end of a love affair and will, therefore, react with frustration.

Saying good-bye to an old love and life style means that you must say hello to an unknown future and a sense of uncertainty. If you have not made future plans, your anxiety will be heightened. Many ex-intimates may know that they want "out" but are really unclear about what they want to do next. "Do I want to jump into another relationship right away?" "Where do I want to live?" "What do I want to do with the rest of my life?" All of these questions, and more, will come up and answering or sometimes even looking at them causes uncertainty, ambivalence, indecision, fear and, surrounding them all, some sense of anger. When these questions are resolved, the frustration level will lessen. But until you have successfully gone through this "Who am I and what do I want next"crisis, your frustration will be greater.

Anger in a relationship creates emotional distance. Obviously, to develop that necessary distance from a dead love affair, you must *not* continue to feel tied to or dependent on your ex-mate for emotional nurturing. Anger, then, as a natural phase in the grief process, helps ex-intimates begin to let go emotionally of their old love affairs. When you are angry at someone or something it means that you care enough to be hurt. You still feel close and connected to him/her but are creating some distance. This is not an end in itself. Ex-intimates who stay stuck in the angry phase *never* fully let go of their old love; but it is an important and a positive step in the direction of letting go. The first person who says good-bye probably has reached this stage in the grief process already. Although he/she may slide back into an earlier phase when the relationship is physically severed, one partner must be at this point to finally end the relationship.

TRAPS THAT REINFORCE ANGER.

Although it is important to feel anger after ending a relationship, it is not necessary or wise to reinforce or build on that emotion. Any trap or pitfall that could reinforce depression, may also increase your anger—depending on whether you hold that irritation inside or spit it back out. According to many ex-intimates, however, the following traps are more likely to promote a reaction of anger than others.

1. *Carrying a "chip" on your shoulder and getting into verbal or physical battles with everyone.* Anger promotes anger or at "best" creates distance. Anytime someone begins venting hostility towards you, you will probably find yourself reacting back with your own anger for protection or avoiding further contact. Although it is easy to understand why an ex-intimate would feel angry at the end of a love affair, those who "take out" their anger on everyone with whom they come into contact will find that

they have more anger at the end of the day than they did at the beginning. An ex-intimate who carries a "chip" on his/her shoulder will find many opportunities to react with hostility: getting "caught" in traffic, a constructive but critical remark from a co-worker, a negative statement from a friend, or a frown from the grocery store clerk. All of these scenes and more provide the perfect chance to overreact. In fact, in my practice as a therapist, I have met many ex-intimates who feel so vulnerable that almost any reaction from me other than smiling support is seen as a "put down" and another reason to get angry. Unfortunately, this spontaneous hostility towards anyone who is not seen as totally supportive creates even more hurt feelings for the person who carries the "chip". Usually his/her "victims' " reaction is to reject any further contact with him/her, thus, leaving the individual feeling even more alone and misunderstood than before.

2. *Attempting to "get even" with ex-mate.* This is a commmon trap to fall into but one that is hard to climb out of. One ex-intimate hurts the other, then the other retaliates, than back to the other, again and again. Ex-intimates sometimes "get even" in very self-destructive ways which promote additional hurt feelings and anger. For example, she dates one of his friends so he dates one of her girlfriends, or he doesn't visit their children at first, so she refuses visitation rights when he finally asks to see them. The trouble with "getting even" is that it's hard to finally stop the cycle and it does not promote any healing effect. One ex-intimate in this cycle really doesn't feel better after he's "gotten even" because he knows it's her "turn" to get back at him and the cycle will continue. The only way to stop promoting your anger in this fashion is to refuse to take your "turn".

3. *Fighting over custody of the children.* This is a very destructive "game" for adults and for children. Happily for all, it is rare. But it does exist. And, those who get involved in this battle over custody reap nothing but additional hurt and anger. It's hard for a parent to lose custody of his/her children (and for the children to physically separate from one of their parents),

but in a divorce someone usually does. And, although it is becoming increasingly popular to "split up" the family and have each parent assume custody for some of the children, only heartache and anger can result from "battles" over this decision.

4. *Fighting over the division of property.* If you're going to "fight" over anything with your ex-mate after the relationship is dead, the safest battleground issues are material possessions: houses, land, cars, furniture and dishes. At least these things won't get hurt in the process, as would a child, and usually there is an end to these battles, though they can be quite drawn out and expensive. Most divorce lawyers will tell you that fighting "tooth and nail" over every piece of property (including who gets the can opener) can lengthen the divorce proceedings and run up the costs. And, while it's important to split property "fairly", when a couple fights each division with vengeance this can promote more anger than it resolves. In fact, you will literally need a referee (the judge) to help you let go of the battle and proceed from that point.

5. *Fighting over whose fault the ending was.* Although it makes absolutely no sense and neither can possibly win in this fight, some ex-intimates battle with their ex-mates about who was the most responsible for the death of their love. This trap can really keep you emotionally "hooked" on your ex-love and prolong your anger. I suppose there may be some amount of satisfaction in hearing your ex-love tell you that you were "right" and he/she was "wrong"—but even if you heard that, what do you do then? To consciously become aware of your own decisions to quit nurturing your love and constructively use that insight is mentally healthy. To argue with your ex-love that he or she killed your love will only keep you emotionally connected, give you an invitation to feel like a victim, and promote more hostility.

6. *Purposely recalling hurtful scenes.* It is not unusual to hear an ex-intimate talk about how he/she reinforces anger by purposely remembering a painful event.

— "Everytime I think about what that Bastard said to me I get angry."
— "It makes me mad, just to think about . . ."
— "I still remember how she used me, what a Bitch!"
— "Each time I think about seeing her in bed with him, I feel like killing them!"

Although it's unhealthy to rationalize away or try to forget your anger before it's resolved, purposely recalling painful events and ruminating about how unfairly you've been treated by your ex-mate will only promote more anger and keep you stuck in that phase.

7. *Trying to pretend it doesn't exist.* It is just as unhealthy to deny that you have any anger from the good-bye as it is to purposely hold on to it with memories—both traps actually build up anger rather than release it. The "nice guy" who never allows himself to acknowledge his anger can be a walking bomb of rage. He can't control a feeling which he doesn't even admit to himself exists. And, people who have nice, friendly divorces often continue to hold grudges against their ex-mates several years after the final decree. Many fail to develop another intimate relationship because they have not truly let go of their last—or have denied so many of their feelings that they no longer feel much of anything for anyone. Some people describe this as "cold" anger because they literally can't feel warmth towards anyone anymore.

8. *Dealing with anger indirectly.* If you deal with your anger indirectly by dreaming of your ex-love's demise, using sarcasm, getting headaches each time you think of him/her, being "super sweet" to your ex-love, taking on the martyr role or any number of other passive-aggressive techniques, your anger will last much longer. One quick outburst is worth several "backbiting" comments to release your anger. The ability to use the energy in anger for constructive change and self-assertion is related to how much you are aware of your own feelings and how directly you deal

with them. The more passive you are with your anger the slower your movement away from the past.

OWNING ANGER: THE FIRST STEP TOWARDS BREAKING AWAY.

I have talked with a number of ex-intimates who admit that they became consciously aware of their anger towards their ex-mate or their old life style but attempted to rationalize it away or deny it because they did not want to break the emotional ties with their ex-love. They knew when they finally acknowledged that anger, if only to themselves, their past love would no longer be quite so treasured in their minds. As one lady shared:

"For the first four or five months of our separation I felt absolutely wretched. John had left me for another woman. My pride was hurt. I felt betrayed, alone and disconnected from everyone. Nothing mattered anymore. I cried myself to sleep every night, dragged through the day, then returned to an empty apartment. I rarely went out. I stayed by the telephone—just in case John called. He didn't, of course. Sometimes I called him, and even though his stance was cold disinterest (mine varied from 'clever and cute' to 'warm and serious'), I felt better when I heard his voice. I refused to believe that I couldn't get him back; I'd change, I decided—'fix' the parts of me he didn't like. Then, when he was through with his new girlfriend, I'd be ready. As near as I could see, my options were to stay alone and be miserable the rest of my life, wait for John to change his mind—or kill myself. I remember telling myself that I *could* just forget him and start over again, but that idea was less appealing than the others. John was the only man I ever really loved and spending my life with someone else seemed flat. I could never love anyone again—it was John or no one!

"I'm not sure when it happened, but gradually I began, first thinking, then feeling, that our 'love' hadn't been all roses anyway. He was a man who 'took' and I 'gave'. At first I shoved those thoughts and feelings aside. I remember telling myself: 'If you really begin feeling like that, you won't want John, even if he does come back'. But, it wasn't very long after that, when I began feeling angry about some of the 'garbage' John dumped on me and I took—not to mention what was I doing to myself. I gave up 'waiting for John' and began living again. It's really a much better spot—even though there are times when I slip back."

Although many may not be so well informed about the purpose of their anger, most discover after they finally allow themselves to feel this reaction, that they are not quite so forlorn about saying good-bye. The sadness will no doubt return, but each time it does, it will be a little less intense and last for shorter periods of time. If you do some constructive things with your anger—like use the energy to help yourself feel better as a "single-againer", your optimism about the future will grow and the grief from the good-bye will diminish.

HOW TO GAIN CONTROL OVER YOUR ANGER.

Many people fear their anger because they hold so much of it inside their own bodies that it only escapes in destructive eruptions. Each "little" frustration they encounter in daily life is kept inside until suddenly, sometimes over a trivial event, they spew like Mt. Vesuvius. Then, the process of swallowing frustrations begins all over again. Ex-intimates often swallow large disappointments, fears and hurt feelings during the ending process for fear of "making things worse" or contributing to an "ugly divorce" and then, when it's finally over, find that they are overwhelmed with their feelings of anger, bitterness and/or depression. This section is designed to help you learn how to keep anger from overwhelming you or turning into self-destructiveness.

1. *Do acknowledge that it exists.* The greater your awareness of your anger in you, the better chance you have of controlling it. No one lives anger "free"; many people say that they do but they are only fooling themselves. Disowned anger turns into depression, high blood pressure, headaches, colitis, self-sabotage (accident proneness), mistrust, a sense of feeling "numb", forgetfulness,

being "super sweet", sadism, overworking, oversexing, "don't worry about me" stances, gossip, sick and dying fantasies to "get even," violent explosions and sometimes, in psychiatric patients, a complete divorce from reality. Obviously, owning the fact that you do experience anger will give you a choice about what you want to do with that emotion. If you deny that you feel it, the anger will continue to exist, only you will have little voice in deciding how to release it.

2. *Don't be afraid of your anger.* Most people who say they are afraid of their anger, really mean that they are afraid if they express how they feel they will no longer appear to be "neutral". But the reality is that we do express how we feel; maybe not directly, but indirectly, the message gets across. If you get angry at your boss because you feel he has treated you unfairly, you will either express that sentiment to him openly, or, you will begin making mistakes at the office, coming in late, forgetting appointments, etc.. Either way, the anger is shown. When it's direct, it can be openly discussed and resolved. Indirectly expressed anger leaves the issue unsettled and builds up some new ones. There are a few people who should be afraid of their anger but aren't. These people usually have a history of violent outbursts and aggressive and/or assaultive acts. They are individuals who resort to primitive techniques to gain control over their environment. Ironically, most of these people are not afraid of their anger, nor, do they feel any concern when they plot to destroy or explode. In general, if you have enough concern to be afraid of your anger, you will not be destructive with it. Ask youself what you're afraid you will do. If the answer is, in fact, a lethal or destructive action, then you should seek assistance from a mental health professional. Otherwise, do *not* be afraid of your anger.

3. *Don't just talk about it, feel it.* Talking about how angry you are—or could be—is of little value. It does not release any energy or get you in touch with your own feelings. Feeling it does. If you have trouble really feeling this emotion, try the suggestions outlined in Chapter 10. Remember that sometimes just expressing your feelings repeatedly out loud will often help you

actually begin to experience them. Once you've felt your anger, you *know* it's there and can then begin doing something with it. Thinking it exists only gives you an invitation to think about how you might deal with it.

4. *Don't reinforce anger.* Often people blow their own anger way out of proportion by reinforcement or exaggeration of their own hurt, frustrations or fears. Purposely setting yourself up for additional anger-provoking scenes may also overload your ability to control that emotion. Any time you direct your life into situations where you have minimal control over what happens, or the chances of "success" are poor, you are setting yourself up for further frustration. Expecting more from yourself or others than your own common sense tells you is realistic will heighten frustration. Ruminating over all the past injustices in your life, from early childhood on, will only give you more anger than you can resolve all at once. You do not need to overwhelm your ability to deal with anger by pulling in extras.

5. *Don't hold it inside.* Many people become overwhelmed with their anger just by storing it up. Each time someone hurts their feelings or they are disappointed, they push back their healthy urge to release their anger by rationalizing that "this isn't a good time" or "so and so probably didn't mean it." How many times have you, yourself, trapped your anger inside by wondering if you had the "right" to feel hurt or upset? Each time you swallow a frustration, you are building up your reservoir of anger. Internalized anger turns into depression, self-hate, guilt, self-destructive behavior and, often, periodic outbursts of rage. The only way to protect yourself from building a "rage reservoir" is to acknowledge your anger and deal with it directly each time you feel it. That way you no longer collect extra anger—to carry around.

6. *Do release your anger through physical activity.* People who have a large reservoir of anger from years of swallowing frustrations find it helpful to "work off" some of the extra energy from their anger. Any activity that involves physical exertion will do. Women often talk about how they give their house "Hell" by scrubbing everything in sight when they're angry. Men

more typically push the lawn mower around the yard or wax the car. Both men and women use recreational sports, such as tennis, handball, badminton, bowling or golf, to release their "tensions". In therapy, I often have patients beat on a pillow or punch a punching bag to help them release excess anger. You can try the same things at home with a pillow or by making your own "punching bag". Incidentally, this is not only a good way to release your rage reservoir but an excellent technique to help you develop constructive insight about the causal factors for your own anger. If you put yourself on a schedule which includes doing physical exercises (taking a brisk walk in the morning, doing some sort of physical activity during your lunch hour or after work, and exercising or punching a pillow just before you get ready for bed) you will be surprised at how much healthier you feel—physically *and* emotionally.

7. *Do learn how to scream.* Expressing your pain, fears and frustrations through screaming can help you to get them out in the open where you can see them and deal with them more directly. Dr. Daniel Casriel, in his book, *A Scream Away From Happiness* suggests that learning how to scream out your feelings can help release inner tensions, break-up your "frozen" emotions and begin the process of becoming a psychologically "open" and healthier being again. If you question the validity of screaming as a therapeutic technique, watch the "rooters'" section at a foot-ball game versus the crowd sitting next to them. The screamers are not only able to openly shout their displeasure about their team's mishaps, but also quite spontaneously show their happi-ness and warmth when the team does well. Whatever happens, those who go away exhausted from screaming rarely pick a fight or are disgruntled after the game; the fans who sat on their feelings or whispered them quietly often are.

8. *Do be prepared for events that frustrate you.* Although we don't always know what scenes are going to cause additional frustration, most of us know some situations that are almost guaranteed to make us angry. I know, for example, that I will start off my day mildly upset if I get up late and rush unpre-

pared to my office, losing my parking space in the process. This is a mild source of anger, but, since I know it exists, I can handle it by making sure I set two alarm clocks or, if I forget to do that, a mild expression of anger before I get in my car releases the tension I could very easily carry into my first appointment. If you take the time to figure out what situations usually give you an invitation to feel frustrated or angry, you will discover that there are some you can totally avoid and others you will be able to handle quite well because you were prepared ahead of time for your anger. It is even possible to predict situations that you have not already experienced but suspect will be "anger provoking", like your ex-love coming back to pick up his/her half of the property, your ex-spouse visiting the children with his/her new love, or meeting with the lawyers (or paying the fees). Since you know all of these situations are an invitation to feel angry, prepare yourself so that you will be able to deal with your anger in a healthy manner.

Gaining control over our anger is something that we all learn how to do. Those who lose control of their anger or express it in destructive ways do so because they were taught by their parents and family that anger is wrong and should not be felt or expressed. This could not be farther from the truth. Anger is a feeling, just like all the others, which does exist and deserves to be acknowledged.

DEALING DIRECTLY WITH WHAT CAUSES YOUR ANGER.

After you have released your anger, take some time for introspection. Ask yourself the following questions:
1. What was I "fighting for"?
2. Is there any way I can obtain it?
3. How?
4. Is that something I'm willing to do?
5. If my goal is unreachable, how can I alter it to something that is realistic?

Answering these questions for yourself can give you a great deal of insight about the causal factors of your own anger, plus additonal information about how to resolve some of your conflict. Let's look at each question specifically.

1. *What was I "fighting for"?* People fight for a number of things: respect, approval, appreciation, sympathy, support, never to be caught "off guard", self-confidence, love, agreement from others, a sense of safety, a feeling of importance and admiration from others. Sometimes it can be "won" through anger, sometimes it can't.

2. *Is there any way I can obtain it?* If you are fighting for something that is possible to "win", your answer will probably be "yes". But sometimes people fight for the impossible and continue to fight because they don't know that or refuse to admit it to themselves. In my opinion, it is impossible to win the following: everything always going exactly the way I would like; all people liking me or giving me their approval/respect; feeling totally "safe" and "secure" in all situations; and never making a mistake again. Somehow knowing that these goals are impossible helps me give up fighting those battles. Sometimes a goal is impossible to "win" because you are fighting in the wrong battlefield. For example, you cannot "win" self-approval, self-respect, or self-acceptance by demanding it from others. Those are goals that only you have the power to give yourself.

3. *How?* If you answered "yes" to the above question, this is the time to figure out how you can obtain your goal. If your goal was to gain approval from your boss, for example, figure out what you would have to do to earn it. Be as specific as you can. If it's worth fighting for, it should be worth your energy to do some problem solving now. If you *still* come up with a blank, ask him/her.

4. *Is that something I'm willing to do?* Once you have figured out what you would have to do to obtain your goal, ask yourself whether it's something you're willing to do. How much effort will it take to earn your boss' approval, for example. If the goal is reasonable and you are willing to earn his/her approval, then

you can use your energy to work for that rather than fight for it through the expression of direct anger.

5. *If my goal is unreachable, how can I alter it to something that is realistic?* If you answered question #2 with "no", this is your chance to begin looking at how you can give yourself permission to give up some of your battles that can't be "won" and replace them with goals that you can obtain. Many people discover that their anger really comes from fighting themselves; fighting to be different than they are—smarter, kinder, warmer, wiser, stronger, braver, etc.. Whatever the fight, the best way to "win" is to start by accepting yourself as you are now. Sometimes this is difficult for ex-intimates because they feel that they are currently alone because there is something "wrong" with them, and, therefore, they do not want to accept themselves as they are; they want to change. But change will only begin after you have accepted where you are now. If you answered "yes" to question #2 and figured out, for example, that you were fighting for your boss' approval but upon further examination, discovered that you would have to literally sell your soul or give up expressing your opinions, you may decide that it is impossible for you to ever gain his approval and still keep your own. If that is the case, you will now need to decide what you are willing to settle for. Is just keeping him/her off your back enough? Or how about learning to accept that all authority figures aren't gods nor is their approval always worth having?

To practice answering these questions for yourself, go back in your memory to the last time you felt your anger. See if you can recall the scene; then try to discover what you were fighting for. If the scene was a battle over what seemed like trivia, look beneath that and see what emotions or issues the trivia symbolized for you at the time.

Use this space to answer these questions for yourself.

1. What was I "fighting for"?

2. Is there any way I can obtain it?

3. How?

4. Is that something I'm willing to do?

5. If my goal is unreachable, how can I alter it to something that is realistic?

CONSTRUCTIVE WAYS TO UTILIZE ANGER.

Everytime you hear someone say "When I finally get 'fed up', I do something," he/she is saying that he/she uses anger for ambition or drive. "I'm too stubborn to quit now" is another phrase often used to express determination for completing a task or reaching a goal. One of my friends uses her anger to help her lose weight: "I never go on a diet until I get angry at myself for being fat—then, I *know* I'll stick to it!" I'm sure if you look at your own life, you'll discover many scenes where you called upon your anger for help—most of us do.

Healthy, constructive anger is an especially valuable resource to help ex-intimates to grow through a life crisis which offers even the most courageous several opportunities to throw in the towel. To help you become more aware of the different ways you can use your anger constructively, let us look at how other ex-intimates have used their anger productively.

1. *Fighting depression with anger.* Turning your anger away from you and directing it outward can change your mood from

sad and lethargic to brighter and active. As one of my patients told me:

> "When I used to come home every evening from work, as soon as I walked through my doorway, I would suddenly feel tired. I knew it was depression and that it depressed me to come home to an empty apartment, but thinking about it really didn't help. What *did* help was hard work. Forcing myself to clean up the apartment, rearrange the furniture, redecorate a room, wash my car, work on a hobby—there are all kinds of things I can do. Sometimes it still amazes me that I have so much energy, once I get going. I sure end up feeling a whole lot better afterwards. In fact, some days I even look forward to coming home and doing something constructive."

A lady talked about how she fought the physical part of her depression by forcing herself to exercise:

> "Not only do I feel better after I start moving again, but I've lost 10 lbs. in the process—a real ego booster!"

2. *Turning anger into ambition, motivation or drive.* Keeping your anger in healthy control can give you the extra strength that you need to keep yourself working towards a new goal.

> "I really have to thank my ex-husband for giving me the motivation to learn how to drive. If it wasn't for his negative attitude about me being 'helpless' and my anger about 'I'll show him', I think I'd still be hiding at home, waiting for someone to take me shopping. My next goal is to get a job —that should be a real challenge!"

One man gave up drinking after his divorce:

> "I'm not sure about all of the fancy psychological reasons, but I do know that I used my anger towards my ex-wife to help me stop drinking. Each time I wanted a drink, I'd remind

myself that that's what Harriet would expect me to do. That's all I needed to put down the glass.''

A lady told us:

"I'd been married 25 years when we finally divorced and I really didn't have very much to show for it. I spent a few months feeling sorry for myself, then decided, 'Now's the time to do something, you aren't getting any younger, old girl!' I ended up becoming a teacher and I love it. Looking back now, I can see how I used my anger to help me get where I am now.''

3. *Using anger to be creative.* Ex-intimates often develop their hidden talents and perfect them through the use of their constructive anger from the good-bye. One man learned to make totem poles after his divorce; first as a hobby and now as a profession.

"I love it. Used to be in the 'rat race.' And all I ever got for work was a thin paycheck and hassles with the customers. I used to carve wood as a hobby—a way to release tension, I guess, and keep me from feeling bored. After my divorce, I couldn't afford to do much of anything extra, so, I just kept on carving. One day I saw a picture of an Alaskan totem pole in a magazine and thought 'Hell—I can do that!' And, sure enough, here I am five years later making a darn good living at something I like. My new wife admires my talent, too.''

4. *Changing anger into self-assertion.* According to Dr. Theodore I. Rubin, author of *The Angry Book*, self-assertion springs from self-esteem, "the spontaneous ability to make a choice and do something in one's behalf without a desire to hurt someone." If you're angry enough to fight for your self-esteem, you have the ability to turn that energy into self-assertion.

"You should have seen the expression on my husband's face when I told him in person, and very matter-of-factly, that he would just *have* to find a way to pay the child support—it was his responsibility and, although I did not want to make it 'hard' for him, neither was I going to let him 'off the hook.' Child support has been a fight for the last nine months and I've vacillated between letting it slide and feeling sorry for myself to shrieking like a banshee about the money he owed us. This time it was different and, I might add, much more effective. He heard me standing up for myself (without putting him down) and so did I. I really felt good about it."

LEARNING TO LET GO OF PART OF YOUR ANGER BY REPLACING LOSSES.

If you are fighting for something or someone you don't have anymore and are frustrated because you feel empty or lost, one good way to win your battle permanently is to replace some of those losses. In fact, many ex-intimates discover that their anger (or depression) subsides quite naturally as they begin refilling some of their emptiness or replacing their old goals with new ones.

It isn't easy to do. In fact, it's very hard to "give up" an old life style, goals and familiar faces and replace them with new "not yet known" ones. But it is possible and often the "substitutes" for your past are mentally healthier and much more rewarding than anything or anyone from the "good old days". But you have to go out and get them—or meet someone new.

Experiments and Exercises.

Role playing is a method in psychological practice (primarily Gestalt) which allows an individual to ACT OUT his problems. This can be a problem the individual has with himself (conflicting feelings) or with another person. The simplest method, created by Fritz Perls, is to set two chairs facing each other. One chair for the ACTOR and the other for the person the actor takes issue with—or in the case of conflicting inner feelings, the opposing feelings. (Sometimes a third chair is used as the "decision making" position—that is, if the conflict appears to need a neutral, decision making position, after both sides have been verbalized, the ACTOR will use this third chair to assess the other two positions and come up with a decision or logical resolution of the conflict.)

Try the two chair role playing technique to express your anger. Stand on a sturdy chair, looking down at the person you are angry at. Tell him/her what you are angry about and why. Make sure you express your feelings to the degree you feel them: don't "soft pedal" your position. Say all the things you've always wanted to say and never dared. Switch to the other chair and allow the person you are talking with to respond as you think he/she would. When you feel "finished" draw the scene to a conclusion.

After this exercise take some time to reflect and ask youself the following:

   *What did I learn from this?

   *Is there any way I can prevent this same thing from happening again?

   *Is there any other way to get what I was "fighting for"?

   *What do I need to do now?

13: How to Lessen Self-Pity

"I hope I didn't sound like I'm feeling sorry for myself"—
"Don't pay any attention to him, he's just wallowing in self-pity"
are both statements we hear or often make ourselves. Martyrs
are not admired: they're scorned. "Self-pitiers" are prejudged as
weaklings and avoided whenever possible. No wonder we try to
ignore or deny our won feelings of self-pity—we are trained to
condemn them!

Yet all of us do feel sorry for ourselves occasionally. Whenever
our feelings are hurt or we're feeling abused and misunderstood
we cry. It's a normal human emotion and a natural part of saying
good-bye to an old love affair. In fact, there is nothing "wrong"
with self-pity. It is a way of nurturing yourself—giving sympathy
and support to someone you care about—someone whose feelings
have been hurt. If you have the warmth to give healthy sympathy
to others, you should also be able to give some to yourself when
you need it.

The problems develop when you wrap yourself in self-pity and
use it as your excuse for giving up on life. "Nothing good ever

happens to me anyway, there's no use in trying" can be the arrow that pierces your hope. Such an attitude creates an emotional trap that immobilizes you within depression much longer than is necessary—or healthy. Sometimes people cannot untangle themselves from self-pity and need professional counseling to help them "unhook". Many people who are prone to self-pity or self-doubt find the ending of an intimate relationship the final "straw" that breaks them—especially if they are not the ones to initiate the good-bye or their fears of the future seem overwhelming.

CAUSAL FACTORS OF SELF-PITY.

There are a number of scenes or circumstances which may trigger your self-pity—especially if you are prone to those feelings anyway. And, sometimes, if you can understand why you feel sorry for yourself or how your own personal traits reinforce your disappointment and sorrow, you can use that insight to lessen your self-pity.

Individuals who have low self-esteem and "give in" constantly to others or do too much to preserve a relationship are prone to self-pity. They end up feeling "used" and may not believe they deserve any better treatment. The following comments were expressed by members in my group who are prone to self-pity.

— "I gave him the best years of my life . . ."
— "My wife used me—She never really cared about me."
— "I always did everything for him—and now look."
— "My wife never understood me."
— "I loved him more than he loved me."
— "I loved my job, and I gave it up for him—"
— "I knew this would happen—I knew she'd leave me."
— "I tried harder than she did."
— "I always knew I'd end up alone."
— "Even after his infidelity I was still nice to him."
— "I could never figure out what she wanted from me; I bent over backwards."

1. "Bending over backwards" to please someone or save a relationship is a sure way to end up feeling used when it's over—and a "natural" for self-pity. Ironically, ex-intimates who uphold the idea of "giving more than you get" have a greater chance of feeling sorry for themselves. The person you bend over backwards for rarely appreciates your sacrifices and, in fact, may gradually come to expect you to always do more than you should. In addition, the other person sometimes resents your sacrificing because he/she looks "bad" in comparison. Ironically, sometimes this dynamic becomes the underlying reason for the dissolution of the relationship.

> One lady I know always felt "used" because she put everyone else's needs before her own. If a friend called and asked her for a favor, she would drop whatever she was doing to help. Her friends rarely appreciated her efforts, but the lady kept on "doing" for others because she did not believe her friends would like her if she didn't. When *she* needed a favor, some of her friends seemed to vanish and the others she wouldn't even ask. Usually she ended up taking care of her own problems and feeling sorry for herself in the process. Through therapy, she learned how not to always sacrifice for others and how to feel confident in her own worth so that she didn't have to "sacrifice" in order to be deemed a worthy friend to others. Once she practiced giving only what seemed "fair" to her, much of her self-pity lessened.

2. Some people are prone to self-pity because they confuse sadness with tragedy. The ending of an intimate relationship with all its painful fallout is not a disaster—it is sad. If you accept your pain and fear as unpleasant and sad rather than tragic, you can learn to heal your wounds and plan for the future. If you treat the death of a love affair as a tragic event that is the irrevocable end to your happiness or the absolute failure of all your relationships, you can only feel sorry for yourself and wallow in pain.

Laurie is a 23 year old bank teller who was recently rejected
by her boyfriend, John. When she first came to my office,
she was overwhelmed with depression. She felt like a loser
and feared that she could not go on living without Jack. "No
one will ever love me—I'll never get over Jack—There's
nothing left in my life!" The longer she talked, the more
evident it became that Laurie equated rejection with disaster.
Once I explained this to her and helped her accept that her
boyfriend's rejection was sad but not a tragedy, she was able
to let go of her self-pity and look at more constructive ways
to deal with her depression.

People like Laurie who overdramatize their painful and scary
feelings have a tendency to overwhelm themselves, "give up"
trying and stay stuck in unhappiness much longer than others
who deal with their feelings more realistically. Friends don't
know how to comfort someone who not only feels so tragic but
who actually refuses comforting from anyone who even hints that
his/her wounds will heal. "Nobody knows the pain that I feel"
is often the lonely theme song for this brand of "self-pitiers".

3. Another group of people prone to self-pity and closely linked
to the "overdramatizers" are those who decide that life is unbearable when they don't get exactly what they want. Most healthy
adults learn to adjust to their disappointments in time and replace
their losses with viable alternatives. A few people, however, refuse
to accept that they cannot always have their own way and, with
the ending of an intimate relationship, may run into unchange-
able disappointments for the first time in their lives—especially
if they did not want the relationship to end, but sometimes even
when it was their own idea.

Polly was immobilized with self-pity after she divorced her
husband of 21 years. As a child, Polly had been spoiled by her
parents. When she married, her husband, Tom, took over
the role of a pampering parent. Polly didn't get everything
she wanted, of course, but when she wanted something badly

enough, Tom would usually get it for her—nice clothes, a pretty house, her own car and "good" schools for the children. In spite of this "spoiling" Polly really didn't feel very satisfied. She decided that if she divorced Tom, she could get what she wanted—a sense of freedom. Unfortunately for Polly, the divorce split Tom's income and it was impossible for her to keep all of her "things" and still have her freedom. But she didn't want Tom back nor could she see any way to give up her "home". Polly began to sink into a well of self-pity and was finally brought to the mental health clinic by a friend. In therapy it was discovered that Polly had become overwhelmed with self-pity because she didn't know any other way to deal with her disappointment. She believed that she should get anything she really wanted and when she learned she could not, she gave up. Gradually, she was able to accept her disappointment and learn how to adjust in a healthier manner.

Every ex-intimate who has trouble adjusting to disappointment is not pampered like Polly, but most refuse to believe that they have to accept something different than what they really want.

4. Sometimes people fall into self-pity because they confuse what they want with what they actually need. We need food, shelter and clothing to physically survive. To be emotionally healthy we need understanding, acceptance and love from ourselves and other people. We may want that love, acceptance and understanding from specific individuals, but it is not really necessary for our emotional health that we get it from any one person specifically. Many ex-intimates get trapped in self-pity because they confuse their need for human love and understanding with their desire to gain it from a specific person (usually someone who is no longer available). As long as their confusion with wants and needs continue, self-pity will prevail when they cannot obtain what they want.

5. Some people who are prone to self-pity add to their sorrow by getting disturbed that they have any frustrations at all.

— "Why should I have to wait in line at the bank?"
— "I'll never learn how to balance my check book."
— "I can never get a seat on the bus."
— "The mailman never delivers anything but bills."
— "I wonder why no one smiles at me first?"
— "How can I ever afford to pay these high prices?"

The list of routine frustrations in daily living is extensive. If you have recently said good-bye to an old love affair, you may find that your frustrations will be heightened and so will your sensitivity to those frustrations. Be aware of your sensitivity so that daily inconveniences don't drain you to the point where you have just enough energy left to bemoan your fate.

6. People who decide that they cannot trust anyone with their feelings are prone to self-pity. We all need someone to care, listen, understand and be concerned about us—especially when we're feeling hurt. But when ex-intimates decide (for their own reasons) that no one cares about their feelings as much as they do, *or* that their feelings would not be accepted by anyone, they are stuck with self-pity. Anytime you find yourself saying that you wish you could talk with someone but no one cares how you feel anyway, you are engaging in self-pity. When you have what you judge as a "wrong" feeling or experience hurt over some situation that you are ashamed of or embarrassed to talk about, you will probably only end up feeling sorry for yourself. And, the more you use yourself as your sole source of sympathy, the sadder you'll feel, the less objective advice you will gain, and the farther down in the hole of self-pity you'll sink.

COMMON TRAPS THAT REINFORCE SELF-PITY.

It isn't easy to pull out of self-pity—especially if you perpetuate that emotion with an exaggerated sense of responsibility and "fairness". Many ex-intimates get caught in self-pity because they are individuals who either attempt to make up for their lack of self-confidence by overachieving or are firmly convinced that if they are "good" they will get what they feel is "fair". But the ending of an intimate relationship with all its painful and often "unfair" fallout is difficult to control and many of these ex-intimates reinforce their self-pity by falling into the following traps.

1. *Trying to take care of all your own hurt feelings by yourself.* Getting trapped in self-pity because you don't want to "bother" anyone else with your sorrow is an easy pitfall for some to slide into. Some ex-intimates immediately isolate themselves and refuse invitations from their friends because they "don't feel up to entertaining and would only be a drag." Others initially reach out to other people for emotional comfort, support and human contact, but after the first few visits decide that their friends have had enough of their sorrow (even though the ex-intimate hasn't) and the "best" thing to do is discontinue visiting with their friends until they feel better. In both cases the ex-intimates do not decide to give up feeling "blue", they merely decide to handle their pain by withdrawal from supportive contact with friends. Thus, their self-pity is reinforced by deliberate isolation from others. Obviously the way to get out of this trap is to encourage yourself and others not to let you withdraw. Naturally there will be times when you'd rather stay by yourself, but don't allow yourself to always decline invitations—pretty soon, you will cease getting them. When a friend invites you to join him— accept. If you're really worried about being a "drag", take the responsibility to give up the "blues" for one evening.

2. *Feeling sorry for yourself because your ex-mate or others can't see their "unfairness".* There are a lot of "unfair" things that happen in the dissolution of a relationship—some are self-imposed, others happen by circumstance or are caused by other people. Self-imposed injustices are caused by exaggerated amounts of guilt or making harsh judgments on yourself. Circumstances like the high cost of living on a presently smaller income, having to give up your home and/or children, or the inequities in divorce courts create "unfair" hardships on ex-intimates. And, finally, other people (friends, family and, perhaps, your ex-love) may judge you unfairly or treat you with malice just because a

relationship with one other individual has died. Obviously, that's not "fair"—but don't expect everyone else to see the "unfairness"; you'll be disappointed if you do. As a matter of fact, many ex-intimates increase their self-pity by expecting their ex-mate and others to see the "unfairness" or be "fair" themselves. One lady was drowning in self-pity because of her unwillingness to accept the fact that her ex-mate apparently did not care whether he was "fair" or not. He had deliberately moved to another state to avoid child custody payments. "Doesn't he know we need the child support money? I just can't understand how he expects us to live. We'll have to go on welfare and that's not fair to the children. I know he's making good money, what'll I do?" Although she was normally a very reasonable adult, self-pity had "jammed up" her ability to solve problems because her ex-mate could not see his "unfairness". One of my male clients got himself in a similar predicament by trying to get his ex-wife to be equitable about splitting the community property. She fought him every step of the way and he sporadically made his life miserable by feeling sorry for himself because his ex-wife wouldn't see that she was being "unfair". Most of us know that we cannot stop others from being "unfair" but we have trouble actually accepting that fact. Once you accept it, you can give up your self-pity and spend your energy learning to deal with life's inequities rather than becoming overwhelmed by them.

3. *Feeling sorry for yourself because you can't be both mother and father to your children.* This is a hard trap to avoid because most parents carry a certain amount of guilt for "splitting up the family" and often try to make up for the missing parent to absolve their guilt. Sooner or later, all "single" parents recognize that it is impossible to completely fill both parental roles. But, in the process, many ex-intimates cannot forgive themselves when they fail.

The first three months I saw Edna, she was almost always in crisis. She and her husband had agreed to divorce in a reasonably "adult" manner—but their seven year old son,

Danny, reacted like a "child". One day he'd be sullen and quiet, the next, he's rage like a madman—fighting in school and screaming at home. Edna accurately assessed that Danny was reacting to his parents' divorce and the absence of his father, but inaccurately concluded that she could absolve Danny's pain and protect him from sadness by filling in for his father. First, she tried to take over the role of a father in addition to her other responsibilities, spending total weekends with her son and playing with him after work each night. For a brief period of time this seemed to "quiet" Danny, but after a couple of weeks, he once again began missing his father and reacting with sporadic upsets. Edna handled her son's behavior and her failure to be both mother and father by feeling sorry for herself and sinking into a depression. Gradually, both Danny and Edna were able to accept his father's absence and learn to adjust in a healthier manner.

In general, any situation which gives you an invitation to feel hurt or disappointed but which you feel helpless to change or accept, may reinforce your self-pity. To get out of any of these pitfalls you must decide that you genuinely want to quit feeling sorry for yourself and get on with the business of living. No one can force you to give up your pain.

ACCEPT THAT YOU ARE FEELING SORRY FOR YOURSELF.

If you really want to give up your self-pity, or learn to lessen it, you must first accept the fact that you *do* feel sorry for yourself. A lot of ex-intimates have trouble accepting that they actually are "self-pitiers". "Yes, but—you don't understand" is often an automatic response. Immediately they begin to defend themselves when confronted with the reality that they are immobilizing themselves with self-pity. (Some people don't even comment at all— they just feel a little more "put down" and sorry for themselves.) But, suggesting to someone that he/she is trapped in self-pity and should accept what he/she is doing is not attacking or judging that reaction. Of course an individual has the "right" or valid reasons to feel sorry for himself; everyone does! But the fact is that self-pity can often be a trap which keeps its owner feeling sad. And, whether an individual prone to self-pity owns his/her emotions and reactions to pain or not—they still exist.

So, if you have decided that sometimes you *do* feel sorry for yourself at the expense of growing or learning, avoid self-condemnation. If you actually have the courage to admit to yourself that you do get overwhelmed with self-pity, you have enough strength to "grow" on with your life.

TAKE RESPONSIBILITY FOR IMMOBILIZING YOURSELF.

After you have admitted to yourself that you are trapped in self-pity, the next step is to take responsibility for being immobilized. This means that you will have to give up all of your favorite "villians"; your ex-love, parents, friends, society's value system and/or your own children. Whatever they have done to you (or continue to do) is miniscule compared to what you're doing to yourself now! Long after the wounds have been inflicted, you can keep them open with self-pity and make your life miserable. One lady I met was still wallowing in self-pity and loneliness six years after her ex-mate had left her for another woman.

When you take the responsibility for your own self-pity, it means that he/she or "they" no longer have so much power to hurt you. Sitting at home night after night waiting for the phone to ring and feeling sorry for your lonely self is far more damaging than the fact that your ex-mate doesn't call. Your ex-mate's infidelity or abusiveness causes you much more pain when you use it as the reason to never love anyone again. Many adults hold on to their hurts from their early childhood and keep themselves much more miserable because of it. Most of them refuse to accept that whatever happened cannot be changed and they can only make themselves feel worse by bemoaning their past abuses.

The sooner you take the responsibility for your own self-pity, the quicker you can lessen it by doing some healthy constructive problem-solving and planning about your "plight"; filling up your emptiness with new friends, doing things to build up your self-confidence and, maybe, even learning how to risk with someone new. Somehow, the telephone *not* ringing becomes less important when you're enjoying those hours with someone else.

GIVE UP THE "DOORMAT" SYNDROME.

A doormat is something people wipe their muddy feet on when they come into a house. Doormats are useful but they are *not* respected or treated with any sort of kindness because they are things without feelings. When they get frayed and worn, most people toss them aside for new ones.

A lot of people put themselves in "doormat" positions. And those who wipe their feet on human "doormats" think no more about them than do the rest of us when we use regular doormats. Human "doormats" are natural self-pitiers, and the only way they can get out of feeling sorry for themselves is to get out of that position. As long as they lie there, someone will wipe his/her feet.

Most "doormats" have trouble standing up—they feel (for various neurotic reasons) that they are destined to stay where they are. Consequently, they are automatically stuck with self-pity and resentment—at the price of respect and kindness. Those who decide to stand up have some trouble at first, but, with practice, they gain respect and kindness from themselves and others while losing their self-pity and resentment about being "used".

If you decide you're a human "doormat" but want to give up that position, let me suggest the following:

1. *Learn to say "no"*. Many people have trouble saying "no" to someone they know who asks for a "favor" or sometimes, even, to salesmen who are strangers. It makes no difference whether they want to say "no" or not, the word just gets stuck in their throats—if they don't feel they have a "good" reason to refuse. Practicing to assert yourself is the only cure. At first, you may have trouble with this. Lots of people shout "no" at everyone

when they first begin trying. Sometimes, people get scared (or feel guilty) when they come on so strong and immediately give up trying to assert themselves anymore. But, if you recognize that you're learning a new skill which will take time to perfect, your clumsiness won't scare you and with practice you will be able to say "no" without putting other people down in the process. Don't be afraid that others will no longer like you. If they care, they'll want to adjust to the "new" you, just as you are adjusting to an acceptance of your real feelings. In fact, you might find others far more comfortable with you now that you don't hide what is really going on inside you.

2. *Don't sacrifice for others or do more than you think is "fair".* If someone asks you to do something for him/her which you feel would cause you a personal hardship or is more than you are genuinely willing to do, don't do it. If you tend to be a "doormat" anyway, it may be hard for you to even recognize that doing the favor is a "sacrifice" until after you've already said "yes". If that is the case, may I suggest that you stall on your automatic compliance until you've had time to think it over. Tell your friend, "I'm really not sure whether I want/can do that, let me call you back." If your friend is not a "feet wiper", he won't be offended. Practice it. If you decide that the "favor" is something you want to do and it is not an "unfair" request, go ahead. If, however, you decide that you would end up feeling "used" and resentful if you do it, politely decline the invitation to be a martyr. Being a "doormat" really doesn't help a healthy relationship, anyway.

3. *Never offer to do something which you really don't want to do—or if there are "strings" attached.* A lot of human "doormats" wave flags with "Let Me Do More!" painted on them, then resent everyone who accepts. These people can always be found at the end of a party, muttering to themselves and cleaning up after the guests have gone, or, weighted down with most of the hors d'oeuvres, sputtering how everyone else is "selfish" for not offering to bring as much as they did. They make life uncomfortable for themselves and everyone else. If someone tells them *not* to do so much, their feelings are hurt. And if other people agree

to the "doormat's game," they are resented unless they accept one of the "strings" of the game, which is usually to praise the "doormat" for "sacrificing" so much, or agree to "sacrifice" too. If you have a tendency to *always* offer to do more in a relationship (or at a party) than others do and/or there are "strings" attached to your "kindnesses", stop! Hold back on your automatic offers to "sacrifice". Whatever your historical reasons for starting this game, remember that you are not perpetuating a mutually satis-fying relationship by continuing to play. Instead, you are only perpetuating your feelings of self-pity.

4. *Own the reality that some "sacrifices" that you make for others are really for your own needs.* Many human "doormats" insist on being used because of their own needs rather than for the "good" of others. Sometimes understanding those needs helps "doormats" decide to stand up or at least give up their feelings of being "used". For example, some people "sacrifice" to avoid feeling guilty. A friend of mine *always* offered to help other people to avoid feeling like a "feet wiper" herself. One of my clients "sacrificed" anytime there was an opportunity to "make up" for using people when he was a teenager on drugs. Some people do "good" so that others will like them. But, usually, others are wary of the compulsive do-gooder. Others "sacrifice" because of their distorted image of giving or kindness. One lady sacrificed for her ex-husband during their marriage because she thought that a "good wife" was always supposed to give and give in. She really felt sorry for herself when he left! But sacri-ficing doesn't mean you love someone—if means you're a martyr! If you are prone to take on the martyr role, spend a little energy looking at what needs it meets for *you*. Maybe you can find other ways to build up your self-confidence or salve your guilt feelings. Being a "doormat" isn't usually every effective.

5. *Do things for yourself.* A lot of "doormats" end up feeling used because they do "little" things for others but *never* do any-thing for themselves. If you're this type of person, spend the extra time and money on *you*. If you are really convinced that you can "buy" friendship, "buy" your own. It's emotionally

healthy to treat yourself as well as you do your best friend. And, you can give much more graciously to others when it's out of an honest desire to do so—not some neurotic need.

OTHER WAYS TO GIVE UP SELF-PITY.

If you have a tendency to overreact to your disappointments and catastrophize your negative feelings and fears, you can lessen self-pity by taking the responsibility to both ask and answer the following questions:

1. Just because I'm feeling this way now, does that mean I will *always* feel like this?

2. Haven't there been times in the past when I've felt equally desperate, but resolved it somehow?

3. Am I being totally honest when I judge myself so critically, or is it possible that this is merely what I'm feeling right now?

4. Could I learn something constructive from this experience?

5. How would I look at this differently if I weren't feeling sorry for myself?

Most of us recognize when we answer these questions that despite sad and fearful disappointments, we are not totally helpless. "When I look more realistically at what I'm reacting to, it isn't nearly so overwhelming—but it does still hurt." There is no doubt about the fact that pain—in any form—hurts. But intensifying that pain by catastrophizing will only lower your self-esteem and immobilize you in self-pity.

GET INVOLVED IN INTERESTS OUTSIDE OF YOURSELF.

Most of a "self pitier's" problem centers on the fact that his primary interest and focal point of attention is himself. *His* problems are the worst in the world, *his* feelings the most intense, *his* sadness the most tragic. No one anywhere has ever suffered as great or lost so dramatically. A "self-pitier" has a narrow point of view. Like the ancient astrologers who believed that the sun and galaxies revolved around the earth: the "self-pitier" feels that the world revolves around him.

Everyone who occasionally feels self-pity and loses interest in other people and events will find it most effective to force him/ herself to notice the rest of the world. Keep reading the newspaper or watching the newscasts on television. Take the responsibility to keep interested in your career, your friends and your family. Develop new interests outside of yourself. Many people find it very healthful to help others when they are feeling sorry for themselves. "Helping other people with their problems helps me forget mine or reminds me that I'm not the only one in the world who has troubles" are common statements to hear from people who were formerly wrapped in self-pity.

As with everything, use some common sense when you encourage your own interest in the rest of the world: totally avoiding your painful feelings can be just as unhealthy as wrapping yourself in self-pity. Most people discover that within a short period of time they are actually letting go of their self-pity as they begin to rebuild their self-esteem and nurture other interests.

Experiments and Exercises.

The following is a list of self-pity reinforcers. Go through it and check whether you are likely or unlikely to use any item on the list. Make sure that you answer them honestly—the first step in solving a problem is to recognize you have it.

	L	*U*
1. Try to take care of "everything" alone.	—	—
2. "Turn the other cheek" when someone hurts your feelings.	—	—
3. Feel sorry for yourself because others can't see their unfairness.	—	—

 4. "Give in" consistently to others.   __ __
 5. Give more than you want to.   __ __
 6. Keep an unwritten ledger of what others "owe"
    you.   __ __
 7. Feel "unloved" or abused when someone doesn't
    automatically offer to help.   __ __
 8. "Bend over backwards" to save a relationship.   __ __
 9. View the loss of your love as a tragedy.   __ __
10. Feel helpless to change your fate.   __ __
11. Blame others for your problems.   __ __
12. View rejection as a tragedy.   __ __
13. Feel that life is unbearable when you don't get
    what you want.   __ __
14. Confuse your wants with your needs.   __ __
15. Get upset when you are frustrated.   __ __
16. View yourself as more "sensitive" than others.   __ __
17. Secretly view yourself as an abandoned child.   __ __
18. Often feel that you were "born to lose".   __ __
19. Secretly feel that no one has it as "bad" as you do.   __ __
20. Secretly feel that no one really cares about you.   __ __

Now go back through this list and study those you are likely to do.

   *How would you honestly rate your degree of self-pity now?

   *Is there a pattern you can see—or a "life theme"?
Make a statement about yourself from this insight:

   "I have always seen myself as _____".

   *How would you like to change the above?

   *Specifically, what would you have to do differently in your everyday interactions with others?

   *When will you begin to change that? Be specific.

Now pick one reinforcer you would like to give up. Using the two chair role-playing technique, go back through your memory and visualize the *last* time you remember doing or feeling this. Remember who was there and what was going on. Allow one chair to be the "abused" part of you and the other to be the rational problem-solving part. Now give the "abused" part of you permission to really feel sad. Give in to all the sympathy you feel for yourself. Express those feelings out loud—including your resentment. When you feel you are "finished" move into the "problem solving" chair. From this position, look at the "abused" part of you and acknowledge your sympathy as a friend. Tell the "abused" part he/she does have a right to feel sorry (and resentful) *but* add your suggestions on what he/she can do to change this behavior or attitude and feel better. Come up with some sort of conclusion which includes plans on how to change.

When you are "finished" with this exercise, take some time to reflect on your experience.

*Make a commitment to yourself to follow through on what you have learned for the next week.

*After a week's period of time, re-evaluate how you are doing and add any new ideas you've discovered.

*Continue this pattern until you feel the issue is no longer a problem.

14: Loneliness Made Easier

Writing about loneliness is like writing about love; it's a difficult concept to understand or even define. Everyone seems to have his/her own definition of loneliness and what it entails. Anthropologist Margaret Mead calls it "being alone when you don't want to be"; psychologist Ira Tanner defines it as the "fear of loving" in his book, *Loneliness*; Freud felt that loneliness had something to do with the fear of death; Dr. David Rubin says it's related to nostalgia and a sense of longing; and my five year old neighbor, Timmy, told me he was lonely because everyone on the block is too old to play with. However, there is general agreement that feeling lonely is sad, that everyone experiences it occasionally and that none of us likes it. You can be lonely in a crowd or by yourself; at age three or one hundred and three; whether you're wealthy or poor; man or woman; single or married; black, white, yellow, red or brown. And, although we may curse our need for others when we're lonely, we revel in feeling "together" with someone.

Telling you that loneliness is part of saying good-bye to an old love affair is probably not very innovative. If you're a sensitive person who acknowledges your needs for warmth and caring from others, you already know that—perhaps, all too keenly. Helping you learn how to lessen your loneliness and offering advice which others have found helpful may be something new.

It is possible for all of us to chisel our own loneliness down in size and frequency—but impossible to ever completely erase it. One thing I've discovered for myself and from others—that there are all kinds of ways to handle our loneliness but only a few which are actually effective overall. You can wallow in self-pity because you feel lonely, get depressed or angry, fill up your stomach with alcohol or "pop" pills to avoid it, gorge yourself with food, pretend that you don't need anyone else and you aren't lonely anyway, or constantly keep busy with "strangers". Those are the ineffective ways to grapple with loneliness. Dealing with your loneliness effectively requires taking the responsibility for how you react to that feeling, developing constructive insight about your loneliness at the time, learning how to be "company" to yourself when you're alone and risking intimacy and close friendships with others.

People who fear inadequacy or intimacy are more prone to loneliness than others, and during times of change, stress or loss, the feeling is stronger. Sometimes ex-intimates find that they are actually less lonely being single than they were when they were "married". And often married couples seek counseling because of their loneliness and lack of intimacy. In a way, ex-intimates are lucky. When you're alone, you *expect* to feel lonely and, often, armed with that knowledge, expect yourself to learn how to handle it. People who do not end an intimate relationship for fear of their loneliness, will experience a mild form of emptiness and dissatisfaction all of their lives, but avoid learning how to lessen it in emotionally healthy ways because they can often deny it exists—or place the responsibility for their feelings on their mates.

ON THE FEAR OF BEING ALONE.

Almost everyone is afraid of being alone and only those who have chosen it or have effectively learned how to cope with aloneness feel comfortable on their own. "I'd get a divorce, but I'm afraid of living alone" is a common statement to hear. Countless unhealthy marriages are held together by two unhappy people who fear being by themselves more than they fear staying miserable. Together and miserable they're used to—alone and ? is unknown.

> *1st person*: "What kinds of things do you have to face when you live alone?"
>
> *2nd person*: "Two things primarily—taking the responsibility for myself and learning to accept that I'm inadequate at times."

Taking responsibility for yourself and your own reactions means that no one else can be blamed. If the house is a mess and you want it cleaner—you must either clean it yourself or take the initiative to get someone else to do it. If you're bored on Wednesday evening or Saturday afternoon, you can't blame someone else for your reactions—you're the one that's bored and you're the one that will either have to do something about it or keep feeling bored. If you're used to depending on someone else to make you feel good or keep you entertained, you will quickly learn the job is yours by default. Many people who begin living alone discover that their panic comes from suddenly discovering that they are dependent people and, in fact, used their ex-mates to take on their own responsibilities, then blamed them when things didn't go well. One man I know discovered that he used his ex-wife to build his self-esteem and blamed her when he felt inferior. When he began living alone, he learned that *he* was ultimately the one who was responsible for how he felt about himself and no other scapegoat was necessary. In fact, it was easier—and much more rewarding to take that control than to dump it on someone else who couldn't be effective anyway.

Learning to accept that you're inadequate at times comes from taking the responsibility for decisions and sometimes goofing in your choices. Remember the times that you slipped out of owning your mistakes by blaming your ex-mate? "It's your fault we live like we do" or "I didn't want to go to this movie, you're the one that dragged us here!" are both statements of irresponsibility. Even if he/she was the one who finally verbalized the decision, it does not excuse your responsibility in agreeing to it—or worse yet, waiting for your ex-mate to make the choice so that you could blast him/her with criticisms. Being alone means you take the credit for your choices that turn out well and the blame for the ones that go poorly.

One of my clients, who is a very insightful woman, got in touch with what Freud felt was the core issue in our fear of being alone.

> "The main thing I learned from living alone was that no one could protect me from death. I'm not even sure why I thought of it, but one of my first weekends alone, I got very depressed and suddenly discovered that I was afraid of dying and no one can save me from it. My panic didn't last very long. I remember feeling grief for a short period of time, then thinking: 'Even if I wasn't alone, I am still going to die.' For some reason that made living more important to me and being alone much less scary."

There is no way of knowing how many people actually get in touch with their unconscious fears of dying and the childlike solution that if you have someone holding your hand, you will stay with them rather than die. But, if you are fortunate enough to become aware of that fear and resolve it constructively, living alone will no longer be so frightening—nor will living "together" again with someone new.

The positive part of living alone is that you have the opportunity to learn how to take the responsibility for your own choices, a chance to become a mature, independent adult on your own. The negative part is periodically failing to attain that goal and having to accept that failure. And, that's where the fear enters —the fear that you cannot survive without someone taking care of you. Feeling lonely when you're alone is not unusual but feeling lonely and being alone are not the same things, nor do they necessarily go together.

UNDERSTANDING YOUR OWN LONELINESS.

Loneliness comes from feeling unloved/unlovable and/or experiencing a loss. Obviously, with all the fallout of dissolution, ex-intimates will experience some loneliness. If you cared at all about your old love or had any sort of emotional commitment to the relationship, you will feel lonely when it's over. The intensity or duration of that feeling depends on a number of factors:
— your own self-esteem before, during and after the "marriage".
— the degree of investment still commited to the relation-ship when it ended.
— your own fears of being loveable or loving again.
— how much of your own identity, friends, family and surroundings you've lost by saying good-bye.
— your ability to adjust constructively to change.

If you've always felt insecure and basically unlovable, you will no doubt feel lonelier than someone who believes in his/her desirability and capacity to love again. People prone to depression or self-pity will stay immobilized in loneliness longer than others, and those who primarily react with anger or bitterness may feel empty for a longer time. Learning to love again (one of the "cures" for loneliness) will take you as long as it does to work through the grief process. However, you will not necessarily feel lonely all that time nor will the intensity remain the same.

"I feel loneliest during the evenings, right after I get home from work."

"Mornings are the worst for me—when I wake up and no one's next to me in bed."

"During the first few weeks I thought I would die from loneliness. After that, it was only at certain times—like after a party when I went home by myself."

"Holidays are the loneliest—that's when I miss my family the most."

"I get the loneliest when things are going really well for me—or really awful. That's when I miss sharing with someone 'special'."

The times and events that remind you of your loneliness will vary. The longer you cherish your old love in your soul, the longer your loneliness will linger. A "romantic" who glorifies his ex-mate's memory (now that she's gone) could be sentencing himself to a lifetime of emptiness. It's natural to miss your old love for awhile and on occasion become nostalgic, but in so doing, your loneliness will linger.

Use this space to jot down the times when you are aware of feeling lonely:

1.
2.
3.
4.
5.

Understanding the reasons for your own loneliness means that *you* will have to take the responsibility to look at both your feelings (or fears) and your immediate surroundings at the time you are feeling lonely. Probably you will find that your loneliness is a combination of your own internal hurt and fear of loving, plus some external scene or upcoming event which has triggered it. For example, you may discover that you have always been slightly afraid to risk loving someone, and, now that you're dating again, that fear has been triggered by the fact that you are just not "turned on" to your current date. It's natural not to fall in love again quickly (although there are exceptions), and some people discover that their loneliness becomes more intense when they try to make themselves love someone new. Or, you may find that when you get your feelings hurt by someone (a friend or a stranger), your loneliness becomes stronger. There are all kinds of situations which get you in touch with your loneliness and whatever the scene that triggers that feeling, the first step towards feeling better is to recognize what set it off.

Internal barriers that stop people from loving and therefore, according to Ira Tanner, lock them in loneliness are:

1. "I don't deserve to be loved and I'll prove it."
2. "I don't trust people who want to give love and I'll prove it."
3. "I've given up trying to give love or receive it."

Whenever you find yourself in any one of these psychological stances (a normal protective reaction when you've been hurt), you will be hesitant to replace your loneliness with sharing. And this apparent self-protection, in combination with hurtful or scary scenes, will make your loneliness stronger.

To develop an understanding of your own loneliness is the beginning of its demise. As one of my clients shared:

> "Once I started looking at how come I'm lonely, my attitude about ever feeling 'safe' or 'together' with someone new changed. It was like I was taking charge of my feelings—deciding that I could work out the ones that were scary. My loneliness no longer 'spooked' me. It wasn't some mysterious blight that could control me no matter what anymore. It was a normal feeling that I could lessen if I choose to."

Anything that is "unknown" can be frightening and feel unsolvable to us. Once you begin to understand why you feel lonely, some of the fear of your own pain will vanish, and then you can begin to develop constructive solutions towards filling up that emptiness.

HOW TO COMBAT LONELINESS BY YOURSELF.

Most experts will tell you that loneliness can be lessened by being and sharing with someone else—a close friend, someone you love, or a relative, for example. And while it is true that loneliness can be eased in that manner, there are also things you can do to combat loneliness by yourself. Probably you will find it most effective to use a combination of both. Many lonely people live alone—but it is also true that many people who live alone are not lonely because they have developed the ability to conquer their fears of being alone and have learned how to be "good company" to themselves. The following hints come from their experiences:

1. *Make your house or apartment a setting you enjoy.* There's nothing more depressing than coming home to a dreary apartment. Most people spend a great deal of time in their homes and how you feel has a lot to do with the setting you live in. If your home looks empty and bleak and you think of it as just a place to sleep, it's quite easy to "catch" that feeling and attitude from your surroundings. A room filled with sunshine, a few plants and a couple of your favorite treasures is much more enjoyable for you to be in than a dark, drab space. Even if you never paid much attention to where you lived or what it looked like when you were living together, now that you're living alone, the setting will be much more important to your psychological state and worth the effort of fixing up. If you're afraid of living alone, make sure that all of the doors have good locks and safety latches. Put sticks or window locks in all of the windows and sliding glass doors—that way you know that you're "safe" to enjoy your home.

2. *Save some alone times to do "fun" or creative things by yourself.* Most people do a number of things with someone else that they could also enjoy by themselves: going to art galleries,

dining out and going to a movie, going window shopping, taking a "hobby" class, going swimming, bowling, golfing, bicycle riding, visiting a park or zoo, painting and redecorating a room, going for a ride in the country, visiting a boat show or an antique auction. Look at some of *your* favorite activities and see if you can come up with a few that you could enjoy by yourself as well as with others; then plan to do them.

3. *Avoid dwelling on your loneliness or scaring yourself with "what ifs"*. Most people who enoy living alone do not spend large amounts of time ruminating about their feelings of loneliness or scaring themselves with "what ifs": "what if I'm always going to be alone?"; "what if I get sick or injured?"; "what if the refrigerator breaks down?"; "what if I don't get an invitation for Thanksgiving dinner?"; etc.. The healthiest and most effective way to enjoy your life is one day at a time—especially if you have a tendency to be pessimistic and "what if" your pleasure away.

4. *Avoid sinking into self-pity*. The quickest way to increase your loneliness (by yourself or in the company of others) is to sink into self-pity. Avoid falling into that trap as much as you can. If you have a tendency to feel sorry for yourself, follow the advice in Chapter 13.

5. *Do things to build up your self-esteem*. Take the effort to keep up your physical appearance and complete projects that will help you feel better about yourself. Avoid constantly criticizing each piece of your behavior, and give yourself extra "pats on the back" when you do something well.

6. *Develop new hobbies and build on old ones*. Most hobbies give their creators the opportunity to build their skills, talents, and sense of accomplishment with the extra bonus of an end-product that can be useful or asthetic. Hobbies almost always have to be done alone and give you the opportunity to direct your interest in something outside of yourself. People who live alone enjoy themselves much more readily (and so do others) when they have interests outside of themselves and their work.

7. *Change your leisure routine.* If you always spent Sunday mornings lying in bed and reading the newspapers with your old love, continuing that routine when you live alone will only increase your loneliness. Changing those "special" leisure routines is an effective way to combat some of your loneliness. Use Sunday mornings to enjoy a new hobby or go on an "outing" you'd like by yourself. The trick is to replace one enjoyable activity with another that you feel could be equally pleasant and satisfying. Don't replace your old "fun" schedule with drudgeries or tasks that are chores.

8. *Turn on the television or a radio for company.* Many people find that quietness in a lifestyle that was once filled with noise deepens their sense of loneliness. A radio or television turned on, even softly, can temporarily fill up some of the emptiness that's felt internally. Statements like:"It doesn't make any difference whether I'm even in the same room or not, having the T.V. on and hearing the voices is 'company' for me at times," or "I often have my stereo on when I'm at home," are common to hear from people who live alone but are not necessarily lonely.

9. *Getting a pet may be helpful.* A dog, cat, bird or even goldfish can be great companions for people who live alone. These animals should not act as substitutes for relationships with others, but can be a warm, supportive addition to any household.

10. *Positive attitude about living alone.* Everyone I have ever talked with who lived alone but did not feel lonely had an attitude of confidence about him/herself—as well as others. Even the ones who would prefer living with someone he/she loved again took the stance that: "This is what I'm doing now, so, it's worth learning how to enjoy." No one can tell you specifically how to develop this attitude for yourself. It's a matter of making the decision to enjoy your life, and then genuinely doing whatever it takes to make sure you attain that goal. Remember: everyone who has ever conquered their loneliness started out feeling empty inside.

FIGHTING LONELINESS WITH ENVIRONMENTAL CHANGE.

Some people discover that their loneliness seems to linger and deepen when they continue to live somewhere that brings back painful memories every day. Curling up in the same bed alone, living in the house where the two of you remodeled the garage— all of these scenes and a hundred more can remind an ex-mate that he/she no longer shares an intimate relationship with his/her old love. Nostalgic longing for someone or a life style that is no longer available can scrape on your wounds and make it more difficult to begin learning to love someone new. And staying in the same environment makes it almost impossible not to remember those "good times"—especially for those who were not the first to initiate the good-bye.

One of the "fortunate" things about divorce is the fact that most ex-intimates are forced to sell their homes which results in both partners physically moving. As awful as that might seem at the time, many people discover that being forced to move out of their old environment is a blessing in disguise.

> When Paul and Marie divorced after ten years of marriage, Marie and the two children stayed in their home for six months until it was finally sold. Marie moved into a duplex reluctantly, but shortly thereafter discovered that she really felt much better. "I don't even try to make my duplex look like our home. I tried that with the house and it was always painfully impossible to do because Paul was missing. It's funny, but I don't feel as lonely in the duplex. It's not our bedroom—it's mine. The garage doesn't look bare without Paul's tools cluttering it up—this garage never sheltered them. I think moving really did help me lessen my loneliness."

As therapuetic as being forced to change your physical environment is, making that move voluntarily is ten times more helpful because it requires a deliberate decision on your part to move on.

FIGHTING LONELINESS WITH THE AID OF OTHERS.

The best way to fight loneliness is to risk intimacy and friendship with others. A difficult thing to do sometimes—especially when you're feeling vulnerable, abused or unlovable—but still the "cure" for getting rid of your loneliness. Nothing thaws loneliness quicker than understanding, which is best gained with the risk of sharing your feelings with others.

Risking should go in stages. Many people refuse to risk closeness and understanding because they have some sort of exaggerated expectation that risking entails baring your soul to someone without any defenses to protect you from hurt. "I freeze when someone says that he wants to get to know me better. I feel like I should tell him everything I've ever done or felt that I'm ashamed of. I know that's silly, but I still feel like I'm not totally honest or really 'close' unless I do." It is natural to share small amounts of yourself at a time. Trust is built slowly by gradual acceptance, *not* in one gigantic step. And the fear of taking one gigantic "soul baring" step can immobilize even the most courageous— not to mention how overwhelming your "here's all my secrets" speech will be to a stranger. To effectively build closeness with others, it is important to mutually risk a little at a time.

Most of us enjoy different levels of friendship with other people. We share parts of ourselves with acquaintances, a little more with friends we have known for a short period of time or only at specific settings like work or school, and close, lasting friendships with only a few "special" people whom we feel we "know" and trust the most. Reaching out to these friends and acquaintances during the times when you feel lonely will automatically fill up some of that emptiness.

"Sometimes when I'm lonely, I just call a friend and, hearing his voice—knowing that someone still cares about me and understands, reassures me that I'm not alone in the world."

"I've become more friendly now that I'm alone—it's like my loneliness forces me to meet people. I even know my neighbors now—they're very nice people. I never knew them when I was married. It was easier to hide in my shell."

"Since our divorce I've made an effort to get closer to my family. For the first time in my life I feel like they love me. I know now that I've always needed them."

"I used to be afraid that I was a 'cold' person, but now I know I need other people and I let them know that too. I'm less lonely now than I've ever been."

PITFALLS TO AVOID IN LONELINESS.

Through this book I have mentioned pitfalls that ex-intimates fall into which increase their depression, self-pity or anger, while keeping them stuck in the grief process longer than is necessary or healthy. All of these traps may heighten loneliness as well, for often these feelings are caused by loneliness even though many people are unable to recognize that themselves. The irony about the following pitfalls is that most ex-intimates who fall into them purposely do so to lessen their loneliness, and, when they discover that they are even lonelier, usually stick to their favorite trap more insistently. The misconception here is that if they only stay longer, their sense of abandonment and emptiness will lessen—like the man who keeps searching in the same dresser drawer for a missing cuff link. The idea that "this *should* work" is difficult to erase—especially if you desperately want *something* to work. Unfortunately these traps will not lessen your loneliness and, in fact, may do the opposite so, don't try to "con" yourself—recognize what you're doing.

1. *Risking with the "wrong" people.* Telling you to be careful and avoid risking your feelings with the "wrong" people may sound absurd, but many ex-intimates literally jump from the romantic frying pan into the fire in an effort to fill up their emptiness.

Sharon is an attractive, intelligent 27 year old secretary who went from one emotionally destructive relationship into another with a married man. After six weeks, her new love affair frizzled, leaving her even more lonely than before. "When I met Bob I knew he was married. As a matter of fact that's what attracted me to him. It seemed 'safe'; he was separated from his wife but she would probably return. I didn't have to worry about making a commitment to him —or falling in love again. Bob could just be someone to be with so I wouldn't be lonely. I certainly didn't expect to feel worse! I guess I started caring about him and then, when he decided to go back to his wife, I felt lonely again *and* ashamed."

This woman is not unusual—many ex-intimates make emotionally unhealthy choices when they decide to risk caring again. And, although it is impossible to know for *sure* whether your new love is "right" for you, it doesn't make sense to risk loving someone whom you know at the beginning will probably be "wrong". If your last love was an alcoholic and that didn't work out, don't set yourself up to fall in love with another one. If you have a tendency to be a martyr and your last relationship died because you felt "used", don't risk loving someone new who seems like more of a "feet wiper" than your last love. And don't risk your feelings with an ex-mate who's already rejected you. Let your own common sense be your guide and listen to your instincts for growth when you begin risking with someone new.

2. *Frantically searching for someone to love you.* "If only I can find someone to love me again, I wouldn't be lonely," is a common "faulty" solution to the problem of loneliness. The "faulty" part lies in the phrase "to love *me*"—implying that the individual need not risk loving again him/herself, only find someone to prove that he/she is lovable. But loneliness has at its root *two* fears: being unlovable *and* being afraid to love. A solution that touches only half of the problem never works, and, in fact, usually increases the loneliness and frustration. For example, if a man actually succeeds in finding someone to love him, his own doubts about himself as a warm, caring person worth loving are heightened. "She loves me but I don't love her" increases

self-doubt, guilt, bitterness and resentment—all of which add to frozen emotions and isolation. There are a number of people who marry someone they don't love with the hope that, in time, they will learn to love that person. Usually this results in a mutually self-destructive relationship which ends with both partners seriously questioning their ability to love and be lovable. (If you've been in this kind of relationship, you know how painful it is.)

To frantically search for someone to love you rarely works out. Everyone senses your panic and emptiness, including you, and the "success" rate for those so desperately searching is minimal. Making yourself available to meet someone new and encouraging him/her (as well as yourself) to see you as lovable is one thing. Rushing out every night after work searching for your savior from loneliness is quite a different matter. Love grows slowly and risking takes time, both of which are necessary in order to truly develop an understanding, intimate relationship. Ex-intimates who decide they don't want to risk loving again but do want someone to love them will stay lonely for a long time— "in" or "out" of a relationship.

3. *Deciding to "kill" your need for love so you'll never be hurt again.* Most experts agree that the loneliest people are those who have decided to stop loving. Yet many ex-intimates mistakenly decide that if they disavow their feelings, no one will ever be able to hurt them again and they'll never be lonely. Someone who chooses this alternative connects his/her loneliness with the loss of a specific person. And while that is partially the cause for his/her loneliness, it is not the cause of loneliness—or even half of it. Each of us has control over how we deal with our emotional needs; we do *not* have control over whether we have them or not. And when an individual decides that he'll deal with his need for warmth and understanding by pretending that he doesn't have it—he's chosen to feel empty or "dead" inside.

4. *Substituting physical closeness for emotional intimacy* Prostituting yourself for physical closeness or money rarely

decreases loneliness, yet many ex-intimates go through a phase of attempting to fill up their emotional needs in this way. "Maybe I'm not capable of living or being loved but I am a good bed partner" has a very hollow ring to it. Sexual intimacy can be the ultimate expression of emotional closeness and caring, but it can also be used in a number of emotionally unhealthy ways—to "get back" at the opposite sex, increase feelings of self-doubt and guilt, or mistakenly try to prove that you're sexually adequate. The trouble with this trap is that it's difficult to get out of. One of my divorced friends is in his fifth year of prostituting his emotional needs for one night stands and he's still just as lonely as he was at the beginning. Evenings, week-ends and holidays are still very empty and planning a vacation with someone "special" six months from now is, of course, out of the question, because his faith in anyone's ability to be honest, caring or faithful (including his own) is quite badly shaken. If you're in this kind of trap, give yourself a time limit on how long you're going to stay in it—then climb out of it when your time is up. That's the only way you'll ever replace going to bed with everyone for making love to someone "special".

Loneliness is not owned exclusively by ex-intimates; the world is full of people "married" and single who are emotionally isolated. Nor is it a mysterious aura that controls how you feel. Loneliness comes from building walls rather than bridges.

Experiments and Exercises.

List the ways you currently deal with your loneliness.

1.
2.
3.
4.
5.

Now reflect on the above:

*After reading this chapter and evaluating from your own experience, would you rate them as "healthy" or "unhealthy" techniques?

*Which ones should be changed or altered to be more effective?

*Are there some that should be "dropped" altogether?

In this chapter, several suggestions on combating loneliness were offered. List one or two "new" ones you are willing to try during the next week:

1.
2.

Now, plan what you will have to do in order to try one of these:

1.
2.
3.
4.
5.

Now, follow through on your plans.

At the end of two or three days, evaluate your progress and add any alterations you may have discovered.
*Keep practicing this exercise until you have chiseled away some of your loneliness.

Transition Exercise.

Making the transition from your old life style and relationship to enjoying single status can be a painful and bumpy process at times. Especially when you get lost in your hurt feelings and fears. The following exercise will help you gain a clearer, more objective, understanding of your past relationship as well as your plans for the future. Do it when you are feeling strong, not "down" and will have *at least* 30 minutes of uninterrupted time for yourself. Choose a setting that is physically and emotionally comfortable. Practice this exercise as often as you need: it may take several rehearsals to actually "experience".

Close your eyes and take a few moments to relax. Practice taking deep, slow, rhythmtic breaths. Once you feel your body relax, imagine that you are in a movie theater.

Tonight you will see one movie plus the preview of "coming events." In the movie you *were* the writer, director, producer and star. Tonight you're the audience. The movie is about your old relationship. The "preview" will be your plans for the future: you are the writer, director, producer, star and audience.

The movie:

1. The title goes on the screen. What is it?
2. What kind of theme does it have?

a) melodrama   f) mystery
b) soap opera   g) adventure
c) fairy tale   h) ?
d) comedy
e) tragedy

3. Is the movie in color or black and white?
4. What kind of background music does it have?
5. Are you viewing certain scenes or do you see the whole picture?
6. Who does the dialogue sound like?
   Who talks and who listens?
   What is talked about? What issues are hidden?
7. Is there a "hero" or a "heavy"?
8. As the viewer how do you feel about your old role in the movie? How were you dressed? Did you stand straight or slump?
9. As the viewer how do you feel about the theme of the movie?
10. What feelings are aroused as you view it?

When you are ready, draw your movie to its conclusion. Then, take some time to reflect.

When you are ready to move on, sit back and view the "preview". Include anything you would like to place in your future.

1. This time, what is the title?
2. What is the theme?

   a) melodrama   e) tragedy
   b) soap opera   f) mystery
   c) comedy   g) adventure
   d) fairy tale   h) ?

2. Are the "coming events" in color or black and white?
4. How is the background music?
5. Are you viewing certain scenes or do you see parts from the total picture?
6. What does the dialogue sound like?
   How is it different/same as the movie?
7. As the "star", what is your role?
   How are you dressed?
   Do you stand straight or slump?
8. Do you have a co-star or several?
   Does it change as the "previews" progress?
   What's your supporting cast like?
9. What feelings are aroused as you view the "previews"?

Conclude the "previews" when you feel the viewer would want to return for the total showing.

Now take some time to reflect:

1. Where are you in the production of your new movie?
2. What steps will you need to take to enjoy single status again?
   a)
   b)
   c)
   d)
   e)

15: Enjoying Single Life

"For the first time in human history, it is finally possible
to be both single *and* whole."

—anthropologist Herbert Passin

Enjoying single life could—and probably should—be an
entire book rather than the concluding chapter in a book on
good-bye. The time between your last love affair and the next
one can be one of the most creative and enjoyable periods in
your life, or it can be empty and desolate—depending on how
you deal with the grief process, your attitude about beginning
again, and your ability to enjoy being alive. The majority of
single-againers, just like their counterparts who are still "married", have both "good" and "bad" days; times when they feel
on top of the world and moments when they feel crushed underneath it. When you're feeling "on top", you'll wonder why you
ever felt badly about saying good-bye; and when you're crushed,
nothing in the present or future will seem half as bright as the
dreariest days in your past—and you will blame being single for

all of your sadness regardless of whether that's true or not. Gradually you will discover that your "up" days are far more frequent and lasting than those that are down. Especially if you genuinely want to feel good and it's worth your effort to make like enjoyable.

GIVING YOURSELF PERMISSION TO BE FREE.

"I know it's silly, but I still feel 'married' to Paul even though we've been separated for months."

It's not unusual for ex-intimates to still feel "tied" to their last love, even when he/she has long ago vanished. And, being emotionally tied to a "ghost"—whether it's a person, an idea ("being single again means I'm a failure") or a fear ("I can't make it by myself, I'm too fragile")—can stop you from truly enjoying your single status. As a matter of fact, the unconscious psychological purpose of feeling tied to a "ghost" is to keep you from feeling alive and self-confident enough to risk enjoying your new life. Like an emotional governor allowing you to progress past your grief period but regulating your desires and actions to join in on the "fun" parts of being single again, the "ghost" appears just as you begin planning or right after you have taken action on an exciting plan.

"I started to plan a vacation to Hawaii by myself and though 'What's with you, you'll never have fun by yourself?' At first I had trouble shaking that fear—but thank God I did. I went and had a fantastic time. I can hardly wait for another vacation. It doesn't even have to be so exotic. I know now that I can go on vacations by myself and enjoy them."

"I told myself I would never join a singles' club—it didn't seem 'right'. Probably I'd just meet a bunch of 'weirdos' there. But I finally shook the idea that there's something 'wrong' with people who go to those places, and joined in. I'm really glad I did—I've made a lot of new friends there."

"After I came home from my first date with a man I met at work, I felt like I was cheating on my 'ex'. It was the strangest feeling. I really had a good time but it was like I was punishing myself. 'I shouldn't enjoy another man's company so soon'—or something like that. I'm glad I got over *that* feeling, I've discovered there are a lot of men I enjoy being with—and several who find me attractive, too.''

To enjoy the fun parts of being single again—dating, going on vacations, being self-indulgent at times, or trying whatever you'd like to try—you will need to give yourself permission to go ahead and risk having fun in spite of your own self-doubts. Unhooking from the "ghosts" that stifle your enjoyment requires:

1. Recognizing which "ghosts" you own.
2. Acknowledging to yourself that you are putting a "damper" on your life by carrying them with you always.
3. Taking the responsibility to give up your "ghosts".
4. Risking growth by taking action and enjoying your new plans in spite of your fears.

Naturally, the more self-confident you are, the easier it will be for you to let go of your fears and fantasies. And nothing builds confidence more quickly than successful experience.

NEW AND EXCITING VACATIONS.

Ex-intimates often dread their first vacation because they've decided that they cannot possibly enjoy it alone. But, nothing could be farther from the truth! As a matter of fact, many single-againers discover that vacations can truly be fun—sometimes for the first time in their lives because the choices about where to go and what to do are totally their own and not a middle of the road compromise that no one enjoys. There are literally hundreds of travel clubs and tours set-up exclusively for singles, and thousands of resorts all over the world cater primarily to single adults. You can find everything from dude ranches in the mid-west, rafting down a river, skiing in the Swiss Alps, sailing on the Carribean or roughing it in a hut in North Africa. A vacation can be short and cheap or long and expensive.

When you decide on a vacation, make sure that your first one is something you would really like to do. Don't settle for filling your time up with something you feel you *should* do—like staying at home and working on the yard, or going to visit relatives you've never been close to anyway. If you feel "funny" going by yourself for the first time, it's probably a good idea to go on a planned tour or resort for singles only. If you're a bit braver, you might try a tour that is not exclusively designed for singles or couples. (Incidentally, according to a travel agent friend of mine, around 50% of all tours or resorts are filled with singles—I guess married couples stay home and remodel their garages!) Some single-againers enjoy treking out on their own in a camper or back-packing up in the mountains by themselves. If you are one of the more pioneer types who really would enjoy a vacation with nature and no other people, feel free to make that your first vacation alone. If the great outdoors "turns you on", but camping alone is less than appealing, ask some of your other single friends to join you. One lady I know loved to go camping but couldn't find any friends to go with her, so she put an ad in the paper inviting strangers who were interested to contact her. Eleven of them joined her for a pot-luck dinner on a Saturday night, and six of them went camping together for a week in the mountains. If art shows, antiques, historical landmarks or beach bumming is your forte, gather together some new friends who enjoy the same interests and organize your own tour. You'll be pleasantly surprised at how many fun-loving people are just waiting around for a leader like you to organize a different and exciting vacation.

FUN IDEAS FOR AROUND TOWN.

You don't have to wait for vacation time to enjoy life or fill part of your leisure with exciting or creative pasttimes. In fact, planning to enjoy the people, activities and sights in your own home town is just as easy as planning a vacation—maybe even easier. You have everything that is already established and available in addition to whatever your own imagination and creative abilities can design and develop.

One woman I know has made it a practice to plan a mini weekend vacation once each month. At first she had all the normal doubts about choosing a "spot" and indecision about where and what to do. But, after the first couple of times, her fears and doubts were happily replaced by enthusiasm and a sense of adventure. Her guideline is to visit some place within a hundred mile radius of her home. There's a map in her study with a red circle outlining the perimeter of her mini vacation land with stars or checks by the areas she's visited so far. Before she chooses a town, she writes to the local chamber of commerce for information and reads up on the different areas. Then, after deciding "where", loads up her camera, film, notebook and week-end wardrobe and is off on vacation again. Over the past year, she has gathered together enough material to write feature articles for the local newspaper—a profitable hobby that pays for her monthly vacations.

If you have less pioneer spirit, but still enjoy physical recreation and outdoors activities, contact your local parks and recreation district office. During the summer and spring time, expecially, the planned activities are usually in full swing—and, contrary to popular opinion, local recreational activities are *not* just for children. Most good city park systems have organized adult acitivties ranging from dances, tennis matches, softball games and open swimming classes. If your system doesn't have one yet, you might want to help your community get one organized.

Many people have "fun" helping others. Volunteer work is available in every area—from convalescent homes to day care centers: the U.S.O. to the Peace and Freedom Party. You can volunteer for as few or as many hours as you want and, happily, for those who have trouble commiting themselves, you can quit anytime you decide. Being a volunteer can help everyone, including the volunteer, feel a little more compassionate about the people he shares his world with. So, check with a volunteer bureau in your community and spend a small amount of your leisure time giving enjoyment and kindness to others. You'll discover how quickly your warmth is returned.

OTHER SINGLES AND WHERE TO FIND THEM.

With the frequency of dissolution, no one who is single again really needs to feel alone or embarrased about his/her status. But, in spite of that fact, many ex-intimates begin their single again status hovered in a corner feeling like they are the only ones who have ever ended a love affair. "Everywhere I look, there are couples—I feel like I'm the only person in the world without a partner" is a familiar lament amongst single-againers.

The best way to prove to yourself that you are not alone in the world is to meet other people who are in the same spot. For ex-intimates this usually means attending singles' clubs, groups or organizations designed specifically for them. Although this may seem like a simple solution for a complex problem, most ex-intimates are extremely reluctant to join *anything* specifically for them.

"I'd feel funny going to a group like that."
"What would everyone say?"
"I wouldn't know what to do."
"What if I met somebody awful?"
"I'm not *that* desperate!"
"No thanks, I'll wait until I meet someone through a friend."

All of these hesitations are natural, but do need to be overcome —for unless you are one of the "fortunate" few who already know a number of single adults, your social life will consist of being alone or tagging along with couples. And, enjoying single life again *has* to include socializing with other single adults.

Because of the rising divorce rate *and* the current popularity in choosing single status as a life-style, there are literally thousands of singles' clubs, groups, bars, resorts, apartments and every other type of organization you can think of for single adults.

Almost every town of moderate size has at least one singles' club —and in many cities it is possible to live in a singles' apartment, socialize at singles' clubs exclusively, and attend a church with a special group for its single members on Sunday.

Many papers have a weekly column announcing singles' club dances, dinners and meetings. Churches often have singles' clubs connected to their parishes and several groups, such as the Sierra Club in the West, have special events for single members only. Community colleges and universities are beginning to conduct classes for living alone effectively, and recently some of the Y.M.C.A. groups have started rap sessions for singles.

Attending any one of these organized activities can broaden your ability to enjoy single status by helping you meet new people and increasing your self-confidence. Although at first it may seem scary, it is important to *force* yourself to attend at least three or four singles' events alone. Once you're there, it won't be so frightening, and it is much easier to maintain flexibility when you don't feel that you have to worry about whether your friend is having a good time. And, best of all, you will be giving yourself another opportunity to prove that you do not have to depend on someone else in order to attend and enjoy social functions.

One of my clients recounted her progress in learning to assert herself and meet new friends by attending a singles' club dances:

> "I had to *make* myself go to a singles' dance alone. The idea seemed easy—but doing it was hard. I almost backed out several times, but kept telling myself that I had to do this —to prove to me that I could. The first time I stayed for about an hour, talked to one other woman, then faded into the woodwork and out the door. The following week I went again. That time I stayed much longer, met several more people and actually forgot how scared I was at times. It boosted my ego to go there by myself and not 'fall apart.' I've gone several times since than and really enjoy it. As a matter of fact I've made several good friends (everyone's not as 'awful' there as I feared) *plus* I've discovered I can go any-where by myself and have a good time. I used to just stay at

home until a friend suggested we do something together. Now, if I hear about something 'special' or get an impulse to go somewhere, I go—whether I can find someone to join me or not."

Once you've increased your self-confidence again, you might want to organize your own singles' group—a lot of innovative people do. For example, one lady I know has a Wednesday night bridge club for singles only at her home. She runs an ad in the local paper, asking bridge players to contact her for reservations. In that way she can pre-screen her guests. The club is growing in popularity and often, I'm told, she has to turn down interested bridge players because all the reservations are filled. Also, a man in the San Francisco area organized a group of tax-payers to lobby for decreased income tax for single adults—at last count he had over two hundred men and women joining together with him to help lower taxes *and* get to know each other.

Regardless of what your favorite pasttime or own "special" cause is, it is possible to continue with it while developing new friendships with other single adults by inviting them to join in the fun. Just remember that there are hundreds of other singles in your community who share your same interests and are just waiting to get things organized. Contrary to popular myth, it is not necessary to go bar-hopping to meet other single-againers, but it is necessary to keep your mind open for new ideas and use your courage to assert yourself.

DATING AGAIN.

For most ex-intimates, dating again produces all sorts of anxieties—a kind of renewed adolescence filled with excitment and frought with self-doubt. The mother of four teenagers getting ready for her first date with a new beau may feel excited and just a little bit foolish while upstairs putting the final touches on her make-up. And downstairs, her middle-aged date may be awkwardly squirming while the "children" inspect their mom's boyfriend. It's a tense time for everyone. And this type of scene, or others which are just as emotionally charged, will happen repeatedly during the time that you're single again. Gradually, the self-doubt and nervousness lessens and the pleasure of dating again grow stronger. But it takes time—and using the constructive insight you've gained through the grief process.

How quickly you are able to adjust in an emotionally healthy manner to the dating scene and enjoy the pleasure of others varies with your own self-image, the insight you've gained through ending, and the length of your last relationship. Ex-intimates normally begin dating again before all of their wounds from their last love affair have totally healed, and, as a matter of fact, dating is the only way you can really know that you are still attractive to the opposite sex and have the ability to love and develop intimacy with someone new. Since most ex-intimates still feel vulnerable, there are several issues and problems that come up with dating again—along with the pleasures.

The major issues that come up usually revolve around:
1. Trust of intimacy (emotional and sexual).
2. Feelings of self-doubt.
3. Unresolved conflicts from dissolution.
4. Fears of vulnerability.

These four questions can come in the form of self-questioning:
1. Will I always be alone?
2. What's wrong with me that I can't "make it" with anyone?

Unconscious decisions:
1. I'm too vulnerable to risk loving again.
2. I don't have the ability to love.
3. No one who knows me could really love me.
4. I'll never love or trust anyone again.

Or actions:
1. Dating several people at the same time.
2. Dating one person at a time—but briefly.
3. Dating someone you know will be a "dead end".

It is natural to ask all of these questions, periodically decide not to risk loving again, and practice these unconscious solutions by dating with emotional distance. Gradually as these issues become less overwhelming (through the pleasures of dating), your need to protect yourself from hurt and disappointment will lessen and your ability to risk intimacy will strengthen. Most ex-intimates fluctuate between actively dating again and doing things by themselves or in the company of "friends".

One of my friends who has been divorced for 3 years recounted his dating experience to me in the following manner:

> "The first four months I did nothing—oh, I went to parties at friends' houses, but for the most part, I just stayed at home and felt sorry for myself. Then, I started going out with some of the other men at work—barhopping and picking up one night stands. I did that off and on for a few months, then quit. In between, I dated a couple of women that I really developed friendships with. For the most part my dating the first couple of years was casual and pretty sporadic—always, in the back of my mind, I was hoping it would work out with my ex-wife. Oh, yes, there was a brief period during the first year when I fell passionately in love with someone. But that only lasted for a couple of months. It's funny after that bombed out, I went into a 'blue funk' for about three days and then snapped out of it. But then, all my love went back to my 'ex' again. It's only been in the last six months (really, since I've decided that I *could* live alone for the rest of my life if I have to) that I've found someone I think I could marry—I'm not sure yet where that will go—but, it's a neat feeling."

Obviously my friend does *not* speak for the whole singles' group—or even the "male" part of it—but, he does recount a fairly typical pattern of dating again. All men and women will need to deal with the issues of trusting intimacy, self-doubt, unresolved conflicts, and fears of vulnerability while dating again. The problems that evolve and sporadic withdrawals from dating are attempts to deal with these four basic issues. The pleasures of dating come from occasional resolution and the melting away of these fears.

And there is also another layer of issues that dating often reveals:

1. *Confusion in sexual self-image.* Contrary to popular myth, *both* men and women suffer blows to their sexual identity when they end an intimate relationship. And dating quickly uncovers those hang-ups. Women are perhaps the most vocal with their frustrations and confusions, but men, too, when they're honest, acknowledge those fears. For both, the issue is how they see themselves now that they are sexually experienced but no longer in a "permanent" relationship—and how others may view them. "I know that I'm not a blushing or rowdy teenager anymore, but does that mean I'm damaged goods or somebody else's rejection?" is an underlying question many will need to resolve. The obvious answer is "No, you are not 'damaged goods' or sexually inadequate" but each individual must discover that answer for him/herself. It is natural to fear your sexuality and ability to enjoy sexual happiness, if your last relationship was sexually destructive or unsatisfying, *but,* happily, most ex-intimates discover their ability to enjoy sexual relationships directly connects with their ability to risk loving and expressing that warmth through touching. Avoid judging yourself harshly when dating again—and go with your feelings *not* your fears. Most ex-intimates discover that they automatically choose dates who reconfirm their own sexual self-image and as they begin feeling better about themselves and their own bodies, they date men or women who see them as sexually attractive and potent.

2. *Ambivalent feelings about sexual intimacy.* It doesn't take more than a few dates for most ex-intimates to discover that they may have very strong feelings about sexual intimacy. Men sometimes feel they are *supposed* to ask their dates to go to bed with them, at least after the third or fourth date, and women often *assume* that "men are only after one thing." In fact, the assumption goes, if you don't go to bed with a man as soon as he asks, (usually after the second or third date) then he'll drop you like a hot potato. I suppose there is some validity in these assumptions —but only among the emotionally immature. Nonetheless, the

fear that these ideas are factual for every potential new love accounts for a great many "short" dating patterns.

> "I dread the scene at my front door. I know as soon as I tell my date 'no'—I'll never see him again—plus, he's liable to be nasty in the process. So, usually I date a man a couple of times—then make excuses about why I can't see him again."

> "Women *expect* you to proposition them. If you don't, they think you're 'weird'. Well, maybe I am 'weird' but I feel guilty about going to bed with someone just because she wants me to—or, it's the thing to do at the end of a date. Furthermore, I've tried that and if I don't feel like making love, I just can't do it. So, I end up dating a lot of different women—but, not for very long."

Both of these comments were made by sexually normal, responsive adults whose fears of sexual intimacy—and others' expectations—kept them from learning to develop caring relationships with their dates. Those who find themselves in this type of "short" dating pattern need to be honest with themselves and their dates about their feelings and fears. Usually, this honesty relieves a great deal of tension and anxiety and opens the door for the development of a closer relationship in addition to helping each individual gain a little more constructive insight about him/herself in the process.

In spite of the widely publicized liberal views on sexual intimacy, the majority of adults over 25 *still* have traditional values. Those who remain married can objectively view our culture's changing attitudes towards sexual freedom. Those who are single again, quickly find they can no longer take an unattached viewpoint. As soon as an ex-intimate begins dating again, he/she discovers that traditional morals about sexual intimacy have been replaced by a more liberal and open attitude, one which values sexual freedom for it's own sake and not necessarily as a way to show love to a "spouse". Anyone who has been "married" for more than six or seven years or came from a sexually conservative heritage will discover that his/her value systems are in conflict. If you add individual fears about sexuality, of being "used", and of not being valued as a total person *and* connect emotional nakedness with sexual intimacy, you can easily see why every ex-intimate will have to constructively examine and probably alter his/her own sexual morality.

Whether *and* how you decide to alter your views on sexual intimacy is a personal choice. But, I believe it is safe to say that you will have a very difficult time finding another "spouse" *if* you refuse to share sexual intimacy while dating again. If you believe that your views on sexuality are really too conservative (even for you) but you don't feel "comfortable" about changing them, examine them carefully. If it is intellectually "okay", act on that acceptance, then deal with your feelings afterwards in a supportive, constructive manner. Most people discover if they wait around until they feel perfectly "comfortable", they never change anything. On the other hand, if you decide, after close examination, that even intellectually, you cannot accept altering your values—better hold off for awhile and stay with the old ones.

3. *Unrealistic expectations of dating again.* Many ex-intimates create extra problems for themselves and hamper their pleasure in dating by expecting too much or too little from their dates. Those who expect too much view each new date as a prospective lifetime partner and judge him/her accordingly. A date is not enjoyed just for the evening, but is seen as the first step towards a life time commitment. It is easy to understand why an individual might proceed so cautiously or place such extraordinary importance on dating again—especially is he/she is feeling vulnerable and feels the need to quickly find a replacement for his/her last "spouse". Unfortunately, such unrealistic expectations usually place too much tension and anxiety on a casual date and doom it to failure at the beginning. Moreover, the "type" of man or woman you are willing to date is thereby automatically restricted, erasing your chances of learning to enjoy different people. Many ex-intimates repeatedly fall "in love" and

then "out again" with the same type of mate because they repeat their first choices in dating and commit themselves to one of the first two or three people they date. If you have a tendency to expect too much from each new date, try to remember that *one drink is not a lifetime commitment!* Enjoy the drink and your date's conversation and avoid daydreaming about what it will be like with him/her ten years from now.

Expecting too little from dating again can rob you of the pleasures of dating just as quickly as expecting too much. Those who expect too little, date for a "free" meal, or to avoid eating alone. Usually these people have very low opinions of themselves, are quick to judge harshly, prone to self-pity and bitterness and carry equally low opinions of anyone who would date them. You or your date may not be Prince Charming or Cinderella, but if you think in terms of "frog" and "scullery maid", you will rob yourself of another opportunity to enjoy the fun in dating.

4. *Confusion and/or acting our unresolved conflicts from past relationships.* Some of the more destructive problems in dating again evolve when a misguided ex-intimate attempts to work through his/her unresolved conflicts (and oftentimes anger) with a past love by confusing current dates or *all* members of the opposite sex with an old love. So called "man" or "woman" haters fall into this category. Women who literally lash out at their dates for no apparent reason, or passively demean them and scoff at their offers of friendship and kindness, are obviously confusing the current men in their lives with someone who is no longer present. Men who literally "screw" every woman they date, then proudly announce their opinion that *all* women are "sluts" are perhaps the most obvious. Others, who are a little more sophisticated, show their anger less openly, but their dates still know they've been "put down". These misguided ex-intimates are emotionally damaging to themselves and whomever they date—for no one can genuinely experience the pleasures of dating if he/she is "getting even" with a "ghost". Most emotionally healthy ex-intimates attempt to avoid these types of games if at all possible because they understand that it is counter-productive for their own

emotional growth and happiness. Unfortunately, many people continue the games through ignorance. If you find yourself making statements like "men (women) can't be trusted" or "no man (woman) will ever hurt me again"—*while* you are dating, you may be robbing yourself and your current date of the fun in dating because of some "unfinished business" for which you still hold your past love accountable.

As an ex-intimate resolves some of the problems in dating again, he/she can start looking around and experiencing pleasure with other people for its own sake and not out of internal anxieties or anger. For most ex-intimates, this is a sporadic process. One moment you'll notice that you're actually listening, talking and laughing with your date and the internal "push" has magically disappeared—only to return an hour later. But gradually the pressure will lessen, and soon (within a few weeks) you will find that most of the time when you're with someone you are actually *with* him/her and not far into what the future might hold or mucking over some pain from the past. You can quicken this process of learning to enjoy the pleasure in the present by deliberately focusing your attention on the here and now and your current feelings—rather than what you might feel later or did feel before.

ASSESSING NEW LOVES.

Some dates will last no longer than one or two evenings, and either you or your "date" will decide (for any number of reasons) that you do not enjoy each other's company well enough to continue. Other "dates" will turn into platonic friendships and, perhaps, one or two will develop into intimate, caring relationships that last for several months. With each of the "endings" you may experience a certain amount of grief but gradually, as you begin feeling more secure about yourself as a separate person, you will be able to understand that every "rejection" is not a rejection of you (or your new love) as an individual—but, rather, normal personality differences which are not compatible.

In dating again it is important to develop the freedom and self-confidence to enjoy different "types" of dates, but equally important to evaluate more serious relationships and reject those which appear to be emotionally destructive for you. This flexibility to accept or reject new "loves" based on your own emotional health and needs can increase your enjoyment of dating—for it gives you the freedom and internal security to risk caring for others without the fears of being emotionally crushed if you pick someone who just isn't right for you.

As a result of the self-awareness gained during the grief process, most ex-intimates have a better idea of what it will take to make them happy than they did before. Use that insight you've gained to assess each new "love". The important thing is to look at what you really need or want to be happy—not what you'd like to want or what someone else suggests you need.

LOOK BEFORE YOU LEAP AGAIN.

Mel Krantzler, author of *Creative Divorce*, suggests that "Divorced men and women, especially after a long marriage, need a period of experimentation with a variety of different people and relationships before they commit themselves to another marriage." It doesn't make any sense to go through all the pain of the grief process (or even part of it) and commit yourself to another relationship immediately. It can be a great temptation, especially during the first few months or year when you may feel overwhelmed with sadness. But avoid jumping into another "marriage" out of desperation or loneliness.

As I commented in the beginning of this book, many intimate relationships end because the lovers failed to realistically assess their relationship at it's beginning—before they made a commitment to each other. Without being *against* commitments in intimacy, I do suggest, however, that you use your common sense and the insight you've gained from saying good-bye to your past love before you commit yourself to someone new again.

Being single again does not mean just going through the grief process or learning how to deal with your pain in emotionally constructive ways. It means enjoyment—and laughter—and excitement—and all sorts of warm pleasantries that help you feel better about *you* as a separate person, your world and the people you share it with. Take the time to enjoy your single status by yourself—with friends—and new "lovers".

Those who have grown through the grief process and learned that they can enjoy themselves as separate people rarely trade in their freedom for anything less than a happy, emotionally healthy commitment the next time around. Many will even tell you that they feel *good* about having struggled through the grief process —even though there were times when they felt like dying.

> "It was like having an operation to remove a poisoned appendix. It hurt like hell! And, the recovery period was agonizing at times. But thank God I did it—and didn't give up salving my hurt."

Experiments and Exercises.
List five things you currently enjoy about being single again.
1.
2.
3.
4.
5.

List five more you would like to begin trying (use your imagination and suggestions from the book).
1.
2.
3.
4.
5.

*What will you need to do to try these?

*Pick one of the above and make a commitment to begin working on it immediately.

Now list five things you value most in life.

1.

2.

3.

4.

5.

Ask yourself:

*How do my values relate to my life now?

*Does the way I am living my life now reflect what I say I value?

*What are my goals for the future?

*What potentials do I have in attaining those goals?

*What are the barriers?

*What am I going to do about the potentials and barriers?

The following exercise was at the end of Chapter 1. Jot down the first words that come into your thoughts as you read the sentences. After you have completed it compare your responses. Pat yourself on the back for the growth you have made. Encourage yourself to continue growing in the areas that could still be improved.

1. If I were to use three words to describe myself, they would be _____, _____, and _____.

2. If I were to use three words to describe my ex-mate, they would be _____, _____, and _____.

3. When I look at my past, the word that comes to mind is _____.

4. When I look at my present, the word that comes to mind is _____.

5. When I look to the future, the word that comes to mind is _____.

6. My three greatest fears are _____, _____, and _____.

7. My three greatest strengths are _____, _____, and _____.

8. The one quality I would like to develop in me is _____.

9. Right now I feel I can look forward to _____.

DEAR READER,

Now that you've finished reading this book, I would like your candid opinions on its contents as well as any other comments you would like to share.

Please send your letter to me in care of:

SCHENKMAN PUBLISHING COMPANY
  3 Mt. Auburn Place, Harvard Square
  Cambridge, Mass. 02138

Although I may not be able to directly respond to your letter, I will read it.